2708

P9-EER-771

NORMAN LEWIS

New Power with Words

EXPANDED SECOND EDITION

Thomas Y. Crowell Company   *New York*

ESTABLISHED 1834

ACKNOWLEDGMENTS

Acknowledgment is made for permission to reproduce the following copyrighted material:

Excerpts from "Political Frustration: Cause and Cure" by Robert and Leona Train Rienow on page 54 and "Cauldron of Creativity" by David Boroff on page 60 by permission of the *Saturday Review*.

The material from *The New Yorker* on pages 58, 60, 213, 222, and 227 copyright © 1943, 1963 by The New Yorker Magazine, Inc.

"Freezing Method in Ulcers Queried" on page 199 and "Colleges Warned on Profile Tests" on page 222 © 1963 by The New York Times Company; reprinted by permission.

Excerpts from *The Old Trails West* by Ralph Moody on pages 206 and 209 copyright © 1963 by Ralph Moody (Thomas Y. Crowell Company, publisher).

Designed by Joan Wall

Manufactured in the United States of America.

Library of Congress Catalog Card No. 64-23135

First Printing of Expanded Second Edition

FOR

Mary, Margie, Debbie

CONTENTS

ONE

Measuring Your Word-Power

The following pronunciation symbols are used in this section:

ə—the obscure vowel sound of the *-a* in *sofa* (SŌ'fə)
ăr—as in *carriage* (KĂR'-əj)
er—as in *very*
o͞o—as in *moon* (MO͞ON)
o͝o—as in *book* (BO͝OK)
ō—as in *go* (GŌ)

A Test for You

YOUR ENGLISH can take you places—or it can hold you back. It can open for you certain doors to social, economic, and professional advancement—or it can slam those doors in your face.

These are facts that you can verify from your own experience. When you speak to the important people of this world, the men and women who give orders, who draw the top salaries, who have a measure of control over their own destinies and the destinies of others—when you speak to these people, you cannot help being struck with the skill they display in handling their native language. Their words are forceful, incisive, full of color and action. Their grammar is free from gross and illiterate errors, but never pedantic; their pronunciation is educated without being affected. *You enjoy listening to them because they know what they want to say and how to say it most effectively.*

This is neither an accident nor a coincidence. Success in life and efficiency in language always go hand in hand; power over people and power over words have ever been two sides of the same coin. And you have only to listen to people of influence and power to realize how true this is. You have only to compare the speech habits of the head of a large organization with those of his lowest-paid employees to understand that the way a man talks and writes is usually indicative of the position he holds.

Power over words can be quickly and effectively increased by intensive training in five areas of language:

1. Vocabulary
2. Pronunciation
3. Correct usage
4. Reading
5. Spelling

The book you now hold in your hands aims to help you develop in yourself vast new powers in these five departments of English. It will show you how to add more new words to your vocabulary every week than most adults learn in a year. It aims to give you complete self-confidence in all matters of pronunciation and grammar. It will explain how to eliminate any difficulties you may have with spelling. It will teach you new techniques for reading with greater skill and understanding.

In short, this book expects to make you so completely a master of words that you will speak and write more effectively, more persuasively, more confidently, and more successfully.

Let us discover first, however, how much power you already enjoy over words. The test which follows will hold up a mirror to your ability in the five vital fields of human language with which this volume is concerned.

I. PRONUNCIATION

If you can check the preferable form of eight or more of the following words, you may feel secure that your general pronunciation conforms to educated patterns.

1. mischievous   *a.* mis-CHEE'-vee-əs   *b.* MISS'-chə-vəs
2. admirable   *a.* ad-MIRE'ə-bəl   *b.* AD'-mə-rə-bəl

3. radiator   *a.* RAY′-dee-ay-tər   *b.* RAD′-ee-ay-tər
4. epitome   *a.* ə-PIT′-ə-mee   *b.* EP′-ə-tōm
5. percolator   *a.* PURK′-yə-lay-tər   *b.* PUR′-kə-lay-tər
6. esoteric   *a.* es-ə-TER′-ək   *b.* ə-SOT′-ər-ək
7. fiancé   *a.* fee-ahn-SAY′   *b.* fee-AHNS′
8. genuine   *a.* JEN′-yōo-wine   *b.* JEN′-yōo-ən
9. impious   *a.* im-PY′-əs   *b.* IM′-pee-əs
10. longevity   *a.* lon-JEV′-ə-tee   *b.* LONG′-və-tee

II. VOCABULARY

The richness of your vocabulary obviously determines how effectively you are able to express yourself. Can you think of just the right words to communicate your thinking to others? Complete six to eight blanks to consider your vocabulary above average, nine to ten to feel that you have an unusually rich vocabulary.

1. The act of compelling or of using force   co———————ion
2. Recollection of past experiences   re———————ence
3. Disposition to be merciful   cl———————cy
4. A sense of superiority which manifests itself in an overbearing manner   ar———————ance
5. A connoisseur in eating and drinking   g———————met
6. A woman who endeavors without affection to attract men's amorous attentions   c———————te
7. One who does not believe in God   a———————ist
8. One who has a morbid and irresistible desire to steal   kl———————maniac
9. Shortness   b———————ity
10. Calm, placid, unemotional   phl———————atic

III. CORRECT USAGE

Grammar, too, is a hallmark of general language effectiveness. Is your speech free of obvious errors and illiterate forms? Does it meet an acceptable standard of educated usage? Score at least eight right before you answer *Yes.*

1. He (*a*. lay; *b*. laid) asleep all morning.
2. Is this the man (*a*. whom; *b*. who) he said was innocent?
3. I (*a*. haven't; *b*. have) hardly any money.
4. Everyone received a number except (*a*. I; *b*. me).
5. Margery and Myrna (*a*. are; *b*. is) here.
6. Neither Rhoda nor Ralph (*a*. was; *b*. were) present last night.
7. Have you (*a*. drunk; *b*. drank) your coffee?
8. She is light- (*a*. complected; *b*. complexioned).
9. You ought to (*a*. have; *b*. of) known better.
10. Mary is much taller than (*a*. me; *b*. I).

IV. SPELLING

Ability to spell according to generally accepted patterns is another prime characteristic of word-power. Can you detect at least six of the ten misspelled words in this list? To consider yourself a superior speller, find all ten.

1. descriminate	11. rediculous
2. discription	12. sacrilegious
3. picnicking	13. inimitable
4. ukelele	14. newstand
5. inoculate	15. accidentally
6. manageable	16. incidently
7. desirable	17. alright
8. wierd	18. analyze
9. seperate	19. proceed
10. arguement	20. precede

V. READING

The final important facet of language skill is the talent to understand what you read. This power can be tested most significantly when you attempt to interpret the mood, feeling, or attitude of a particular selection. Three right in the following exercise shows ability somewhat above average; five right indicates real power.

1. Life's but a walking shadow, a poor player
   That struts and frets his hour upon the stage

And then is heard no more. It is a tale
Told by an idiot, full of sound and fury
Signifying nothing.

SHAKESPEARE

The speaker is expressing a feeling of
   a. hopelessness   *b.* optimism   *c.* wonderment

2. The year's at the spring
   And day's at the morn;
   Morning's at seven;
   The hillside's dew-pearled;
   The lark's on the wing;
   The snail's on the thorn;
   God's in his heaven—
   All's right with the world.

ROBERT BROWNING

The mood of this poem is
   a. depressed   *b.* confident   *c.* puzzled

3. Hardly a man takes a half hour's nap after dinner, but when he
   wakes he holds up his head and asks, "What's the news?" as if
   the rest of mankind has stood his sentinels. Some give directions
   to be waked every half hour doubtless for no other purpose; and
   then, to pay for it, they tell what they have dreamed.

THOREAU

The writer implies that people are too
   a. inquisitive   *b.* selfish   *c.* highstrung

4. In the fell clutch of circumstance
   I have not winced nor cried aloud.
   Under the bludgeonings of chance
   My head is bloody, but unbowed.

   It matters not how strait the gate,
   How charged with punishments the scroll,
   I am the master of my fate;
   I am the captain of my soul.

WILLIAM E. HENLEY

The poet's attitude is one of
   a. fear   *b.* defiance   *c.* complaint

5. Poverty demoralizes. A man in debt is so far a slave; and Wall Street thinks it easy for a millionaire to be a man of his word, a man of honor, but, that, in falling circumstances, no man can be relied on to keep his integrity.

EMERSON

Indirectly, the author shows toward money an attitude of
a. reverence   *b.* cynicism   *c.* delight

ANSWERS:

Test I
1—b, 2—b, 3—a, 4—a, 5—b, 6—a, 7—a, 8—b, 9—b, 10—a.
Test II
1—coercion, 2—reminiscence, 3—clemency, 4—arrogance, 5—gourmet, 6—coquette, 7—atheist, 8—kleptomaniac, 9—brevity, 10—phlegmatic.
Test III
1—a, 2—b, 3—b, 4—b, 5—a, 6—a, 7—a, 8—b, 9—a, 10—b.
Test IV
1, 2, 4, 8, 9, 10, 11, 14, 16, 17.
Test V
1—a, 2—b, 3—c, 4—b, 5—b.

You have now arrived at a preliminary estimate of your power with words. The diagnosis you have made indicates to you those sections of the book that will prove most valuable for you. Pay special attention to Section Two if you have found a weakness in vocabulary; Section Three if your pronunciation score was low; Section Four if the grammar test was difficult; Section Six if your ability in the spelling section was not adequate; and Section Five if you found that your comprehension of the final section was not up to par.

If you have made a better than average score in all five parts of the test, then you have developed your word-power to a degree greater than that attained by most adults. You are bringing to this work a better than average background in English; as a consequence, your rate of improvement will be swifter than that of the person in whom there are major weaknesses, and the speed and ease with which you will be able to apply the suggestions contained in the remaining chapters of this book will be correspondingly greater.

You know where you stand now. Whether you are good, poor, or mediocre, you can confidently expect to improve long before you've turned the last page.

TWO

How to Enlarge
Your Vocabulary

The following pronunciation symbols are used in this section:

ə—the obscure vowel sound of the -*a* in *sofa* (SŌ′-fə)
ăr—as in *carriage* (KĂR′-əj)
er—as in *very*
o͞o—as in *moon* (MO͞ON)
o͝o—as in *book* (BO͝OK)
ō—as in *go* (GŌ)

ONE

~~~~~~~~~~

Waking Up to Words

THERE IS NOT a quicker nor a happier road to effective speech than a large vocabulary. Nothing will add so certainly to your self-confidence when you speak as the knowledge that you have * enough words at your command to express creditably (1) * the thoughts that course through your mind.

These points are so obvious that it seems almost unnecessary to state them. But did you also know that the extent of your vocabulary has a measurable relationship to your potentiality for success in life? This is a fact, not an abstract theory. Tests at the Human Engineering Laboratory have conclusively proved that the *one* factor inevitably accompanying progress in business and the professions is a better than average vocabulary. In the words of Dr. Johnson O'Connor, director of the Laboratory, "An extensive knowledge of the exact meanings of English words accompanies out-

* The numbers in parentheses after certain words will be explained at the end of the chapter.

standing success in this country more often than any other single
characteristic which the Human Engineering Laboratory has been
able to isolate and measure."

"Why do large vocabularies characterize executives and possibly
outstanding men and women in other fields?" continues Dr. O'Connor's account. "The final answer seems to be that words are the instruments by means of which men and women grasp the thoughts of
others and with which they do much of their own thinking. They
are the tools of thought."

Granted, then, that it is worthwhile improving your acquaint-
anceship with words, what can you personally do about it? The
usual, but not very satisfactory, answer to this question is that you
must "get the dictionary habit." You must learn to look up new
words when you meet them; you must read with a dictionary at
your side; you must browse through a dictionary at odd moments;
you must keep a notebook and faithfully and conscientiously record
therein one or two or five or ten new words every day, according
*to the extent of your ambition and the heat of your fervor (2).
Now, theoretically, this is the best advice in the world; what makes
it unsatisfactory is that, *by itself,* it is supremely impracticable. I
*know of no authenticated (3) instance in which any human being
*followed such a dry regimen (4) for longer than two weeks. I
*know of no zealot (5) who possessed the fortitude (6) and tenacity
to initiate such a program of self-improvement and follow it through
religiously despite more pressing claims that were made on his time
and energy. And as a teacher I have had the opportunity to discuss
the matter with thousands of adults intent on improving their vocabularies.

*Happily, a start at vocabulary improvement can be made with-
out "getting the dictionary habit."* When you were born you knew
no English words at all; now you probably use five thousand or
more and can doubtless recognize three times as many as you actually use. And I believe it is safe to say that you learned very few
of these thousands of words by looking them up in a dictionary. You
acquired the words now in your vocabulary because you were exposed to them; if you hadn't managed to master them, you would
have found it difficult to carry on the affairs of your life. Then the
time came when you were out of school, and were established in

*some business or profession or social stratum (7); when you knew enough words to get by on, when it was no longer imperative to learn more in order to communicate adequately with your friends and business associates. And having learned enough words for that, your mind automatically closed to new ones, in the same way that your eyes automatically close when you need sleep, or in the same way that thirst automatically vanishes when your need for water has been satisfied.

(The average adult learns fewer than twenty-five new words a year, these being almost exclusively the words which gain sudden popularity in the news of the world.)

When I say that your mind automatically closes to new words once your communication needs have been satisfied, I am referring especially to a phenomenon which occurs in your daily reading. If you come across an unfamiliar word, say in a magazine article, what do you generally do? If you are superhuman, you rush to the dictionary and find out exactly what that word means. Otherwise, you conveniently ignore the word, because the rest of the sentence makes adequate sense without it. Or, if it does not, you shake your head angrily and proceed with your reading, making a mental note that you dislike authors who use words you don't understand. Or possibly, if you are of a more violent frame of mind, you either turn to the next article, or just throw the magazine down impatiently.

Yet it is in these very magazines, or in books or newspapers, that the secret of practical vocabulary improvement lies.

Words are generally meaningless except as they add to the thought of a phrase or sentence; hence, increasing your vocabulary *from your daily reading is the most logical and functional (8) plan you can possibly follow. This method demands no change of your daily schedule. It involves no special activities. All it requires is a change in your *attitude* to words. It is, hence, a plan that can be put into operation immediately, painlessly, and without inconvenience. Indeed, as will be explained shortly, you can take a long step toward improving your vocabulary even before you come to the end of this chapter.

So simple is this natural approach to vocabulary improvement that it can be described in a single sentence: *In your reading, learn to let your mind linger on the words whose meanings are partially or completely unfamiliar to you.*

It is a human characteristic to pay little heed to things that are constantly under our very noses. Doubtless you ride up and down the elevator of your apartment house or office building a hundred times a month—but have you ever noticed the name on the control mechanism? You may have been eating your lunch in the same restaurant every day for years—but can you recall the color and design of the dishes?

Don't let your ignorance in these matters embarrass you. You cannot answer these questions for a good reason: your brain is too economical and efficient! It refuses to waste energy registering information that seems unessential—*unless some external stimulus forces it to.*

The same phenomenon is at work while you read. Your eyes may see an unfamiliar word, your inner ear may hear its pronunciation, but your mind will refuse to register it if it decides that you can go on living comfortably without knowing that word. Indeed, you can encounter the same word a dozen times over, and your mind will continue to balk at grasping it—*until some external stimulus compels it to.*

To increase your vocabulary at a very rapid rate, you have only to form the habit of providing that external impulse—the habit of compelling your mind to linger for a few seconds on each new word it meets. You have only to say to your mind, "Hold on to that word; I may find some use for it." Note that you need not say, "I must find out at once what that word means." The meaning of each word you force your mind to register will come—not at once, perhaps, but eventually. Eventually, and slowly—but inevitably and unforgettably. For having once recorded the word (remember, you never totally forget anything you have learned) your mind will recognize it at every subsequent encounter. Each new experience your mind has with that word will make the meaning just a little clearer. And as the meaning gradually unfolds, the word will burrow deeper and deeper into your vocabulary, until finally you will understand it so well that—perhaps to your own amazement—you will find yourself making use of it, *quite casually,* in your thinking and conversation.

Thus your vocabulary will be growing, gradually and uniformly and almost without effort, in the same way that every other part of your mind and body grows.

Let us apply the plan specifically. Here is a sentence from a recent issue of *The New Yorker:* "All the girls had . . . that special fixity around the mouth and eyes so apt to be found in any *woman who feels that she is being *arbitrarily* (9) kept waiting in line by insect officials." You do not, we will say for the sake of argument, know the exact meaning of *arbitrarily*. It's a simple word, easy to pronounce. It fits in pleasantly with the rhythm of the sentence. But what, precisely, does it mean? In this particular pattern of words *arbitrarily* could signify a number of things, all with equal logic: *unnecessarily, annoyingly, unhappily, despotically,* or *wrongfully*. If the word were omitted entirely, the sentence would convey enough meaning to permit you to continue reading without undue discomfort. But when you enjoy the inimitable flavor of the *word, when you can respond fully to its rich connotations (10) and undertones, the sentence comes alive for you as it never could with a dead and meaningless word dangling uselessly from it.

Go back for a second and stare at the word. Let your mind, your eyes, linger on it. What do you think it means, now that you stop to consider it? Which one of the adverbs suggested seems most likely to be its synonym?

Learning to stare at the unfamiliar words that you meet in your reading, learning to spend a few seconds puzzling them out, is the secret of developing the kind of word-consciousness that will rapidly enrich your vocabulary. That extra bit of attention devoted to *arbitrarily* will lodge the word securely in your mind. The next time you meet the adverb, you will recognize it as an old friend. And you will be startled how soon you will meet it again! The word will not have gained any sudden and inexplicable currency among writers; but, because your mind is now trained to look for it, *arbitrarily* will strike you sharply each time you see it, even though, under other circumstances, you might have casually ignored it a dozen times in a week. Now, as you continue encountering it, *each time in a different context (11), its meaning will gradually and correctly unfold. As you become increasingly familiar with the word, any misconceptions you may have had will slowly dissolve.

And because you are learning new words in the natural way, by hearing and seeing them in many different sentence patterns (which is, fundamentally, the way you learned all the words at present in your vocabulary), your acquisitions will become lifelong members of your speaking and recognition vocabulary.

With a few days' practice, word-consciousness will become a habit. From that point on, every day that you read will bring its quota of new words. The process is cumulative, as all natural processes are. Each day the habit will become more and more a part of you, each day your competence will sharpen. Too, your reading itself will become more skillful, for nothing so contributes to the ease of absorbing a page of print as an acute sense of the precise meanings of the words on that page. If you devote about the same time to your reading as most people do, you will, on an average, add twenty-five words a month, three hundred words a year, to *your vocabulary—a truly prodigious (12) feat considering that many adults learn fewer than twenty-five new words a year!

You can make a start at developing your word-consciousness even before you've finished this chapter. You may have noticed that certain of the words in these paragraphs were followed by a number in parentheses. You can find them by looking for the identifying asterisk at the left margin of the page. They are words not commonly found in the poor vocabulary. Go back and find the numbered words and let your mind linger for a few seconds on those you don't already know. Puzzle out their probable meaning, as far as you can, then compare your conclusions with the definitions given below. How successfully your ideas match these definitions is of no consequence; what is important is that you have already begun to improve your vocabulary—you have already started to become word-conscious. And just notice, in the next few days, how frequently these same words bob up in your reading. The flush of recognition and the thrill of accomplishment which you will feel will more, far more, than compensate for the time consumed by this type of verbal calisthenics. More to the point, the habit you've begun to develop today will remain with you as a lifelong acquisition.

If you sincerely do want to improve your vocabulary, start today to make this attitude a permanent part of your reading habits.

When you meet a new word, train your mind to register it. From then on, things happen by themselves—automatically!

KEY TO NUMBERED WORDS IN THIS CHAPTER

1. creditably—in a praiseworthy manner
2. fervor—intensity of feeling
3. authenticated—proved genuine
4. regimen—a systematic diet, as of food, exercises, words, etc.
5. zealot—a fanatic
6. fortitude—resolute endurance
7. stratum—a layer, as of rock or society
8. functional—able to be put into practical use
9. arbitrarily—despotically
10. connotations—suggestive significances of words apart from their actual meanings
11. context—the passage in which a word occurs, and which helps explain the meaning of a word
12. prodigious—extraordinary; out of the ordinary; marvelous

HOW GOOD IS YOUR VOCABULARY?

If you know the meanings of most of the words in List I, your vocabulary is average; in List II, good; in List III, superior.

List I	*List II*	*List III*
candid	inveigle	prognosticate
placid	recumbent	antithesis
sulky	mercenary	nebulous
engross	coquetry	adamant
morose	gruff	vicissitude
cumbersome	respite	efficacy
sinister	dilapidated	proclivity
timorous	implicit	exigency
idiosyncrasy	convivial	anomaly
feign	virile	phlegmatic

TWO

~~~~~~~~~

Stop, Listen, and Learn

A CHILD'S VOCABULARY increases with breathtaking rapidity; an adult's vocabulary increases at a rate that would make a turtle seem like a speed demon.

From that time in your infancy when you first learned to talk in connected syllables, you added hundreds of words to your vocabulary every year of your preschool life; [1] indeed, if you were an exceptional youngster, you entered the first grade able to understand and use over four thousand words.

For the next eight years of your grade-school life, you absorbed another three to four thousand words. In high school and college, if you continued your education, you became acquainted with a minimum of two to four thousand more.

[1] According to Lovisa C. Wagoner, Chairman of the Department of Child Development, Mills College, California, the average child of two knows and uses 300 words; at the age of two and a half, he knows 450; at three, 1,000 words; and at four, 1,800 or more.

Thus, 95 percent of your vocabulary was gained in your formative period—over twenty times as much in those first school years as in all the rest of your life. For, as an average adult, you have learned about twenty-five words annually, such additions being mainly those new words mentioned in Chapter I which deal with world affairs.

Weigh the contrast. The minimum vocabulary increase of a child of four is many times larger than your maximum, and for a single reason: A child knows how to listen for new words; an adult has stopped listening. Without knowing the meaning of "vocabulary improvement," a child conscientiously and unceasingly goes about improving his vocabulary, for he knows, instinctively, that he must learn words if he wishes to be able to communicate his thoughts to, and understand the thoughts of, the people around him. An adult, on the other hand, has reached that point described in the previous chapter at which he knows enough words to communicate adequately with his friends and business associates; hence, to learn more does not seem of critical enough necessity for him to take any great pains at doing so.

Increasing your stock of words is tied up, intimately, with increasing your knowledge, with broadening the horizon of your understanding of the world about you. A word is not an empty combination of syllables. Indeed, it is more, much more, than what its mere definition states it to be. *Psychiatry,* for example, is defined as "the medical study of mental disorders." But when you can recognize and use this word, you show that your knowledge of life is great enough to encompass an understanding that disease can attack the mind as well as the body, and that mental illnesses can be cured just as bodily illnesses are—an understanding, by the way, which the wisest men in the world did not have five hundred years ago.

Phlegmatic is defined, simply, as "dull, sluggish, unemotional." Your recognition and use of the word, however, shows that you realize the vast differences that exist in personality development—a realization, also, that very few people had five hundred years ago.

A child is eager to learn new words because they help explain to him the puzzling world he finds himself in. When he hears a new word for the first time he repeats it—he tastes it on his tongue, listens to the odd sound it makes in his ears. If he understands its meaning, or likes its sound, he is tickled pink, and will probably use the word so continuously that he drives everyone crazy with it.

A child is always asking questions. What is snow? What makes light? Where did the sun come from? Why are you my mother? Now actually, the child is indirectly asking, "What does *snow* mean? What do *light, sun, mother,* mean?" He is adding these words to his vocabulary, and doing so in a way which adults might well copy.

This brings us to a second step in our vocabulary-improvement program.

The first rule, as you remember from Chapter I, was to take note of the new words you meet in your reading. Or, phrased more graphically: Keep your eyes open!

The second rule: Keep your ears open!

When you hear a new word from your friends, or on radio or television, or in the theater or movies, or from the lecture platform, react the way a child does; for, remember, a child is the greatest expert there is at vocabulary improvement. Repeat the word to yourself. Listen to the sound it makes. If possible, ask the person who used that word, "What does it mean?" Logically, the only time you can pose this question is when you hear the word from a friend. Do not expect that the answer you receive will always be accurate. A person can understand the meaning of a word perfectly, can use it correctly, and can still be unable to give a precise definition. You should see lexicographers tearing their hair and gnawing their fingernails to compose a suitable definition even for a simple word. (In fact the simple words are harder to define than the more complex ones. Can you imagine trying to explain *if* to a foreigner whose language you do not speak?) But the accuracy of the definition you receive is not important. You can imagine that a child receives very few exact definitions for the words he inquires about. He learns the words nonetheless. Eventually, by constantly listening to how the words are used, his mind arrives at a suitable understanding of them. And your mind will do the same. The purpose of your question is not so much to discover the meaning of a word as to impress on your mind the need for registering the word. This is another facet of the phenomenon described in Chapter I. The important thing is solely to force the word into your consciousness—the definition will unfold eventually. And even if your friend gives you a totally incorrect definition, nothing is lost in the long run. You will discover the true meaning in time, and the only possible casualty will be your faith in your friend's knowledge.

The suggestion to keep your ears open is merely another weapon in your battle to develop word-consciousness. In the last analysis, the best, if not indeed the only practicable, way to increase your vocabulary is to become alert to the power and richness of words. This attitude, once developed, will mirror a rebirth of intellectual progressiveness and curiosity which will give you power over words and effectiveness in speaking and writing such as merely poring over a dictionary never can hope to.

PUTTING THE METHOD INTO PRACTICE

Yes, you can radically improve your vocabulary merely by listening more acutely and analytically to the words you hear all about you.

Pretend, as an experiment, that you were listening to the people quoted below, and imagine how they might define some of the words they use if you asked them to do so.

1. Conscience can back up the worst kind of conduct as well as the best. The reason for this *ambiguity* is plain. Conscience says: "You ought to do right!" But conscience by itself does not tell us what is right. HARRY EMERSON FOSDICK

If Dr. Fosdick were here now, we could say to him: "What, exactly, does *ambiguity* mean?"

What do you think his answer would be? Perhaps you already know the word—or possibly you think you know it. Or maybe it is entirely unfamiliar to you, in which case you will have to guess at its meaning from its use in Dr. Fosdick's sentence. After all, your understanding of all the new words you hear is based on their use in context.

Write in the following lines a simple definition of *ambiguity* as it is used above. Guess as much as you like from context.———

---

2. Little business is ordinarily less conservative and more venture-some than big business with its huge investments in existing plant equipment. . . . Unless pushed by small enterprises . . . [big business] tends to become static and *immobile*.

PAUL V. MC NUTT

How do you think Mr. McNutt would explain *immobile?*——

---

3. Solitary reading is not so much fun as bookish *conviviality*. There is too little talking about books with others who have read the same books. I say a great pleasure and a great source of fruitfulness comes from reading books with others and discuss-ing them. MORTIMER J. ADLER

If you were Professor Adler, how might you define *conviviality?*

---

4. The era of great fortunes, new or hereditary, is coming to an end; for even the tax-exempt bond, that last citadel of great wealth, the writing on the wall is to be seen, and at any time it may fall into the arms of the *insatiable* tax-collector.

JAMES ROWLAND ANGELL

Conjecture how Mr. Angell would explain *insatiable*.————

---

5. I know of no better place to start in providing security than with a home which belongs to you. If one owns a home, and really owns it, that is if he does not fool himself by having such a mortgage on it that someone else owns it, he has the most valu-able, the most absolute, the most *inviolate* property in the world. . . . For while in times of disturbance a house here or there may be burned, or invaded, or foreclosed, it is just impossible for

any movement, however radical, to take away homes, because they are more than property.   OWEN D. YOUNG

What does *inviolate* mean?————————————————

————————————————————————————————————

6. The future is always *inscrutable,* and nothing is permanent, but we can only act with reason, logic, and experience, plus our idealism translated into will.   DOROTHY THOMPSON

What does *inscrutable* mean?————————————————

————————————————————————————————————

7. Public Opinion, or, to be more accurate, *articulate* Public Opinion, is the most powerful force in the world today.
                                        GEORGE V. DENNY, JR.

What does *articulate* mean?————————————————

————————————————————————————————————

8. There are those who fear the age of *chivalry* . . . is over; as one who rides in the New York subways several times a day, I am sometimes tempted to share in their pessimism.

                                        SANFORD BATES

What does *chivalry* mean?————————————————

————————————————————————————————————

9. Men can be *nominally* free and actually slaves.
                                        ROBERT HUTCHINS

What does *nominally* mean?————————————————

————————————————————————————————————

10. Ours is a civilization of hubbub where *raucous* voices drown out the still, small voice of reason.   FELIX FRANKFURTER

What does *raucous* mean?————————————————

————————————————————————————————————

11. Years ago, when Henry Ford was *fulminating* against woman suffrage in his weekly journal, 'The Dearborn Independent,' . . . [he said] that a woman putting a baby to sleep was a hundred times more attractive than a woman putting an audience to sleep. ERNEST M. HOPKINS

What does *fulminating* mean?————————————

————————————————————————

12. It seems to be the *prerogative* of a democracy to make some errors. J. HOWARD MC GRATH

What does *prerogative* mean?————————————

————————————————————————

By listening carefully to what other people have said, you have made a start at adding as many as a dozen new words to your vocabulary, assuming, of course, that some or all of the words discussed in this chapter are relatively unfamiliar to you.

How well did you puzzle out these words? Here are the correct definitions—check them with your own to see how close you got. Say each word aloud as you read its definition; nothing so helps to fix a new word firmly in your mind as hearing it in your own voice.

1. *ambiguity* (am-bə-GYOO'-ə-tee)—the quality of being able to be understood in two or more different ways. Conscience is *ambiguous* (am-BIG'-yoo-əs) in that it can be understood to back up both good and bad conduct. A statement or sentence is *ambiguous* when its phrasing permits various interpretations. For example: *The farmer told the hired man to take his car out of the garage.* Whose car?

2. *immobile* (im-MŌ'-bəl)—unable to change or move. Big business tends to repeat old patterns, to stay, figuratively, in one place. The noun is *immobility* (im-mō-BIL'-ə-tee).

3. *conviviality* (kən-viv'-ee-AL'-ə-tee)—sociability; tendency to enjoy participation with others in an activity rather than doing something alone. The adjective is *convivial* (kən-VIV'-ee-əl).

4. *insatiable* (in-SAY'-shee-ə-bəl)—never satisfied with what one gets, but always greedily wanting more and more. No matter how much

the tax collector is fed, he is still hungry. The noun is *insatiability* (in-say'-shee-ə-BIL'-ə-tee).

5. *inviolate* (in-VY'-ə-lət)—sacred against violation, seizure, destruction, etc. The noun is *inviolacy* (in-VY'-e-lə-see).

6. *inscrutable* (in-SKROO'-tə-bəl)—beyond understanding, fathoming, or puzzling out; so mysterious as to be utterly incomprehensible or unknowable. The noun is *inscrutability* (in-skroo'-tə-BIL'-ə-tee).

7. *articulate* (ahr-TIK'-yoo-lət)—As used here, the word is an adjective meaning *able to express oneself clearly, forcefully, understandably*, etc. The verb *articulate* (ahr-TIK'-yoo-layt) means *to say or pronounce*.

8. *chivalry* (SHIV'-əl-ree)—courtesy, respect, and protectiveness on the part of men toward women. The adjective is *chivalrous* (SHIV'-əl-rəs).

9. *nominally* (NOM'-ə-nə-lee)—in name only, but not in fact.

10. *raucous* (RAW'-kəs)—harsh and rough in sound.

11. *fulminating* (the first syllable is accented, and rhymes with DULL—FUL'-mə-nay-ting)—shouting denunciations and censure; attacking violently in speech or writing.

12. *prerogative* (prə-ROG'-ə-tiv)—a right or privilege exclusive to a particular group, class, type, etc.

You've made contact with these twelve words as actually used by real people to express their thinking and opinions, you've heard them in your own voice, and you've studied their meanings according to specific contexts.

Now you are ready to discover how successfully you can acquire new words by listening to what other people say.

As an acid test of your learning, I ask you to recall one of the twelve words when I offer you a brief definition and an initial letter.

1. never satisfied (adj.)   i_____
2. able to express oneself (adj.)   a_____
3. in name only (adv.)   n_____
4. special privilege (n.)   p_____
5. motionless, unchanging (adj.)   i_____
6. courteous and attentive to women (adj.)   c_____
7. not to be violated (adj.)   i_____
8. harsh-sounding (adj.)   r_____

9. sociable; enjoying the company of others
   (adj.)   c————
10. to shout denunciations (v.)   f————(against)
11. able to be interpreted in two or more ways
    (adj.)   a————
12. unknowable; unfathomably mysterious
    (adj.)   i————

ANSWERS: 1—insatiable, 2—articulate, 3—nominally, 4—prerogative, 5—immobile, 6—chivalrous, 7—inviolate, 8—raucous, 9—convivial, 10—fulminate, 11—ambiguous, 12—inscrutable.

THREE

~~~~~~~~~~~~~~~~

Putting Books to Work

THE TWO METHODS so far suggested are *indirect* methods of vocabulary improvement. They are the best methods there are, because:

1. They are a natural extension of the principles by which you learned all the words at present in your vocabulary.
2. They can remain in operation almost all the waking hours of your life—whenever you read, or speak, or listen.

They are called *indirect* methods in that they are by-products of intellectual living—by-products usually lost unless habits are developed to save them. Once you have developed these habits, once you have become word-conscious, vocabulary improvement will be as integral and unobtrusive a part of your life as washing your teeth or eating your breakfast or reading the morning paper. And when that time comes, as it will shortly, you will be eager to employ more direct and forthright methods of increasing your word stock.

Would you like to add, in twenty or thirty minutes some evening, a dozen new words to your vocabulary merely by taking two volumes down from your bookshelves? Settle yourself in a comfortable chair at your desk, have your dictionary and *one* other book within reach, arm yourself with a pencil and some scrap paper, and you're ready to begin.

In this method of vocabulary improvement, you use a book purely as a means of finding words which a particular author knows and uses and which you, perhaps, do not. You use your volume not as a reader, but simply as a vocabulary syllabus. There are six simple steps to follow:

1. *Choose a book of the type you ordinarily read for enjoyment or information.* The books you generally enjoy and are accustomed to are always a little higher in vocabulary level than your own speech is. Not too much higher—for then they would prove so difficult that you would not enjoy them. And not inferior in vocabulary level to your own, for then they would be so immature that you would be annoyed by them.

2. Start your reading anywhere at all in your volume.

3. Jot down on the paper beside you any words which are not completely familiar. You will come across a host of these. When you read for meaning alone, the unfamiliar and the slightly familiar words blend with the fully familiar, thus at least partially conveying the thought of the passage before you.

4. Now, examining the way a word is used in its sentence, write as intelligently as you can a definition of that word. You may have to guess wildly in many instances. Go right ahead and guess. Training yourself to figure out the meaning of an unfamiliar word will benefit you immensely in many ways. It will help make your speech more accurate, and you more word-conscious. It will teach you to appreciate the beauty and richness of your language. More, it will help you remember and spur you to use your new words as no mere reference to a dictionary ever can.

5. Stop when you have followed this procedure with twelve words. A dozen new words is all you should attempt to learn at any one

time. Vocabulary improvement is one field in which gluttony hits back quickly. Try to learn too rapidly and all will be confusion. Taper your rate down to a comfortable amount, but learn *frequently* and *intensively* and your vocabulary will keep enlarging beyond your fondest hopes.

6. After you have recorded your own definitions, use the dictionary to check on any misconceptions or inaccuracies. Make the necessary changes. Look your words over. Be certain that you can pronounce them correctly. Say them aloud several times.

HOW THE METHOD WORKS

Let us use as our source book Clifton Fadiman's *Reading I've Liked*.[1] In a prefatory critique on literature called "My Life Is an Open Book: Confessions and Digressions of an Incurable," Fadiman uses words that are vibrant and dynamic. Let us see whether we can find some for ourselves. The material that follows will show you how to organize your own work when you follow this plan. As you come to the blank lines where the definitions belong, write your own. When the answers are given to you later, as they will be, you can check on your ability as an amateur lexicographer.

Is it some constant nervous need for reassurance that makes human beings so alert to point out the capacities that separate them from the lower animals? Thus, we have *rationality* (1) (I am hastily wiping that silly grin off my face), and the beasts do not.

rationality: ————————————————————

————————————————————

We use tools; they don't. Man, some solemn ass once pointed out, is an animal that laughs; animals do not laugh. We have long memories; beasts, save for the proverbial elephants, do not. We make war on each other and have at last, after much trial and error, learned how to exterminate our species, whereas the animals have to depend for their own destruction largely on the mere accidents of nature.

[1] Simon and Schuster.

These are some of the *criteria* (2) which man has set up to demonstrate his superiority.

criteria: —————————————————————————————

—————————————————————————————

Criteria being cheap, I should like to add another. Man, modern man, is a word-making and word-reading animal. Both of us, I who compile this book, you who read it, are engaged in specifically human acts. Writing, and more especially reading, represent habits that we engage in constantly almost from the cradle to the grave. Civilized man is a reader. *Irrevocably* (3) he would appear to be committed to the scanning of small black marks on plane surfaces.

irrevocably: —————————————————————————

—————————————————————————————

It is, when you come to think it over, an odd gesture, like the movement the camera catches of the heads of a tennis audience. But there it is—we are readers, and it's too late to change.

. . . There is no doubt . . . that a fox-slaughtering man makes love in a manner subtly different from the way a non-fox-slaughtering man does. The same must be true of an *omnivorous* (4) reader and a more *desultory* (5) one. In some cases the impulse to read (and reflect on what one has read) dominates completely.

omnivorous: —————————————————————————

desultory: —————————————————————————

—————————————————————————————

Then you get queer but interesting specimens like Robert Burton, who wrote *The Anatomy of Melancholy*. In such a case reading has become a kind of disease, a fascinating, *proliferating* (6) cancer of the mind.

proliferating: ———————————————————————

—————————————————————————————

. . . The *Overall Boys* was and doubtless still is a rousing tale of two devoted brothers, aged five and seven, and their *monosyllabic* (7) adventures on a farm.

monosyllabic: ―――――――――――――――――――――

―――――――――――――――――――――

The style was of transparent *lucidity* (8).

lucidity: ―――――――――――――――――――――

―――――――――――――――――――――

. . . Everything after the *Overall Boys* has been *anticlimax* (9). The same new world can never be discovered twice. One's first book, kiss, home run, is always the best.

anticlimax: ―――――――――――――――――――――

―――――――――――――――――――――

Between the ages of four and ten I read but moderately and with absolute *catholicity* (10).

catholicity: ―――――――――――――――――――――

―――――――――――――――――――――

We had in our household the usual meaningless *miscellany* (11) that accumulates if the parents are not specifically literary.

miscellany: ―――――――――――――――――――――

―――――――――――――――――――――

Now check up on yourself. Here are the answers. See how closely they tally with what you yourself wrote:

1. *rationality* (rash′-ə-NAL′-ə-tee)—quality or state of being able to reason. (adj.: *rational*)

2. *criteria* (kry-TEER′-ee-ə)—standards for judging; rules or tests by which anything is tried in forming a correct judgment respecting it. (singular: *criterion*)

3. *irrevocably* (i-REV′-ə-kəb-lee)—in a manner incapable of being revoked; unalterably. (adj.: *irrevocable*)

4. *omnivorous* (om-NIV′-ər-əs)—devouring or absorbing everything without discrimination (intellectually, as used here).

5. *desultory* (DES'-əl-taw-ree)—aimless; planless.

6. *proliferating* (prō-LIF'-ər-ay-ting)—growing wildly by rapid production of new parts. (verb: *proliferate*)

7. *monosyllabic* (mon'-ə-sil-AB'-ək)—containing just one syllable.

8. *lucidity* (loo-SID'-ə-tee)—clearness; intelligibility. (adj.: *lucid*)

9. *anticlimax* (an-tee-KLY'-maks)—a sentence or passage in which the ideas fall off in dignity or importance at the close; any event, especially the last of a series, that is strikingly or ridiculously less important than one immediately preceding. (adj.: *anticlimactic*)

10. *catholicity* (kath'-ə-LIS'-ə-tee)—state or quality of being liberal or comprehensive in sympathies and understanding. (adj.: *catholic*)

11. *miscellany* (MIS'-ə-lay'-nee)—a mixture of various things; especially a collection of writings on various subjects.

As in the previous chapter, study how these words were used in context, pronounce them aloud several times in order to gain greater ease and familiarity with them, then test your learning by recalling the word that fits each brief definition.

1. without aim, plan, or purpose (adj.)   d―――――
2. one-syllable (adj.)   m―――――
3. unchangeable (adj.)   i―――――
4. collection of writings (n.)   m―――――
5. suddenly dropping in importance (adj.)   a―――――
6. standard of judgment (sing. n.)   c―――――
7. clear, understandable (adj.)   l―――――
8. all-devouring (adj.)   o―――――
9. to grow wildly (v.)   p―――――
10. liberal in sympathies (adj.)   c―――――
11. able to reason (adj.)   r―――――

ANSWERS: 1—desultory, 2—monosyllabic, 3—irrevocable, 4—miscellany, 5—anticlimactic, 6—criterion, 7—lucid, 8—omnivorous, 9—proliferate, 10—catholic, 11—rational.

FOUR

~~~~~~~~~

Browsing Through the Dictionary

IT SHOULD SEEM supremely logical to go to the dictionary as the primary source book in enlarging your vocabulary. It must undoubtedly have occurred to you that if you could simply "read" the dictionary you would eventually know as many words as anyone else in the country. But a device as simple and logical as this must have a catch.

If vocabulary improvement resulted most effectively from a mere perusal of dictionary pages, there would be little point in your reading this section of the book. To my knowledge, no one has successfully "read" the dictionary. Much value, however, can be obtained from an occasional browsing through it. You might make it a habit, whenever you find yourself obliged to look up a particular word, to glance at some of the other interesting words on the same page. Gaining power with words presupposes becoming word-conscious. Obviously a person interested in words will take every available opportunity to increase his knowledge of them, especially when he can do so economically and painlessly. With the dictionary already open in front of you, it seems economically wasteful not to glance at a few of the other entries on the page.

Let us say that you require the exact meaning of *cogitate*. Well, you find it and discover that it means *to think over, to plan*. But wait, don't be so eager to close the book. Just an inch or so above *cogitate,* you will find *cogent,* and as you run your eye over the page, you will meet *cognizance, cognoscenti, coherence, cohesive,* and *coign:* all good usable words with interesting definitions. *An extra moment or two before you put your dictionary away and you've added six fresh words to your vocabulary.*

Some evening you may be tempted to spend ten or fifteen minutes browsing through the dictionary. Give in to that temptation. Open the book at random, and glance through the columns of just one page.

For example, so we can try this activity together, suppose you turn in your dictionary to that page, more or less, containing the following eight words:

octogenarian	odalisque
octoroon	ode
octuple	odium
oculist	odoriferous

Technical or obscure words like *octonary, octroi, oculomotor, odograph,* etc. may also be found on the page—these are deadwood, obviously, and you need pay no further attention to them.

Very common words like *octopus, odd, odor,* etc. will also appear—these you already know and need spend no more time on.

But the eight words listed are interesting and useful and may be partly or completely unfamiliar to you. Read the definitions carefully, pronounce the words aloud, note their derivations, think about them, then check your learning by taking this test.

DIRECTIONS: Without further reference to the dictionary page, write next to each definition the correct word.

1. eightfold   ———————
2. person with one-eighth Negro blood   ———————
3. yielding an odor   ———————
4. state of being hated   ———————
5. eye specialist   ———————
6. a female slave   ———————
7. a person who is between eighty and ninety years of age   ———————
8. a poem suitable for singing   ———————

ANSWERS: 1—octuple, 2—octoroon, 3—odoriferous, 4—odium, 5—oculist, 6—odalisque, 7—octogenarian, 8—ode.

You have either added to your vocabulary, or refamiliarized yourself with eight words. The time consumed was possibly five or ten minutes. Do this only occasionally—say once a month—and you add about a hundred words to your vocabulary in a single year. By this practically painless method, *you are more than doubling the average rate of vocabulary improvement.*

Suppose we try another page in your dictionary, the one containing the words *polytheism* to *pontiff*. Decide for yourself which words are either so technical or so common that they can be ignored, then concentrate on the rest—you'll find ten or so worth considering. As before, study the meanings and derivations, pronounce them aloud, and when you feel in complete mastery, test your learning.

1. red fruit with hard rind   ——————
2. self-important; pretentious   ——————
3. hairdressing   ——————
4. dagger   ——————
5. rounded projection on the front of a saddle   ——————
6. Pope   ——————
7. cloaklike garment worn as a raincoat   ——————
8. belief in many gods   ——————
9. ostentatious display   ——————
10. heavy and unwieldy; figuratively, heavy and dull   ——————

ANSWERS: 1—pomegranate, 2—pompous, 3—pomade, 4—poniard, 5—pommel, 6—pontiff, 7—poncho, 8—polytheism, 9—pomp, 10—ponderous.

Below are the eighteen words discussed in this chapter. Can you match the words with their definitions?

1. polytheism	a. red fruit
2. pomade	b. ostentatious display
3. pomegranate	c. weighty; heavily dull
4. pommel	d. Pope
5. pomp	e. offspring of white and quadroon
6. pompous	f. eye doctor
7. poncho	g. person in his eighties
8. ponderous	h. poem
9. poniard	i. belief in many gods
10. pontiff	j. female harem slave
11. octogenarian	k. self-important
12. octoroon	l. raincoat
13. octuple	m. hatred
14. oculist	n. unguent
15. odalisque	o. eightfold
16. ode	p. having an odor
17. odium	q. dagger
18. odoriferous	r. part of a saddle

ANSWERS: 1—i, 2—n, 3—a, 4—r, 5—b, 6—k, 7—l, 8—c, 9—q, 10—d, 11—g, 12—e, 13—o, 14—f, 15—j, 16—h, 17—m, 18—p.

FIVE

~~~~~~~~~~

Every Word Has a Past

WHEN YOU HAVE BECOME word-conscious, when you have become expert at using your eyes and ears to add to your vocabulary all the new words you hear and see, and when you have learned to enjoy an occasional browsing through the dictionary, your next step in gaining power with words is to begin to dig behind the meaning of a word into its source and history.

To discover, for example, that *misogynist* (woman hater) is made up of three Greek particles (*misein,* hate, *gyne,* woman, and the suffix *-ist,* one who) gives you an understanding of the word that the speaker who merely knows its definition does not possess. You know not only what *misogynist* means—more to the point, you know why it means what it does. You are no longer a word apprentice, who sees only the outside of the machine he's driving; you are a word *technician,* who understands the vast intricacy of all the parts that make it possible for the word to go.

If you wish to increase the richness of your vocabulary, learn to probe beneath the surface. Not, *what* does *silhouette* mean, for example, but *why* that particular combination of syllables for such a meaning? Here's the story: Étienne de Silhouette, finance minister of France before the revolution, agitated for greater austerity in the lives of the nobles, so that money usually spent for luxuries could be donated to the treasury. At this time the blacked-in profile was originated in Paris. It was only logical that the name of the man who asked for a simplifying of life should be attached to a type of portraiture that was reduced to the simplest of lines.

You doubtless know that a *chauvinist* is an overzealous and exaggerated patriot. Do you know the story behind the word? Nicholas Chauvin was a soldier in the army of Napoleon. So fervently and fulsomely did Chauvin praise the emperor that his name became a by-word for the very thing he was doing.

You know that a *prediction* is a statement about the future. But why? Let's take our etymological scalpel and dissect the word. The parts are all from the Latin: *pre-*, before; *dict,* from the verb *dico,* to say or tell; *-ion,* a suffix signifying the act of. Hence, *the act of saying or telling beforehand,* with every letter accounted for.

We have a similar word derived from the Greek: *prophecy.* The parts *pro-, phe,* and *-cy* are almost identical in meaning with the corresponding Latin members found in *prediction.* And in Anglo-Saxon *foretelling* we possess a third word of similar composition: *fore-, tell,* and *-ing.* Yet the three words are slightly different in flavor, are they not? Well, there you have one reason for the fascination of words, for the genius of language.

You cannot deny that *prediction* is a more useful member of your vocabulary once you know its family history. Now, let's explore a bit further into its family tree. Do we know any other words which use the prefix *pre-,* "before"? We've just tripped over one, *pre*fix, a particle fixed to the front (or "before" part) of a word. Some more?

*pre*face—speak beforehand
*pre*fer—bear before something else
*pre*historic—before history
*pre*judice—beforehand judging
*pre*lude—a playing or preparation beforehand

*pre*mature—ripening before the proper time
*pre*natal—before birth
*pre*pare—make ready beforehand
*pre*pay—pay before
*pre*position—a word placed before another word

When you encounter new words, be more than just a *sponge*. Be a *prober*. Find out the *why* of all words; any dictionary will help you. Become an amateur *etymologist;* your vocabulary will then be not only extensive, it will be rich and meaningful.

PUTTING THE METHOD INTO OPERATION

Let's go on a journey of exploration. Let's adventure into new fields of etymology, and discover the reasons behind the meanings of some exciting and useful groups of words.

Caedere in Latin means *to kill* or *to cut*. (The two thoughts *are* somewhat related, aren't they?) This verb is found in English words in one of two spellings—either *-cis* or *-cide*.

Let us try, first, to find six words containing the *-cis* stem. Each dash represents a single letter and the meanings enclosed in parentheses will give direction to your thoughts. Fill in as many as you can before checking with the answers.

1. i-cis— (n.)   (a cutting, especially in surgery)   ————
2. d-cis— (n.)   (a cutting off of argument by reaching a conclusion)   ————
3. p--cis- (adj.)   (cutting, sharp; hence, to the point)   ————
4. c--cis- (adj.)   (cut into pieces; hence, much condensed into little)   ————
5. -cis—— (pl.n.)   (instrument for cutting)   ————
6. c-is-- (n.)   (a metal tool with a cutting edge)   ————

ANSWERS: 1—incision, 2—decision, 3—precise, 4—concise, 5—scissors, 6—chisel.

Now let us try the *-cide* road.

1. s--cide (n.)   (killing of oneself)   ————
2. i-----cide (n.)   (killing of a newborn babe)   ————

3. f——cide (n.)   (killing of one's brother—think of
                     fraternity)   _____

4. p——cide (n.)   (killing of one's father—think of *pa-*
                     ternal)   _____

5. m——cide (n.)   (killing of one's mother—think of *ma-*
                     ternity)   _____

6. r——cide (n.)   (killing of one's king or ruler—think
                     of regal)   _____

7. s——cide (n.)   (killing of one's sister—think of *so-*
                     rority)   _____

ANSWERS: 1—suicide, 2—infanticide, 3—fratricide, 4—patricide, 5—matricide, 6—regicide, 7—sororicide.

From a Latin verb *loquor,* to speak or talk, and its participial form *locutus,* we derive nine expressive English words.

1. loqu—— (adj.)   (talkative)   _____
2. g——loqu— (adj.)   (talking in grand or flowery terms)   _____
3. -loqu— (adj.)   (talking expressively)   _____
4. s—loqu- (n.)   (a talking to oneself)   _____
5. c–loqu- (n.)   (a talking together, or a confer-
                      ence)   _____
6. -locut— (n.)   (the art of talking expressively)   _____
7. ven—loqu— (n.)   (one who talks apparently from his
                      stomach, i.e., one who can throw
                      his voice)   _____
8. circ–locut— (n.)   (a talking around, rather than to
                      the point)   _____
9. mag–loqu— (adj.)   (talking in high-flown terms)   _____

ANSWERS: 1—loquacious, 2—grandiloquent, 3—eloquent, 4—soliloquy, 5—colloquy, 6—elocution, 7—ventriloquist, 8—circumlocution, 9—magniloquent.

Now let us take stock of the words we've discovered.

1. incision (in-SIZH'-ən)
2. decision (də-SIZH'-ən)
3. precise (prə-SICE')
4. concise (kən-SICE')

5. scissors (SIZ'-ərz)
6. chisel (CHIZ'-əl)
7. suicide (SOO'-ə-side)
8. infanticide (in-FAN'-tə-side)
9. fratricide (FRAT'-rə-side)
10. patricide (PAT'-rə-side)
11. matricide (MAT'-rə-side)
12. regicide (REJ'-ə-side)
13. sororicide (sə-ROR'-ə-side)
14. loquacious (lō-KWAY'-shəs)
15. eloquent (EL'-ə-kwənt)
16. grandiloquent (gran-DIL'-ə-kwənt)
17. soliloquy (sə-LIL'-ə-kwee)
18. colloquy (KOL'-ə-kwee)
19. elocution (el-ə-KYOO'-shən)
20. circumlocution (sur'-kəm-lə-KYOO'-shən)
21. magniloquent (mag-NIL'-ə-kwənt)
22. ventriloquist (ven-TRIL'-ə-kwist)

Notice how simple these fairly difficult words seem when we learn what their major parts mean. Note, also, how rich and full those meanings are when the words are more than just combinations of syllables.

Now test your learning. For each definition below, choose the proper word from the preceding list and write it in the space provided.

1. a conference   _____
2. a surgical cutting   _____
3. sister killing   _____
4. condensed   _____
5. self-destruction   _____
6. father killing   _____
7. talking in flowery language   _____
8. a talking around, instead of to the point   _____
9. killing of newborn child   _____
10. brother killing   _____
11. expressive   _____

12. talkative   _____
13. king killing
14. mother killing   _____
15. to the point, exact   _____
16. talking to oneself   _____

ANSWERS: 1—colloquy, 2—incision, 3—sororicide, 4—concise, 5—suicide, 6—patricide, 7—magniloquent, *or* grandiloquent, 8—circumlocution, 9—infanticide, 10—fratricide, 11—eloquent, 12—loquacious, 13—regicide, 14—matricide, 15—precise, 16—soliloquy

SIGNIFICANCE

Words will become more alive for you when you know *why* they mean what they do. Whenever you have occasion to find a word in the dictionary (and to develop real power you should make these occasions frequently), notice its derivation. The etymology of a word is too often neglected by people eager to learn a word's definition, yet ironically its etymology is the most effective key to understanding and remembering what a word means.

SIX

~~~~~~~~~

New Words for Old

POWER WITH WORDS depends as much on the accuracy of your vocabulary as on its size. After you have developed in yourself the habits which will increase and enrich your vocabulary, your next logical interest is in invigorating it.

The one thing which puts pep and vigor into your speech is the ability to choose that correct, that exact word from your store which will most advantageously express your subtlest shade of meaning, your most delicate nuance of thought. A varied, accurate vocabulary permits you to choose *le mot juste,* the one single word which will drive home your message with telling effectiveness.

In how many ways can you express the action of *annoyance?* Note these: *torment, plague, pester, vex, exasperate, irritate, harass,* and *bother.*

Unskilled speakers generally restrict themselves to the first and last words in this list. The richness and variety of the other synonyms are completely lost to their speech. Hence, most of what they say is flat, banal, uninteresting.

How varied is your own vocabulary? Would you like a yardstick to measure its variety and effectiveness?

TEST OF VARIETY

INSTRUCTIONS: Here are five ideas, each of which can be expressed in five different ways. One or two initial letters are offered to guide your thinking. Fill in as many as you can, taking all the time you need. Do not hurry.

GRADING: Each correct answer scores four points. Sixty or better shows adequate variety and power; 40 or less indicates a need for improvement.

1. *To be sad*
a. gr—————
b. m—————
c. de—————
d. la—————
e. be—————

2. *Desire* (noun)
a. wh—————
b. l—————
c. y—————
d. cr—————
e. han—————

3. *Educated*
a. w—————
b. sch—————
c. er—————
d. en—————
e. l—————

4. *A going out*
a. e—————
b. de—————
c. em—————
d. ev—————
e. w—————

5. *Love of self*
a. e—————
b. s—————
c. c—————
d. b—————
e. nar—————

ANSWERS:
1. a—grieve, b—mourn, c—deplore, d—lament, e—bewail.
2. a—whim, b—longing, c—yearning, d—craving, e—hankering.

3. a—well-informed, b—schooled *or* scholarly, c—erudite, d—enlightened, e—learned.
4. a—exit *or* egress, b—departure, c—emergence, d—evacuation, e—withdrawal.
5. a—egoism *or* egotism, b—self-absorption, c—conceit, d—braggadocio *or* boastfulness, e—narcissism.

Being acquainted with synonyms is, of course, only the beginning. Knowing how to choose the *best* word is your next step. Let us take that step together. In the next test you will find three possible descriptive words that can be used for each item to be described. Now, to avoid arguments later, let me admit beforehand that each possibility is perfectly *adequate,* but one of those choices is far and away a more powerful word for its context than the other two. Can you choose powerfully in at least six instances?

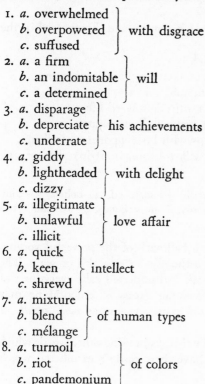

1. *a.* overwhelmed
   b. overpowered } with disgrace
   c. suffused

2. *a.* a firm
   b. an indomitable } will
   c. a determined

3. *a.* disparage
   b. depreciate } his achievements
   c. underrate

4. *a.* giddy
   b. lightheaded } with delight
   c. dizzy

5. *a.* illegitimate
   b. unlawful } love affair
   c. illicit

6. *a.* quick
   b. keen } intellect
   c. shrewd

7. *a.* mixture
   b. blend } of human types
   c. mélange

8. *a.* turmoil
   b. riot } of colors
   c. pandemonium

9. *a.* his competitor ⎫
   b. his contestant ⎬ in love
   c. his rival ⎭
10. *a.* a risky ⎫
    b. a perilous ⎬ business
    c. a dangerous ⎭

ANSWERS: 1—a, 2—b, 3—a, 4—c, 5—c, 6—b, 7—c, 8—b, 9—c, 10—a.

Here is another test that will sharpen your ability to choose the *exact* word. In each of the sentences below, both choices are conceivably correct, but one is definitely, if not always obviously, more powerful. Check the one you prefer:

1. The heat was (oppressive, burdensome).
2. She made a (feverish, fiery) and confused attempt to hide her embarrassment.
3. The thief (grasped, snatched) her purse and disappeared in the crowd.
4. He (gulped, bolted) his food.
5. That is a perfectly (mediocre, commonplace) occurrence.
6. That is a (noteworthy, memorable) fact.
7. You have a (gloomy, glum) attitude toward life.
8. The (superfluous, needless) water will evaporate.
9. The policeman came to grips with his (opponent, assailant).
10. Our production this year will (outrun, outstrip) that of any year in our history.

ANSWERS: 1—oppressive, 2—feverish, 3—snatched, 4—bolted, 5—commonplace, 6—noteworthy, 7—gloomy, 8—superfluous, 9—assailant, 10—outstrip.

There is no more distinctive hallmark of the powerful vocabulary than the ability to express a thought in a wealth of ways. The speaker whose vocabulary is weak and underfed calls everything of reduced size *small* or *little,* or in an excess of emotion he may actually achieve such heights of expressiveness as *very small,* or *very, very, little!*

You may wonder what value there is in using other words which mean *small* or *little* when we have these easily remembered words always so close at hand. One answer might be that one should not use the same words over and over again; excessive repetition makes for boredom. But that answer is not only inadequate; it is also inaccurate, and, to an intelligent reader, unsatisfying. For a moment of thought will convince you that we repeat many useful words to the point where, even if they were of the hardest steel, they'd show wear around the edges in a busy day's conversation. It is scarcely possible to talk for five minutes without using *the* and *it* and *I* and *see* a dozen or more times. Just go back over this page and count the number of times the words *of* and *if* and *word* and *is* and *are* appear. If there is any boredom on this page it is certain that the fault does not lie with the quintet of words italicized in the previous sentence.

No, there is a more intelligent and credible reason for knowing more than two words to describe reduced size. That reason is that *little* and *small* are *dead* words. They express a thought without flavoring it. Note the lack of emotion in the phrases in column *A* below, and the wealth of interest in the synonymous phrases in column *B*.

A	*B*
a *small* babe	a *wee* babe
a *small* tree	a *stunted* tree
small in stature	*puny* in stature
of *small* size	of *pigmy* size
a *small* intellect	a *Lilliputian* intellect
a *small* model	a *miniature* model
a *little* woman	a *petite* woman
small means	*scanty* means
small in usefulness	*limited* in usefulness
a *small* wardrobe	a *meager* wardrobe

The adjectives in the second column are *picture* words: they are forceful because they appeal to your ears, and eyes, and heart, not to your intellect alone. With a fund of synonyms at your command, your words can possess *warmth* and *color* and *depth* as well as meaning. They can contain *lights* and *shadows* instead of being of uniform dullness. Briefly, they can breathe life and vigor into your speech. And you have only to refer once again to column *B* to realize that they can do all these things despite the fact that few of them contain more than two or three syllables.

Of all the aspects of your vocabulary worth developing, this is the most valuable. So let's go right on with our exercises. Below you will find five "dead" or "intellectual" words. Can you fill in a "live," or "picture" synonym for each?

1. *to wrap*   4. *secret* (adj.)

_____   _____
_____   _____
_____   _____

2. *unusual*   5. *to take hold*

_____   _____
_____   _____
_____   _____

3. *to say again*   6. *to see*

_____   _____
_____   _____
_____   _____
_____   _____

ANSWERS: 1. to envelop, wind, muffle, swathe, enfold, cloak, inclose.

2. rare, uncommon, infrequent, scarce, sparse, sporadic, occasional, exceptional, singular, extraordinary.

3. repeat, reiterate, echo, re-echo, harp on, hammer, recapitulate, reword, retell, reproduce, duplicate.

4. concealed, hidden, confidential, unrevealed, undisclosed, untold, privy, private, unknown, veiled, screened, masked, cloaked, disguised, enigmatic, cryptic, occult, mysterious.

5. to seize, grasp, snatch, grab, clutch.

6. to mark, note, notice, perceive, apprehend, comprehend, realize, behold, discern.

SEVEN

~~~~~~~~~~~~~

Putting Magazines to Work

BOILED DOWN to its essentials, vocabulary improvement is nothing more than being on the alert for new words that you can see and hear all around you. The person whose ears and eyes bring him only words that he already knows has an absolutely stagnant vocabulary.

But there are very few literate people today in such a fix. Radio and television and the movies and books and newspapers and magazines are too common and important a part of American life for any citizen to be reduced to intellectual starvation. Too often, however, as one reads books and periodicals, or listens to the radio or to lectures, he lets effective words do no more than flavor the thought of the writer or speaker. He makes no conscious effort to let these words influence his mind. For it is quite possible, as has so often been stated in these chapters, to read a page out of a book or magazine, and, despite half a dozen unfamiliar words in it, to get enough of the thought to go on to the next page.

Now I do not for a moment advocate putting down your reading matter and scurrying to your dictionary every time you meet a new or puzzling word. Getting what you can out of context, letting your mind linger for a few seconds on the new words so that you will recognize them at your next encounter, is the most intelligent and natural way to improve your vocabulary with books and magazines as aids. However, occasionally making a direct and serious effort to add words quickly will appeal to those readers who wish to do more than let nature take its course.

Written language is made up entirely of words: the more accurate your understanding of these words, the more sustenance you can get from them. Just as you will absorb more vitamins from food properly cooked, so you will gain more mental stimulation from words properly understood.

The very first time you meet *panacea, nostrum,* and *plethora* in your reading, your reaction to them can scarcely be more than a weak one. But if you find these words in a magazine, as I shall prove in a moment that you do, it will take you less than a second to underline them. Then go right on with your reading—the primary purpose of a page of print is to communicate a message, not to increase your vocabulary. The fact is, nevertheless, that you can train yourself to derive a secondary benefit, in addition to information or entertainment, from periodicals.

Magazines, rather than any other type of printed matter, are the suggested aids in this chapter because on the one hand they are less impermanent than newspapers, and on the other you will be less reluctant to mark them up than you would a book.

When you're ready to discard the magazine because you've read everything of interest in it, turn back to those pages in which you've underlined the words with which you wish to become better acquainted. Haul out your dictionary. Look up the first word, find the definition that fits the context in which you discovered the word, then read over carefully the sentence in which it occurred. (Notice, by the way, how the sentence now packs a greater wallop than it did when one of its words was vague and almost meaningless.) Then go on, in similar fashion, with the other words you've underlined.

If you're very methodical, you may wish to copy the definitions in the margin of the page. This is not strictly necessary, but will be helpful to people who are particularly eye-minded.

After you've followed these suggestions a few times, you'll be startled to discover that:

1. Your reading habits will be revolutionized. You will be amazed at how much more critically you have learned to peruse a page of print.
2. Words that you have looked up will begin to catch your eye whenever you read. For a time it will seem that you and half a dozen writers discovered a word simultaneously, so frequently and in so many different places will you see it. What is actually happening, of course, is that your mind is now psychologically set toward that word. Where previously your eye and brain would have skipped over it negligently, you now pause to greet a familiar face. The feeling of warmth and confidence this will give you is practically indescribable.
3. As you continue meeting the word and it becomes more and more a part of your thinking processes, you will one day begin to use it in your own speech and writing. That will be a great day, for the word has now passed from your recognition into your functional vocabulary.

Let us test the truth of some of the statements made above. Note these excerpts from *Newsweek*:

In the summer of 1932 an economic *panacea* (1) called Technocracy swept the country like gin rummy. In the depths of its depression the United States needed a *nostrum* (2), and the Technocrats' offer of plenty for all, based on integrated production by those between the ages of 21 and 45, had a greater appeal to Americans than foreign isms.

. . . The *plethora* (3) of pictures with international settings is a boon to linguistic actors, with such varied accents as Turkish, Polynesian, Hindu, Chinese, Japanese, and French in demand.

And these from an article by Robert and Leona Train Rienow in the *Saturday Review*.

Our awe of bureaucracy is suggested by the fanatic way in which almost all the citizens in the vicinity of our country home at Selkirk, New York, pause at high noon to *synchronize* (4) their watches with the shriek of the noon whistle at the railway yards. Few of them know that the man who daily sets off that whistle does so by referring to a dollar watch he has carried for some thirty years.

Our *credulity* (5) as a nation is boundless. Let the Forest Service put its blessing on the term "multiple use" of forest land and the phrase becomes sacred and a cover for any abuse. Because we cherish the image of the Park Service as a dedicated part of this awesome governmental apparatus most of us never question the construction of noisy marinas in national parks, or of wide super-highways that scar natural beauties.

We can, in the first place, make an immediate change in our attitude toward officials. They are not supermen. They are not *omniscient* (6).

Now consider the applicable meanings and derivation of the six italicized words:

1. *panacea* (pan-ə-SEE′-ə)—a cure-all; a so-called remedy for all ills, evils, or diseases. From Greek *pan,* all, and *akeisthai,* to cure.
2. *nostrum* (NOS′-trəm)—a pet remedy, cure, plan, or scheme to solve a political or social problem. From the Latin pronoun meaning *ours,* since the advocate is, in a sense, calling it *our* remedy—originally the word referred to a patent medicine, and then, disparagingly, to a quack medicine, and today it is always used derogatively.
3. *plethora* (PLETH′-ər-ə)—excess, overabundance. From Greek *plethos,* fullness.
4. *synchronize* (SIN′-krə-nize)—to cause to show the same time, as a watch. From Greek *chronos,* time, and *syn-,* together.
5. *credulity* (krə-JOO′-lə-tee)—a tendency to believe too easily; complete lack of doubt, suspicion, or skepticism; gullibility. From Latin *credere,* to believe.
6. *omniscient* (om-NISH′-ənt)—all-knowing, knowing everything. From Latin *omnis,* all, and *scire,* to know.

Read the sentences from *Newsweek* and *Saturday Review* once again. Note how much clearer and more alive and significant they are now that the difficult words are familiar to you.

Tonight, when you turn to a magazine for a somewhat lighter

form of reading than this book affords, keep your pencil close at hand. I am going to donate the next page to your effort. Don't waste it. On that page, jot down the words you learn tonight from *The New Yorker, Life, Time, Harper's, The Atlantic,* or whatever your literary tastes lead you to. Jot them down after you've referred to the dictionary for applicable meaning and for etymology; then close the dictionary and try defining the words in your own language. Through this procedure you'll gain such close contact with your new words that they'll become strong, active additions to your personal vocabulary.

Interesting words (with meanings) from

_____

(Name of magazine)

1.

2.

3.

4.

5.

6.

EIGHT

~~~~~~~~~~~~~~~~

New Words:
Where to Find Them

POPULAR PERIODICALS are a prolific source of interesting words.

Let us pick up some random copies of *The New Yorker*. A constant source of delight to readers of this magazine is the Talk of the Town department, the items of which owe their piquant freshness and puckish humor to its editor's uncanny flair for words. The reader's enjoyment is in direct proportion, of course, to his full understanding of the paragraphs before him—and that understanding is based, in turn, on the richness and accuracy of his vocabulary.

You will find below some sentences from the Talk of the Town which will give you an opportunity of testing your own appreciation of subtle shades of meaning. Check *a, b,* or *c,* according to which definition you think most closely fits the italicized word.

1. Mr. Kao *disabused* his little class of announcers (and us) of the comic-strip notion that the Chinese language depends so much on inflections that circumstances beyond the speaker's control can turn a compliment into a fighting insult.
   a. undeceived *b.* scolded *c.* confused

2. Mr. Kao pointed out that he was really more a guest of New York than a New Yorker, and that this therefore constituted a *bilingual* pun.
   a. subtle *b.* two-language *c.* significant

3. We're pleased to report that this affair was conducted without *rancor* and that the losers are muddling through with their old sinks and a can of Drano.
   a. vehement ill will *b.* error *c.* fear

4. On his own time, he did a mural for the main floor, which twenty or thirty of the partners remarked on favorably, and the firm has rented him a studio on the fifty-eighth floor at 70 Pine and given him *carte blanche* to decorate the whole place; they gave him a raise, too.
   a. a charge account *b.* freedom to do as one wishes
   c. freedom from other responsibilities

5. We wouldn't have been so *complacent* if we'd known where all this was leading.
   a. self-satisfied *b.* worried *c.* delighted

6. The jumbo historical novel would seem, at first glance, to have reached something of an *impasse.*
   a. lack of popularity *b.* maximum size
   c. predicament affording no escape

7. Rushing into print with the week's hottest *exposé,* we would report that you can buy airplane bomb sights down on Canal Street.
   a. scoop *b.* uncensored news
   c. an exposure of something discreditable

8. A young lady social worker from Boston recently joined the staff of the New York Hospital, and was given a small blue identification card with her name and address on it. This proved of no help to her when she tried to cash her first pay check at a bank, and since she had no driver's license, she was in danger of starving to death for lack of liquid funds. Then, resourcefully, she

neatly printed six *arbitrary* numerals along the top of her identification card.
   a. consecutive   *b.* chosen by caprice or whim   *c.* imaginary
9. After that, her checks were cashed without any ado, the bank
   tellers dutifully copying down the *bogus* numerals.
   a. printed   *b.* useless   *c.* false
10. She likes to think of her six figures' being copied by the central
    bank clerk, punched into monster I.B.M. machines, and *im-
    mortalized* on magnetic tape.
    a. transcribed   *b.* set down for all time
    c. given special importance

ANSWERS: 1—a, 2—b, 3—a, 4—b, 5—a, 6—c, 7—c, 8—b, 9—c, 10—b.

Let us assume that you came through this first test fairly successfully (say at least seven correct choices), and that you are ready
for a more challenging problem. What I ask you now requires a
measure of linguistic sophistication and will demand a more active
role in regard to magazine words than you've played so far.

Once more I shall present you with random quotations from
the Talk of the Town. Will you do your best patiently and
thoughtfully to write a concise, clear definition of each *italicized*
word? When you compare your results with those at the end of the
chapter, consider yourself verbally skillful if your definitions contain some of the elements in the ones offered. Work faithfully and
honestly, checking with the answers only after completing the test.
This activity has great benefit in making you conscious of the value
and importance of choosing your words carefully.

We live in a time of signs and wonders, of vast mystical *por-
tents* (1) that change the very sky above our heads. A few days ago a

portent (PAWR′-tent) means: ─────────────────────────

──

large and unusually *virulent* (2) spot appeared on the face of the
virulent (VIR′-ə-lənt) means: ─────────────────────────

──

sun, disrupting radio communication, scrambling telephone calls, turning the aurora borealis on and off, and in general disorganizing a *terrestrial* (3) life that wasn't too orderly in the first place. A few

terrestrial (tə-RES'-tree-əl) means: —————————————
——

nights ago there was blood on the moon, a moon like the one that should have warned Caesar centuries before, now lighting a world in which the techniques of assassination have been considerably improved. We incline to feel that these heavenly signs have some meaning greater than what the *prosy* (4) scientists tell us of lunar eclipses

prosy (PRŌ-zee) means: ——————————————————
——

and *magnetic* (5) particles in space. Coming to work this morning

magnetic (mag-NET'-ək) means: ————————————————
——

we took a chance and asked the elevator boy what he made of them.
   "Just means Market Wise finished eighth at Hialeah," he said, *leering* (6) at us like envious Casca.

leer means: ————————————————————————————
——

   Let us turn now to an article from *The Saturday Review,* "Cauldron of Creativity," by David Boroff, from which the first two paragraphs are reprinted with permission.

   With appropriate irony, Bennington College, where the most popular course is Myth, Ritual, and Literature (reduced in local shorthand to Myth-Rit-Lit), is itself the victim of *luxuriant* (7)

luxuriant (lug-ZHŎOR'-ee-ənt) means: ———————————
——

myths. According to tenacious folklore, Bennington is a self-expression boudoir, a *bucolic* (8) outpost of Greenwich Village where *bucolic* (byoo-KOL′-ək) means: ————————————

————————————————————————

spoiled daughters of the rich perform modern dance exercises on the greensward, daub paint with *anarchic* (9) glee, and experiment

anarchic (an-AHR′-kək) means: ————————————

————————————————————————

with sex in their quest of self-fulfillment.

Generally overlooked in this riot of fancy is that Bennington College is the setting for unremittingly hard work where more than two-thirds of the students major in social science and literature, not the arts. If the tuition is steep ($3,450 for all expenses, probably the highest of any four-year college in the country), one-third of all students receive some financial aid, and the trappings of upper-class living are singularly absent from Bennington's *austere* (10) living quarters and playing fields.

austere (aw-STEER′) means: ————————————

————————————————————————

ANSWERS: 1. *portent*—something that warns of coming events, often of future misfortunes. From a Latin verb meaning "stretch forth."
2. *virulent*—harmful, injurious. From Latin *virus*, "poison."
3. *terrestrial*—having to do with, living on, referring to, etc. the earth as a planet. From Latin *terra*, "earth."
4. *prosy*—unimaginative, uninspired, unglamorous, dull, etc.
5. *magnetic*—able to attract iron, steel, etc. to itself.
6. *leer*—to look (at) in a sly, sidelong, sometimes lustful, malicious, triumphant, or gloating manner.
7. *luxuriant*—tending to rich and exaggerated invention or imagination. From the Latin verb *luxuriare*, "to be too fruitful, grow too richly."
8. *bucolic*—rural, rustic; having the characteristics of the country rather than the city. Generally used somewhat depreciatively or condescendingly. From the Greek *boukolos*, "herdsman," which itself comes originally from *bous*, "ox."
9. *anarchic*—totally lawless, uncontrolled, disorganized; devoid of order, method, rule, system, etc. From Greek *an-*, "without," plus *archos*, "leader."

10. *austere*—severely simple, without luxuries, ornamentation, etc. From Greek *austeros,* "harsh."

Whatever success you achieved in this test is helping you gain power over words. The important fact is not the correctness of your definitions so much as the value and discipline you gained from writing them.

And now a final test of your learning power in this chapter. You have, supposedly, either added to your vocabulary or clarified in your mind the meanings of the twenty words in this chapter. Can you choose from column *B* below the definition or synonym which fits each of those words in column *A?*

	A		*B*
1.	arbitrary	*a.*	bitterness
2.	complacent	*b.*	cause to endure forever
3.	impasse	*c.*	a bringing to light of something bad
4.	exposé	*d.*	excessively rich
5.	bogus	*e.*	ominous sign
6.	disabuse	*f.*	earthy
7.	bilingual	*g.*	malevolent
8.	rancor	*h.*	make free from error
9.	carte blanche	*i.*	capricious
10.	immortalize	*j.*	attractive
11.	luxuriant	*k.*	of two languages
12.	portent	*l.*	lecherous look
13.	virulent	*m.*	blind alley
14.	terrestrial	*n.*	self-satisfied
15.	prosy	*o.*	lawless, uncontrolled
16.	magnetic	*p.*	false
17.	leer	*q.*	severely simple
18.	bucolic	*r.*	freedom of action
19.	anarchic	*s.*	dull
20.	austere	*t.*	rustic, countrylike

ANSWERS: 1—i, 2—n, 3—m, 4—c, 5—p, 6—h, 7—k, 8—a, 9—r, 10—b, 11—d, 12—e, 13—g, 14—f, 15—s, 16—j, 17—l, 18—t, 19—o, 20—q.

Your word sense is developing acceptably if you matched sixteen or more items correctly.

Don't let your magazines go to waste. People with excellent vocabularies write for you every time you open a periodical. Your own vocabulary can be developed to an equal state if you will let it. Indeed, your own word sense can eventually surpass that of any *single* writer, for you will be taking the best from a host of writers and combining all the elements in one single vocabulary—your own!

N I N E

A New Way to Exercise

AS WE NEAR the end of our plan for vocabulary improvement, let us review certain principles which should motivate your work:

1. The number of words you add to your vocabulary, though important, is less vital than your *comparative* rate of improvement. If in previous years you have been in the habit of increasing your vocabulary by some twenty-five words annually (the general rate for adults) and if this year you add some five hundred or more words as a result of the suggestions in these pages, then your rate of improvement has risen 2,000 percent. It is not difficult to imagine how this sudden acceleration of tempo will cause a radical change in your intellectual atmosphere, in the way you think and speak. By analogy, the carpenter with a full and increasing kit of tools is going to work more efficiently than the fellow who must rely solely on a hammer and saw. The machinist with a thousand dollars' worth of fine precision instruments available to him will turn out a better

64

product than a man of the same skill who must rely on a handful of monkey wrenches.

2. These changes in intellectual atmosphere will be due not so much to the new words that you begin to recognize and use as to the fact that you are becoming alert to the nuances and values of all words. Do not think for a moment that the speaker with a rich and healthy vocabulary necessarily uses long and incomprehensible words. Quite the contrary. You will notice, as your own vocabulary refines, that you tend to avoid cumbersome words as so much intellectual deadwood (though, of course, you'll understand them when you see them in print) and choose simpler words which are more pointed and forceful. The most valuable effect that an improved vocabulary can have on your mind and speech is the sharpening of the faculty of discrimination.

3. Your work in this book will incidentally make you conversant with many words about whose existence you may once have been unaware. Note, however, that this section is not designed solely to *increase* your vocabulary (that is a fortunate incidental value) but also to make you a *master* of words, to give you a feeling of supreme self-confidence in spoken and written language.

And so you will be asked to go through a kind of muscle-building exercise in this chapter. You know how muscles atrophy with disuse but flourish with exercise? Let us, speaking metaphorically, refer to your vocabulary as a "muscle." By exercising it well and frequently you can make it strong and supple.

These exercises will demand of you an intensive search in your mind for simple words. This is harder than it may at first sound, and for a while you may be dismayed to discover how "creaky" your vocabulary "muscle" is. For it takes a fluent, sophisticated speaker to be able to dart quickly into the recesses of his mind and emerge quickly with the words that are buried there. But as you keep exercising you will feel new power and tone in your vocabulary, so take a deep breath, keep your pencil handy, and begin:

I. There are at least fifteen common words ending in -*aver*. How many can you think of? A hint is offered in each instance to guide your thinking, and the words are arranged in alphabetical order.

1. ————aver (refers to courage)
2. ————aver (caused by death)
3. ————aver (he's wishing)
4. ————aver (he corrupts)
5. ————aver (he cuts into the surface)
6. ————aver (he subjugates)
7. ————aver (heavy and serious; in fact, even more so)
8. ————aver (it covers the roadway)
9. ————aver (it's tremulous, or contains trills)
10. ————aver (he's mad)
11. ————aver (he's thrifty)
12. ————aver (he must have a beard)
13. ————aver (he sells people; pronounced another way, it's a synonym of *drool*)
14. ————aver (smoother, slicker)
15. ————aver (be indecisive)

Percentage correct

———————

7% for each answer

II. Let us probe in your mind for words ending in *-ensive*. The definition is offered to give direction to your thoughts. Try to get at least five right. *The initial letters of your answers will be in alphabetical order.*

1. ————ensive (fearful)
2. ————ensive (full, complete)
3. ————ensive (warding off attack)
4. ————ensive (costly)
5. ————ensive (covering much ground)
6. ————ensive (causing no annoyance)
7. ————ensive (to an extreme degree)
8. ————ensive (attacking; unpleasant)

Percentage correct

———————

12½% for each answer

The criterion of your success with this method of vocabulary improvement is *progress in proportion*. In each test, as your introspective faculty becomes sharper, the percentage of correct answers should increase. If in Test I you scored 42%, Test II should give you a score a little higher, and Test III should continue that upward swing.

III. Now let us look for one-syllable words ending in *-ink*. There are fifteen common ones. Try for nine at least.

1. ————ink	6. ————ink	11. ————ink
2. ————ink	7. ————ink	12. ————ink
3. ————ink	8. ————ink	13. ————ink
4. ————ink	9. ————ink	14. ————ink
5. ————ink	10. ————ink	15. ————ink

Percentage correct

———————

7% for each answer

IV. Now think of words ending in *-ture*. Two initial letters are offered to help you. Try for ten out of seventeen.

1. ar————ture	10. im————ture
2. ca————ture	11. li————ture
3. ca————ture	12. mi————ture
4. co————ture	13. ov————ture
5. cu————ture	14. po————ture
6. di————ture	15. pr————ture
7. ex————ture	16. si————ture
8. fu————ture	17. te————ture
9. ga————ture	

Percentage correct

———————

6% for each answer

V. By adding *one* or *two* letters only, write words ending in *-air* and *-are* to fit the following hints. Try for ten or more.

1. ————air (sit)	7. ————air (up and
2. ————air (weather)	down)
3. ————air (liking, taste)	8. ————are (conscious)
4. ————air (on a head)	9. ————are (caution)
5. ————air (for animals)	10. ————are (naked)
6. ————air (in poker)	11. ————are (on a horn)

12. ———————are (only a
fool takes one)

13. ———————are (on a
train)

14. ———————are (strong
light)

15. ———————are (and the
tortoise)

16. ———————are (the old
gray one)

17. ———————are (cowards
do this easily)

Percentage correct

_____

6% for each answer

VI. Next to each word, write another of *similar* meaning, beginning with the letter *l*. Try for nineteen or more.

  1. work   l———————
  2. varnish   l———————
  3. woman   l———————
  4. loiterer   l———————
  5. pool   l———————
  6. sheep   l———————
  7. crippled   l———————
  8. spear   l———————
  9. earth   l———————
 10. speech   l———————
 11. thin   l———————
 12. robbery   l———————
 13. big   l———————

 14. rope   l———————
 15. whip   l———————
 16. soap   l———————
 17. praise   l———————
 18. lawful   l———————
 19. to place   l———————
 20. to drip   l———————
 21. go   l———————
 22. glass   l———————
 23. permit   l———————
 24. flat   l———————
 25. generous   l———————

Percentage correct

_____

4% for each answer

VII. After the six exercises you've just finished, your vocabulary
"muscle" should have gained enough strength to pull you
through this final difficult exercise. Write next to each word
another of *opposite* meaning, still starting with the letter *l*.
Try for twelve or more.

  1. slavery   l———————
  2. truth   l———————
  3. death   l———————

  4. dark   l———————
  5. solid   l———————
  6. figuratively l———————

7. big	l_____	14. misfortune	l_____
8. to open	l_____	15. sanity	l_____
9. low	l_____	16. plain	l_____
10. senseless	l_____	17. more	l_____
11. short	l_____	18. follow	l_____
12. find	l_____	19. idleness	l_____
13. hate	l_____	20. water	l_____

Percentage correct

_____

5% for each answer

ANSWERS: I. 1—braver, 2—cadaver, 3—craver, 4—depraver, 5—engraver, 6—enslaver, 7—graver, 8—paver, 9—quaver, 10—raver, 11—saver, 12—shaver, 13—slaver, 14—suaver, 15—waver.

II. 1—apprehensive, 2—comprehensive, 3—defensive, 4—expensive, 5—extensive, 6—inoffensive, 7—intensive, 8—offensive.

III. blink, brink, chink, clink, drink, link, mink, pink, rink, shrink, sink, slink, stink, think, wink.

IV. 1—armature, 2—candidature, 3—caricature, 4—comfiture, 5—curvature, 6—discomfiture, 7—expenditure, 8—furniture, 9—garniture, 10—immature, 11—literature, 12—miniature, 13—overture, 14—portraiture, 15—premature, 16—signature, 17—temperature, texture.

V. 1—chair, 2—fair, 3—flair, 4—hair, 5—lair, 6—pair, 7—stair, 8—aware, 9—care, 10—bare, 11—blare, 12—dare, 13—fare, 14—glare, 15—hare, 16—mare, 17—scare.

VI. 1—labor, 2—lacquer, 3—lady, 4—laggard *or* loafer, 5—lake *or* lagoon, 6—lamb, 7—lame, 8—lance, 9—land *or* loam, 10—language, lecture, *or* linguistics, 11—lanky *or* lean, 12—larceny *or* looting, 13—large, 14—lariat *or* lasso, 15—lash, 16—lather, 17—laud, 18—legal *or* legitimate, 19—lay, 20—leak, 21—leave, 22—lens, 23—let, 24—level, 25—liberal *or* lavish.

VII. 1—liberty, 2—lie, 3—life, 4—light, 5—liquid, 6—literally, 7—little, 8—lock, 9—lofty *or* loud, 10—logical, 11—long, 12—lose, 13—love, 14—luck, 15—lunacy, 16—luxurious, 17—less, 18—lead, 19—labor, 20—land.

This chapter has given you practice in calling words forth from your mind when you want them. It is doubtful if a single word required in these pages was unfamiliar to you. Your problem was not to know difficult or obscure terms, but to dart into the recesses of your vocabulary and haul out the one simple word which the occasion required.

If you were uniformly successful, with a constantly rising score, you may feel quite cheerful about your word aptitude. If, on the other hand, you found the going rough, do not despair— the exercise was of great value to you and, in combination with other exercises to come later, will make you a more fluent, more confident speaker. Win or lose, keep at it. Nothing can so sharpen your word skill as actually working and struggling with and pitting your wits against words.

TEN

~~~~~~~~~~

New Words:
Making Them Stick

THIS CHAPTER is organized on the principle of "gradual unfolding." The theory was advanced in Chapter I, you will recall, that once you have learned to be on the alert for any new word which comes up in your reading, your eye will catch that word at each successive encounter, and, more important, your mind will gradually grasp its meaning, use, and emotional flavor.

The drills in these pages will give you the opportunity of actively and immediately putting that theory into practice; of testing, functionally, whether it is a principle that will work for you.

In each of the following sections (there are ten of them) you will find five words and five incomplete sentences into each of which one of the words will fit. Match words to sentences as intelligently as you can, then check with the answers. If you find

71

that you have been trying to push some square pegs into round holes, don't be alarmed. Any errors you make and then correct will serve to help your mind become more and more familiar with words that once may have been completely unknown to you.

In these sections you will meet the same words over and over again; and the meaning, use, and flavor of the words will gradually unfold from meeting to meeting.

I.

a. phlegmatic (fleg-MAT′-ək)
b. misanthrope (MIS′-ən-thrope)
c. ingenious (in-JEEN′-yəs)
d. malinger (mə-LING′-gər)
e. lucrative (LOO′-krə-tiv)

1. For the few top names in the field, writing is a —————— profession.
2. His misfortunes have made a —————— of him.
3. Sally is too —————— to be worried over so small a matter.
4. There is a tendency in all of us to —————— when there is a hard job to do.
5. He invented a truly —————— system for predicting the ups and downs of the stock market.

ANSWERS: 1—e, 2—b, 3—a, 4—d, 5—c.

II.

a. phlegmatic (fleg-MAT′-ək)
b. misanthropy (mə-SAN′-thrə-pee)
c. erudite (ER′-ə-dite)
d. garrulous (GĂR′-ə-ləs)
e. malignant (mə-LIG′-nənt)

1. He was a —————— old man, and listening to his unceasing flow of meaningless words was no pleasure.
2. His —————— attitude to the world has left him friendless.
3. Professor Clark delivered an interesting and —————— lecture on Elizabethan literature.
4. He is a —————— person, content to watch the world go by.

5. Warm, affectionate people can never quite understand the ———— of the few who thoroughly hate mankind.

ANSWERS: 1—d, 2—e, 3—c, 4—a, 5—b.

III.

a. ingenuity (in-jə-NOO′-ə-tee)
b. malingerer (mə-LING′-gər-ər)
c. erudition (er-ə-DISH′-ən)
d. gullible (GUL′-ə-bəl)
e. enervating (EN′-ər-vayt-ing)

1. The doctor spent a completely ———— vigil at the sick man's bedside.
2. His numerous degrees testify to his great ————.
3. I do not believe you were really ill; I choose to think that you are a ————.
4. The ———— with which a modern electronic computer is built is truly amazing.
5. You are surely not ———— enough to believe that nonsense.

ANSWERS: 1—e, 2—c, 3—b, 4—a, 5—d.

IV.

a. acumen (ə-KYOO′-mən)
b. dudgeon (DUDJ′-ən)
c. redolent (RED′-ə-lənt)
d. enervation (en-ər-VAY′-shən)
e. garrulity (gə-ROO′-lə-tee)

1. He is a man of such great ———— that your most ingenious plan to deceive him will surely fail.
2. I cannot stand his ————; he is the most windy and tiresome talker I have ever met.
3. He was overcome with ———— after two successive nights of sleeplessness.
4. Your plan is ———— of all the cheap trickery of the strong-arm gangster.
5. After his public humiliation, he left in high ————.

ANSWERS: 1—a, 2—e, 3—d, 4—c, 5—b.

V.

a. vindictive (vin-DIK'-tiv)
b. caprice (kə-PREECE')
c. querulous (KWER'-ə-ləs)
d. gullibility (gul'-ə-BIL'-ə-tee)
e. lucrative (LOO'-krə-tiv)

1. He left a ———— job to work for the government.
2. He has such a reputation for ———— that his friends tease him unmercifully.
3. It was just a moment's ————, but see the havoc it wrought.
4. In a ———— tone she bitterly assailed her misfortune.
5. She feels ———— enough to go to any lengths to avenge the insult.

ANSWERS: 1—e, 2—d, 3—b, 4—c, 5—a.

VI.

a. vicarious (vy-KAIR'-ee-əs)
b. panorama (pan-ə-RAH'-mə)
c. malignantly (mə-LIG'-nənt-lee)
d. acumen (ə-KYOO'-mən)
e. dudgeon (DUDJ'-ən)

1. The disgruntled member left the meeting in great ————.
2. He experiences ———— delight when he reads about other people's triumphs.
3. Below him stretched a vast ———— of rolling wheat fields.
4. His eyes glowed ———— as he told his story.
5. Men of ———— have no difficulty carving out lucrative careers for themselves.

ANSWERS: 1—e, 2—a, 3—b, 4—c, 5—d.

VII.

a. redolent (RED'-ə-lənt)
b. vindictiveness (vin-DIK'-tiv-nəs)
c. caprice (kə-PREECE')
d. querulously (KWER'-ə-ləs-lee)
e. formidable (FAWR'-mə-də-bəl)

1. His wife spoke ———— of the furs which other women wore.
2. In a spirit of mean ———— she refused to give her maid the references which would help her find another job.
3. She is a creature of ————; no one knows what she will do next.
4. It was an atmosphere ———— of the early part of the century.
5. She presented a ———— array of reasons for not attending the reception.

ANSWERS: 1—d, 2—b, 3—c, 4—a, 5—e.

VIII.

a. gratuitous (grə-TOO'-ə-təs)
b. cacophony (kə-KOF'-ə-nee)
c. agile (AJ'-əl)
d. gala (GAY'-lə)
e. virago (və-RAY'-gō)

1. She gave a ———— and completely unnecessary recital of her friend's scarlet past.
2. She is as ———— as a monkey.
3. She was entranced by the ———— of the city noises.
4. Christmas is a ———— occasion.
5. Do not clash with Mrs. Brown if you can avoid doing so; she is a ———— if ever there was one.

ANSWERS: 1—a, 2—c, 3—b, 4—d, 5—e.

IX.

a. formidable (FAWR'-mə-də-bəl)
b. virago (və-RAY'-gō)
c. vicariously (vy-KAIR'-ee-əs-lee)
d. panorama (pan-ə-RAH'-mə)
e. cacophony (kə-KOF'-ə-nee)

1. The sea was a huge ———— of foaming whitecaps.
2. She has the reputation among those who know and fear her of being a ————.
3. That is a ———— task; do you think we are capable of accomplishing it?

4. Though he had never left his immediate neighborhood, he traveled ——————— all through the world, for he spent his evenings immersed in books that told of faraway places.

5. To many people jazz is the extreme in ———————.

ANSWERS: 1—d, 2—b, 3—a, 4—c, 5—e.

X.

a. agile (AJ'-əl)
b. phlegmatic (fleg-MAT'-ək)
c. vindictive (vin-DIK'-tiv)
d. enervating (EN'-ər-vayt-ing)
e. misanthropic (mis-ən-THROP'-ək)

1. He swung with ——————— grace from tree to tree.
2. If you catch him in a ——————— mood he will refuse absolutely to help you.
3. He felt just ——————— enough to refuse to recommend him for the post.
4. ——————— people are usually happier than those who are highstrung.
5. He found twelve hours of work too ———————.

ANSWERS: 1—a, 2—e, 3—c, 4—b, 5—d.

HAVE YOU LEARNED THE WORDS?

If you can check the correct definition or allusion in at least nineteen of the following instances, your ability to learn words from alert contact with them is topnotch. A perfect score shows an unusual and superior degree of word-consciousness.

1. *Phlegmatic* people are a. stupid; b. uninteresting; c. unemotional.
2. A *misanthrope* hates a. good food; b. mankind; c. liberty.
3. *Ingenious* means a. out of date; b. useless; c. cleverly contrived.
4. A *malingerer* shirks a. responsibility; b. work; c. friendship.
5. A *lucrative* undertaking results in great a. profit; b. prestige; c. wisdom.
6. An *erudite* person is a. learned; b. frightened; c. cowardly.

7. *Garrulity* is a great deal of *a.* weight; *b.* talkativeness; *c.* love.

8. *Malignant* means *a.* useless; *b.* menacing; *c.* hateful.

9. A person of great *acumen* is *a.* intelligent; *b.* foolish; *c.* happy.

10. *Enervation* is lack of *a.* energy; *b.* fear; *c.* emotion.

11. *Gullible* people are easily *a.* intimidated; *b.* misled; *c.* annoyed.

12. *Dudgeon* is a state of *a.* delight; *b.* puzzlement; *c.* anger.

13. *Redolent* means *a.* evil-smelling; *b.* sweet-smelling; *c.* remindful.

14. A *vindictive* person seeks *a.* revenge; *b.* money; *c.* fame.

15. A *caprice* is *a.* a feeling of regret; *b.* a sudden unusual desire; *c.* a type of food.

16. *Querulous* people are *a.* quarrelsome; *b.* discontented; *c.* unwelcome.

17. *Vicarious* experiences come *a.* at night; *b.* secretly; *c.* without actual participation.

18. A *panorama* is *a.* an unobstructed view of a region; *b.* a plan of action; *c.* the agenda for a meeting.

19. Anything *gratuitous* is *a.* unwarranted; *b.* petty; *c.* useless.

20. *Cacophony* is *a.* a musical crescendo; *b.* harsh and unmusical sound; *c.* a system of communication in code.

21. An *agile* animal is the *a.* elephant; *b.* monkey; *c.* crocodile.

22. A *gala* occasion is *a.* an important one; *b.* a festive one; *c.* a recurring one.

23. A *virago* is a woman who is *a.* gentle and sweet-tempered; *b.* loudmouthed and turbulent; *c.* alluring and mysterious.

24. Anything *formidable* excites *a.* pleasure; *b.* fear; *c.* doubt.

ANSWERS: 1—c, 2—b, 3—c, 4—b, 5—a, 6—a, 7—b, 8—c, 9—a, 10—a, 11—b, 12—c, 13—c, 14—a, 15—b, 16—b, 17—c, 18—a, 19—a, 20—b, 21—b, 22—b, 23—b, 24—b.

ELEVEN

~~~~~~~~~~~~~~~~~~~~~~~~~~

Nine Five-Minute
Vocabulary Fresheners

HERE ARE nine quizzes, each with a twofold purpose:

1. To give you a yardstick by which to measure the strength and extensiveness of your vocabulary.
2. To show you how easy it is to learn new words.

To derive the greatest benefit from these tests do each one carefully; compare your answers as soon as you finish. (Your aim is to reach or exceed par in each test.) Then study the words whose meanings proved unfamiliar to you, referring, where necessary, to a good dictionary. The notes following each quiz contain sidelights on those words whose derivation and meaning are interesting. Make sure to pay especial attention to these.

A little time spent on these pages can add fifty to a hundred excellent, usable words to your vocabulary. *The profit from exercises of this nature is practically incalculable.*

I.

Is a baby frog a *catalogue,* a *demagogue,* a *polliwog,* an *epilogue,* or a *pedagogue?* Of course you can't be fooled by an easy one like that, but how about some that are a little more difficult?

Scoring: Each item counts 10 points.

Par: 50

Your Score:—————

1. To exclude, by common consent, from the rights and privileges of the group.

   a. gormandize
   b. ostracize
   c. evangelize
   d. epitomize

2. Conforming to the structure peculiar to any language.

   a. phlegmatic
   b. axiomatic
   c. climatic
   d. idiomatic

3. To improve.

   a. abominate
   b. ameliorate
   c. annihilate
   d. asseverate

4. A loiterer.

   a. canard
   b. foulard
   c. petard
   d. laggard

5. Glaringly and notoriously bad.

   a. flagrant
   b. vagrant
   c. fragrant
   d. migrant

6. Extreme astonishment or bewilderment.

   a. benefaction
   b. detraction
   c. stupefaction
   d. putrefaction

7. A rising up against civil or political authority.

   a. circumspection
   b. defection
   c. insurrection
   d. dissection

8. Pertaining to the West.

   a. detrimental
   b. oriental
   c. occidental
   d. transcendental

9. Withheld from public consumption; designed for the specially initiated only.

   a. atmospheric
   b. chimeric
   c. esoteric
   d. mesmeric

10. Dissipating like a vapor; impermanent.

   a. acquiescent
   b. convalescent
   c. effervescent
   d. evanescent

ANSWERS: 1—b, 2—d, 3—b, 4—d, 5—a, 6—c, 7—c, 8—c, 9—c, 10—d.

Notes on the Words in Test I

1. The ancient Greeks used *ostrakons* or white shells on which to vote for the banishment of an unpopular office holder.

2. *Idiom* and *idiot* are related, both coming from the same Greek root. In *idiot,* the root means "peculiar," and is found also in *idiosyncrasy.* In *idiom,* the root signifies "peculiar to one language."

5. *Flagrant* comes from the same root as *flame.* In a way the adjective means "flaming into notice," as a *flagrant* error, a *flagrant* breach of faith, etc.

6. *Stupid* originally meant "stunned" or "bewildered." Compare the noun *stupor.*

8. The sun sets in the west and rises in the east. The Latin verb to set or fall is *occido;* to rise, is *orior:* hence, our words *occidental,* "western," and *oriental,* "eastern."

9. Rarely used antonym of *esoteric* is *exoteric.*

10. *Evanescent* and *vanish* are from the same Latin root, *vanus,* "empty" or "vain."

II.

In each group match the words in the left column with their categories in the right column.

Scoring: 4 points for each correct choice.

Par: 50
Your Score:————————

A. 1. concertina
   2. arena

   a. sphere of action
   b. disease

3. hyena   *c.* woman
4. scarlatina   *d.* musical instrument
5. signorina   *e.* animal

B. 1. maize   *a.* part of the body
   2. maze   *b.* waste ground
   3. mow   *c.* labyrinth
   4. moor   *d.* place for hay
   5. maw   *e.* food

C. 1. octoroon   *a.* storm
   2. monsoon   *b.* coin
   3. baboon   *c.* musical instrument
   4. bassoon   *d.* animal
   5. doubloon   *e.* partly Negro, partly white

D. 1. cocoa   *a.* vegetable
   2. rococo   *b.* design
   3. sirocco   *c.* military headdress
   4. okra   *d.* wind
   5. shako   *e.* beverage

E. 1. siren   *a.* dullard
   2. moron   *b.* rabbit pen
   3. heron   *c.* Ireland
   4. warren   *d.* bird
   5. Erin   *e.* flirt

ANSWERS: A. 1—d, 2—a, 3—e, 4—b, 5—c.
B. 1—e, 2—c, 3—d, 4—b, 5—a.
C. 1—e, 2—a, 3—d, 4—c, 5—b.
D. 1—e, 2—b, 3—d, 4—a, 5—c.
E. 1—e, 2—a, 3—d, 4—b, 5—c.

Notes on Test II

C. *Monsoon* is also the name given to the rainy season of India.
D. *Rococo* was popular in Europe in the eighteenth century. The style was florid and complicated and quite the antithesis of what we call "modern."
E. A *moron* is the most intelligent of the feeble-minded; he has

the brain power of a twelve-year-old. Next in descending order is the *imbecile,* with the intelligence of a child of six, followed by the *idiot,* who has the mental age of a baby of two.

III.

Scoring: 10 points for each correct choice.

Par: 50
Your Score: 50

1. If you have been keeping up even slightly with your history, you will recall that one of the following was most delighted when Prohibition was repealed:

   a. the kleptomaniac *b.* the dipsomaniac *c.* the hypochondriac *d.* the chauvinist

2. Those of you who remember the late Harry Houdini know that he was skilled in:

   a. thaumaturgy *b.* chiromancy *c.* seismology *d.* oligarchy *e.* necromancy

3. If the seasons of the year are of any great influence in your life, you will doubtless be able to spot at once the *one* word below which does not fit in with the rest.

   a. estival *b.* autumnal *c.* hiemal *d.* sumac *e.* vernal

4. A man with *polygamous* tendencies is asked to express his fondest desire. His answer, characteristically, would be:

   a. "I long to be a millionaire and live a life of ease!"
   b. "If only I could evade the lures of the opposite sex and remain a bachelor all my life!"
   c. "Just put me on a deserted island with a hundred beautiful women!"
   d. "Let me lead a life that will earn me the respect and esteem of my fellow men!"

5. Which one of the following is now in *limbo?*

   a. horseless carriage *b.* the short bob *c.* political honesty *d.* the bustle *e.* the one-piece bathing suit

6. Two of the following haven't even a remote connection with weather conditions or seismic disturbances.

   a. typhoon *b.* lampoon *c.* cyclone *d.* hurricane *e.* temblor
   f. squall *g.* the doldrums *h.* cataclysm *i.* tycoon *j.* tornado

7. One of these "maniacs" has a persistent neurotic impulse to steal, usually without any economic motive.

   a. dipsomaniac *b.* megalomaniac *c.* egomaniac *d.* pyromaniac *e.* kleptomaniac

8. There is an instrument which records the shocks and motions of earthquakes. It is a:

   a. mimeograph *b.* hectograph *c.* geometer *d.* phonograph *e.* seismograph *f.* chronometer

9. A beautiful actress tells you confidentially that her whole life has been a *fiasco*. She is trying to evoke:

   a. love *b.* trust *c.* admiration *d.* fear *e.* sympathy *f.* resentment

10. "These are *halcyon* times," you hear someone say during a period of ferment and unrest. The statement is:

    a. encouraging *b.* absurd *c.* discouraging *d.* an exaggeration *e.* ambiguous

ANSWERS: 1—b, 2—a, 3—d, 4—c, 5—d, 6—b, i, 7—e, 8—e, 9—e, 10—b.

Notes on Test III

2. Harry Houdini was especially noted for his dexterity in the performance of wonders, miracles, and feats of magic, to paraphrase the definition of *thaumaturgy*.

3. *Vernal, estival, autumnal,* and *hiemal* are adjectives referring to spring, summer, autumn, and winter, in that order. *Sumac,* however, is a kind of shrub.

4. *Polygamy* is the state of having a plurality of wives at the same time. To a person of polygamous tendencies the deserted island would probably be unusually attractive.

5. The bustle has fallen into a "condition of neglect or oblivion," to quote the definition of *limbo*.
6. *Lampoon,* an abusive satire in writing, and *tycoon,* colloquial for "business magnate," have no connection with the other words.
8. Earthquakes are called *seismic* disturbances.
9. *Fiasco* means "a miserable or ridiculous failure."
10. *Halcyon* means "calm and peaceful." According to Greek mythology, the halcyon, a kind of kingfisher, was supposed to nest at sea about the winter solstice and, by thus doing, calm the waves.

IV.

Choose one of the several possibilities given under each question. Scoring: 10 points for each.

Par: 50

Your Score:————

1. A *thespian* would be more than likely to

    a. treat minor foot ailments
    b. appear behind the footlights
    c. dance a fandango
    d. pull a rabbit out of a hat

2. A *terpsichorean* would like to be a member of

    a. Barnum and Bailey's
    b. The Corps de Ballet
    c. Piccadilly Circus
    d. A scientific expedition to excavate the tomb of an ancient Egyptian king
    e. A political caucus

3. A modern *nimrod* would most enjoy using

    a. a fiddle *b.* a fountain pen *c.* a gun *d.* an egg beater
    e. fishing tackle

4. A *lothario* spends his time pursuing

    a. money *b.* happiness *c.* women *d.* fame *e.* business success

5. A *narcissist* is very much in love with

   a. his wife *b.* women in general *c.* himself *d.* his mother
   e. his king

6. You should be most afraid of your *nemesis*

   a. on Friday the 13th
   b. when trying to draw to an inside straight
   c. after having committed some misdeed
   d. during any period of mental depression

7. As the victim of an *Oedipus complex,* you are unduly attached to

   a. playing cards and other games of chance
   b. archery and other games of skill
   c. your parent of the opposite sex
   d. vain and empty boasting
   e. attaining your ambition in the field of political demagoguery

8. A girl who possesses an *Elektra complex*

   a. is vain and snooty
   b. feels inferior without reason
   c. is excessively attached to her father
   d. believes in a single standard of morals

9. A *jeremiad* is

   a. a song of lamentation
   b. a written request for an increased salary
   c. a cowardly act
   d. a legal, but unethical, act

10. A *circe* is

   a. a very beautiful woman
   b. a woman who lures men to their destruction
   c. a woman with a sharp and malicious tongue
   d. a woman of strict morals

ANSWERS: 1—b, 2—b, 3—c, 4—c, 5—c, 6—c, 7—c, 8—c, 9—a, 10—b.

Notes on Test IV

These words are all derived from mythology or literature.

1. Thespis was the founder of Greek Drama.
2. Terpsichore was the Greek muse of dancing and choral songs.
3. Nimrod was the mighty hunter named in the Bible.
4. Lothario was the name of a gay and unscrupulous fellow in Rowe's drama *The Fair Penitent*.
5. Narcissus was the young chap in Greek mythology who saw his own reflection in a pool and promptly fell in love with himself.
6. Nemesis was the Greek goddess of retributive justice.
7. Oedipus, son of Laius and Jocasta, King and Queen of Thebes, fulfilled an oracle's prophecy that he would someday kill his father and marry his mother.
8. Elektra avenged the murder of her father, Agamemnon, by helping her brother to kill her mother.
9. Jeremiah was the Hebrew prophet of denunciation.
10. Circe, in the Odyssey, turned her admirers into beasts (literally).

V.

Fill in the proper word for each definition. Your answers must end in *-et* or *-ette*. Scoring: 4 points for each answer.

Par: 52

Your Score:————

1. We need it for writing.   a————
2. He bears a hereditary title.   b————
3. It is a wood or ivory instrument used for beating an accompaniment to music or dancing.   c————
4. It is played by two people.   d————
5. It is worn on the shoulder.   e————
6. It is the opposite of remember.   f————
7. It is a jewel.   g————
8. It is a small village.   h————
9. It is something placed within.   i————
10. She is a character in one of Shakespeare's tragedies.   J————

11. It is a small kitchen. k———
12. It is a pair of spectacles with a long handle. l———
13. It is a puppet. m———
14. It is longer than a short story, but not quite book length. n———
15. It is a prepared egg dish. o———
16. It is a dancing step. p———
17. It is made up of five. q———
18. It is a small river. r———
19. It is made up of six. s———
20. It is a device for arresting bleeding. t———
21. It is a disarrangement of plans. u———
22. It is a flower and a color. v———
23. He is a knave. v———
24. It means to sharpen. w———
25. It means *still.* y———

ANSWERS: 1—alphabet, 2—baronet, 3—castanet, 4—duet, 5—epaulet, 6—forget, 7—garnet, 8—hamlet, 9—inset, 10—Juliet, 11—kitchenette, 12—lorgnette, 13—marionette, 14—novelette, 15—omelet, 16—pirouette, 17—quintet, 18—rivulet, 19—sextet, 20—tourniquet, 21—upset, 22—violet, 23—varlet, 24—whet, 25—yet.

VI.

In each of the ten sentences below one word is required to complete an intelligible thought. This word should be chosen from the list which immediately follows:

1. incredulity
2. coquetry
3. propensity
4. penury
5. prostration
6. rectitude
7. chicanery
8. carrion
9. compunction
10. anomaly

Scoring: Each correct choice counts 10.

Par: 50
Your Score:———

1. The bewildering events of the morning left Myrtle in a state of nervous ———.

2. Some men find Susan's ———— attractive; other women abhor her for it.
3. Ronald has no ———— about telling the most barefaced lies.
4. Vultures generally enjoy feasting on ————.
5. Ralph is a man of great ————; he has never committed an illegal act in his life.
6. After several years spent in ———— Tom suddenly made a fortune.
7. I do not trust Martin; he is a master of double-dealing and ————.
8. Your story fills me with ————; how could such a thing have happened on this earth?
9. His ———— for figures explains his ability as an accountant.
10. An ostrich is a (an) ————; although it has wings, it cannot fly.

ANSWERS: 1—prostration (complete exhaustion), 2—coquetry (art of playing with men's affections), 3—compunction (conscience pang), 4—carrion (dead flesh), 5—rectitude (adherence to moral standards), 6—penury (extreme poverty), 7—chicanery (subtle trickery), 8—incredulity (disbelief), 9—propensity (leaning toward), 10—anomaly (irregularity).

Notes on Test VI

2. Ironically, *cock* and *coquette* come from the same French root. The connection is found in the way a cock struts to show off his fine plumage.
3. *Compunction* and *puncture* are also related, and in a much more obvious way. Thus the puncture of an automobile tire which might cause a flat is similar to the prick of the heart or conscience that might cause uneasiness.
4. *Carrion* refers only to rotting flesh.
5. *Incredulity* should not be confused with *incredibility*. The latter describes a story that cannot be believed, the former a person who does not believe. A similar relationship is found between the adjectives *credible* and *credulous,* and their negatives, *incredible* and *incredulous.*

9. Etymologically, *propensity* is a "hanging toward." Other words with the same root are *pendant, pendulous, depend, impend,* etc.

10. Most interesting word in this test is *anomaly*. Anything that is contrary to normal occurrence or procedure is an anomaly. All child prodigies are *anomalies,* as also, in a way, was Wendell Willkie, who ran for the Presidency with no previous political experience. An odorless skunk would be an anomaly of nature, and when the lion does finally lie down with the lamb, you'll have the greatest anomaly of all. The adjective is *anomalous*.

VII.

The italicized word makes each statement either true or false. Scoring: 10 points for each item.

Par: 60

Your Score:————

1. A *laconic* person is talkative.   True   False
2. Conscientious people generally do their work *cursorily*.   True   False
3. America is composed of a *heterogeneous* population.   True   False
4. Stern people are usually *inexorable*.   True   False
5. College graduates are more *erudite* than country yokels.   True   False
6. The Chinese are known as an *imperturbable* race.   True   False
7. War is a *panacea*.   True   False
8. The *opulent* usually ask for charity.   True   False
9. Diabetics must *eschew* sugar.   True   False
10. We *incarcerate* our criminals.   True   False

ANSWERS: 1—false, 2—false, 3—true, 4—true, 5—true, 6—true, 7—false, 8—false, 9—true, 10—true.

Notes on Test VII

1. The inhabitants of Laconia, ancient name of Sparta, were famed for their economy and terseness of speech. *Laconic* means "sparing in the use of words"; the noun is *laconism*.

2. *Cursorily*—"in a careless or superficial manner." The accent is on the first syllable.

3. *Heterogeneous*—"of many different kinds"; opposed to *homogeneous,* "of one kind."

4. *Exoro,* in Latin, means "to beseech." The person whom entreaty and beseeching will not move is *inexorable.*

5. *Erudite* means "learned, wise in book lore." The noun is *erudition.*

6. *Imperturbable*—"not easily disturbed or excited." While the definitions seem similar, you can appreciate the great difference in the atmosphere of *inexorable* and *imperturbable.* The Chinese are supposedly *imperturbable;* they mask their feelings. The governor was *inexorable* when we begged for a pardon; he would not change his mind.

7. Well-known *panacea* of early days was the snake oil sold by itinerant medicine men; it cured every disease known to man. Today the antibiotic group of drugs actually does seem to be a panacea. This meaning of cure-all may also be applied in a figurative manner. Thus Socialism was once offered as a a panacea for man's economic ills.

8. *Opulent*—"extremely wealthy." This word, and its synonym, *affluent,* connote great abundance of wealth and possessions.

9. *Eschew*—"to abstain from something wrong or distasteful." The noun is *eschewal.*

10. *Incarcerate* is the more bookish term for imprison. Another synonym is *immure,* which implies imprisonment behind walls (Latin *murus*—wall; think of *mural,* a wall painting).

VIII.

Answer *yes* or *no* to each question.
Scoring: 10 points for each item.

Par: 80
Your Score:——————

1. Would you, as a mother, wish to expose your child to *pernicious* influences?   ——————

2. Is *matricide* a common crime in America?   ——————

3. Do you enjoy having your speech corrected in a *pedantic* way?   ——————

4. Does a judge try to keep the evidence *relevant?* _____

5. Do gossipers *calumniate* the people about whom they talk? _____

6. Do you *commiserate* with your friends on their misfortunes? _____

7. Do you *condone* the actions of a murderer? _____

8. Do you find *prolix* speakers interesting? _____

9. Do you enjoy working under a *martinet?* _____

10. Do you consider *obsequiousness* an indication of a subservient character? _____

ANSWERS: 1—no, 2—no, 3—no, 4—yes, 5—yes, 6—yes, 7—no, 8—no, 9—no, 10—yes.

Notes on Test VIII

1. *Pernicious*—"highly destructive or harmful."
2. *Matricide*—"killing of one's mother."
3. A *pedant* is one who makes an ostentatious display of his learning. His *pedantry* is annoying. He is *pedantic.* A *pedant* is similar to a purist: he insists on strict conformity to minute and usually unimportant rules. Another name for him is a *precisian.* Usually, however, only a teacher of some sort is called a *pedant* (and then the word has the same derogatory flavor as *pedagogue*), though *pedantic* and *pedantry* can be applied to anyone.
4. *Relevant*—"to the point; bearing on the question in hand."
5. *Calumniate*—"spread malicious scandal." The noun is *calumny.*
6. *Commiserate*—"sympathize with." The same root (Latin *miser* —"wretched") is found in *miserable* and *miser.* Literally, the word means "to feel wretched with someone."
7. *Condone*—"forgive." Takes a direct object: *condone his misbehavior.*
8. *Prolix*—"long-winded, verbose, wordy." Noun: *prolixity.* The word implies wearisome attention to trivialities.
9. *Martinet*—"a strict disciplinarian." Inspector General Jean Martinet, of the French army, was wont to drill his soldiers until they were letter perfect in every detail.

10. *Obsequious*—describes currying favor with one's superior by a show of excessive, and usually insincere, politeness.

IX.

In each line are exactly *two* words of similar meanings. Copy the letters of the synonymous words in the space at the right of that line. Scoring: 10 points for each.

Par: 50

Your Score:———

1. *a.* euphemistic; *b.* dulcet; *c.* melodious; *d.* blunt; *e.* eugenic; *f.* flavorful   ———

2. *a.* repudiate; *b.* convalesce; *c.* hinder; *d.* gainsay; *e.* savor; *f.* impede   ———

3. *a.* risible; *b.* contemptible; *c.* portable; *d.* laughable; *e.* credible   ———

4. *a.* reminiscent; *b.* volatile; *c.* nostalgic; *d.* avuncular; *e.* obdurate   ———

5. *a.* showy; *b.* pastoral; *c.* urbane; *d.* possessive; *e.* ostentatious   ———

6. *a.* contrite; *b.* satisfied; *c.* bucolic; *d.* rustic; *e.* contumacious   ———

7. *a.* complaining; *b.* querulous; *c.* quarrelsome; *d.* depressed; *e.* flighty   ———

8. *a.* renegade; *b.* apostate; *c.* novitiate; *d.* pasquinade; *e.* repartee   ———

9. *a.* sensual; *b.* sepulchral; *c.* professional; *d.* amateur; *e.* funereal   ———

10. *a.* earthy; *b.* futile; *c.* mundane; *d.* lactic; *e.* concentric   ———

ANSWERS: 1—bc, 2—cf, 3—ad, 4—ac, 5—ae, 6—cd, 7—ab, 8—ab, 9—be, 10—ac.

Notes on the Words in Test IX

1. The adjective *dulcet* is generally applied to sounds or other things that can be heard, as *a dulcet voice, a dulcet melody.* It means "sweet, soothing to the ear, agreeable." The musical in-

strument *dulcimer* comes from the same Latin root as *dulcet* (*dulcis*—"sweet").

2. To *impede* is derived from a Latin verb meaning "to entangle the feet." The root for *foot* (*ped*) is also found in *pedal, pedestrian, pedicure, pedestal,* and *pedometer.* The noun is *impediment.*

3. *Risible* means "disposed to laugh, or pertaining to laughter," as *a risible fellow,* or *a risible moving picture. Deride* (to laugh at) comes from the same root. *To tickle the risibilities* is a common expression.

4. *Nostalgia* is homesickness, a longing for pleasant sensations, associations, or places of the past. The *-algia* part, which means *pain,* is also found in *neuralgia,* pain along the nerves, and other less well-known diseases.

5. Anything *ostentatious* has an unnecessary amount of empty decoration, is gaudy or excessively pretentious. *Ostensible,* from the same root, means *shown to the eye,* hence *apparent* or *evident.*

6. *Bucolic* and *rustic* are pleasant words referring to the country as opposed to the city. Other words with similar meaning are *rural, pastoral,* and, with a slight variation, *suburban.* The verb to *rusticate* means "to spend time in the country." *Bucolic* is more of a literary word; *pastoral* has overtones of the simple life of shepherds.

8. *Renegade* and *apostate* both refer to people who have forsaken earlier commitments. A common synonym is *turncoat. Apostate* is a religious term, signifying one who has deserted his faith.

10. *Mundane* refers to this world, rather than to spiritual or ethereal things. It has overtones of realism and practicality as opposed to dreaminess and flights of fancy. Questions of food and shelter, soap, bedsheets, gas ranges, for example, are mundane; music and art are not mundane.

TWELVE

~~~~~~~~~~~~~~~~~~~~~~

℞ *For Vocabulary Improvement*

A RESTATEMENT OF THE
PRINCIPLES

WITHIN SIX MONTHS after reading this chapter you can add
to your vocabulary a thousand new words—if you really want to.
You can do this painlessly and with a minimum of inconvenience.
And by means of this sudden spurt in your word knowledge you
can accomplish a complete revolution in your speech and writing, a
radical change in the way you think, and a startling extension of
the number of things you are interested in. These accomplishments
depend on only two things: your will power and your mental attitude.

The actual size of your vocabulary is of considerably less importance than the rate at which it is growing. If five or ten years ago
you were able to recognize thirty thousand words, and if today you
have either lost contact with many of those you once knew, or have

become familiar with, at best, an additional hundred or two, then your vocabulary is in a state of near stagnation. It does not have the richness nor the power of the vocabulary of (for example) a person of eighteen whose vocabulary has been increasing at the rate of five hundred to one thousand words a year for the previous four years of his life. The new words he has picked up are fresh and alive to him. He writes and speaks and thinks with them. He is still interested in the things they represent. The fact that he has been learning new words every week and every month shows that he is intellectually alive, that his curiosity about the world around him is daily demanding and receiving fulfillment.

Similarly, the stagnant vocabulary, no matter what great stature it might have reached before it stopped growing, forebodes an unhealthy diminution of intellectual alertness and curiosity. When knowledge of words has become static, so has interest in the phenomena of life. In general, vocabulary approaches its maximum size in the early twenties, for beyond that age, when we have settled into a definite and seldom-changing routine of living—when the world no longer presents a picture of never-ceasing wonder and puzzlement—when we begin to realize that the thirties, or perhaps the forties, are inescapably advancing upon us—when a certain mental complacence begins to twine its fingers around our minds—why then, that is the time that our interest in new words begins to lose its youthful sharpness. Young people are in love with new words (provided these words are not beyond the scope of their understanding), not as words, but as symbols of the wonderful mysteries of life: which, fundamentally, is what words are before they are anything else. That is why children and adolescents increase their vocabularies at a rate truly prodigious in comparison with their more sophisticated and phlegmatic elders.

Older people may often seem to be greatly interested in increasing their vocabularies—but for a reason worlds apart from the one that motivates youngsters. Young people are avid for new words because these words represent growth and experience and life—three vital needs of those exciting years before maturity is reached. *Older people, on the other hand, generally want consciously to increase their vocabularies simply because they want larger vocabularies.*

I refer, of course, to the average adult who has passed his or her middle twenties. There are many exceptional people to whom the previous statements do not by any means apply, even remotely. You may be one of these exceptional people. At the Human Engineering Laboratory, Dr. Johnson O'Connor has found, by scientific testing, that these exceptional adults whose vocabularies never stop growing, no matter what their age, are the most successful people in the country: the business executives and the top names in professional fields. Their vocabularies continue to grow because their interest in life never ceases growing; and it cannot be doubted that this attitude is one of the potent factors that contribute to their success. The *only* common quality that Dr. O'Connor was able to isolate in studying these thousands of successful men and women was not, surprisingly enough, any such thing as tenacity, or progressiveness, or imagination, or honesty, or ruthlessness, or even luck. Dr. O'Connor found, somewhat to his own astonishment, that every successful person whom he tested had an unusually large vocabulary. In no other particular were all these people identical!

The facts reviewed on the preceding pages offer the key to successful vocabulary improvement. Six steps, if followed faithfully, will bring you to the point where you can continue to grow at the same rate as when you still considered life your oyster and were having so much fun trying to pry it open.

STEP I. CONSIDER WORDS AS SYMBOLS OF LIFE

It was suggested at the outset of this chapter that you could, within six months, learn a thousand new words with a minimum of pain and inconvenience. This can, indeed, be accomplished quite easily, provided you get yourself out of the frame of mind which inhibits so many earnest seekers after vocabulary improvement. Too often an adult who has made a definite resolution to learn new words has failed at the outset because his ambition was solely to "learn new words"—a task which can become deadly monotonous after a very short time. Many are the valiant souls who fill notebooks with unending columns of words, only to be enmeshed in a confusion and tedium of their own making. Words, as separate entities, can become very dull and tiresome. Words are symbols; and symbols, when viewed apart from the things they symbolize, are wearisome and unstimulating things. If you wish to improve your vocabulary solely because you wish to have a larger vocabulary, success will in all likelihood elude you.

But if you wish to improve your vocabulary because you expect thereby to extend your mental horizon, because you intend to become acquainted with all the things that the new words will symbolize, then you will be letting your vocabulary grow in the same natural and purposeful way in which it grew when most of the words you now know first came into your vocabulary.

STEP II. SHARPEN YOUR DESIRE FOR A LARGER VOCABULARY

The second step too is a matter of attitude. Do you wish *seriously* and *earnestly* to improve your vocabulary—so seriously and earnestly that you can keep the desire constantly in mind while you are developing the habits that will permit your vocabulary to continue expanding? Or is the wish just strong enough to occur to you every once in a while, and then to vanish before you can decide to do anything about it?

Vocabulary can, indeed, be increased with a minimum of pain and inconvenience; but a *maximum* of desire and will power is necessary. Ask yourself how keen your desire is. Until it is so keen that it takes permanent root in your mind, you cannot expect to succeed in improving your vocabulary.

STEP III. BECOME WORD-CONSCIOUS

Now you must learn to become aware of the new words you meet. As I have pointed out earlier, you can read a page with half a dozen unfamiliar words in it, and pay so little attention to them that it is just as if your eyes had never seen them. On the other hand, as soon as you determine to pay particular attention to the new words you meet in your reading or hear from your friends or from radio or television, you will be amazed to discover what a great wealth of diamonds has always been in your backyard waiting for you to get started with your digging. This is perhaps the most important step of all: forcing your mind to store away for future reference whatever new combinations of syllables your eyes or ears bring to you every day.

STEP IV. LOSE YOUR FEAR OF THE DICTIONARY

Learn next to make occasional excursions to the dictionary. It is not necessary to look up every word you meet, or even the majority of them. Many words will be quite clear from context; those whose meanings are not discernible the first time you see them will gradually become more and more understandable at each new encounter. No, you must not ask yourself to go to the dictionary for *every* new word you encounter; that is setting out a superhuman task for yourself. On the other hand, you should, as quickly as possible, get into the habit of thumbing through your Webster with a certain frequency—say once a day, or a few times a week.

When was the last time you looked a word up in the dictionary? And how much time elapsed between that occasion and the one preceding it? If your answers to these two questions make you realize how little use you make of the dictionary, then it is up to you, at once, to resolve to change your habits. The dictionary, obviously, is the most powerful ally you can use in your search for victory over new words—but it is of help only if you turn to it frequently.

STEP V. LEARN TO READ THE DICTIONARY

Using the dictionary need not be a chore. On the contrary, you can get the same enjoyment from it as from your morning newspaper. The secret is simply to apply your newspaper-reading technique every time you open the dictionary to find the meaning of some word. Just as you let your eyes dart over the headlines of world news, pausing to read those items which pique your interest, so also glance at every word on the dictionary page open in front of you. Read the definitions of those words that look interesting. There is a truly prodigious wealth of information on any page you can turn to: facts about psychology, art, medicine, law, mythology, sociology, physics, chemistry, and so on without end. No other volume in existence contains so many jewels of varied enlightenment in so small a space as the dictionary. Indeed, were you to read every page in the dictionary, you would know a little bit about every field of knowledge ever explored by man.

Do not be content with the one specific item of information for which you came to the dictionary. Be greedy. Be a glutton. Absorb as much as time and interest permit before closing the book. In this way, every time you take the dictionary off the shelf, you can begin to make the acquaintance, not merely of one word, but of a dozen or more. Thus, if you open the dictionary only once a day, you will be adding over three hundred and fifty fresh words to your vocabulary every month—making one thousand words in a six-month period a ridiculously easy goal to achieve.

STEP VI. DROP YOUR INHIBITIONS ABOUT NEW WORDS

Your last step is the one which takes you over the line that divides "learning words" from "improving your vocabulary." Partly this step will be automatic, partly it will require a certain amount of conscious attention. *Words, like dollars, are useless except as they are put into circulation.* You have not genuinely pushed back the frontiers of your vocabulary until you have begun to think and speak and write with the new words you have learned. In one sense, you need not worry too much about this—as you learn more and more new words your interests will become so manifold, so many new ideas will crowd your mind, and your mind itself will become so increasingly alert to new concepts, that you will find your thoughts being translated in language that is fresh and forceful and virile. But in another sense, you will want to work a bit on this, for if you consciously determine to shed your inhibitions, you can hasten the process considerably. The distinguishing characteristic of the effective speaker and writer is the ability to express ideas in imaginative and colorful language, so don't ever hesitate to phrase your thoughts in new words whose meaning and emotional flavor you thoroughly understand.

Rephrased briefly, these are the steps that will bring you success and satisfaction from a six months' vocabulary improvement program:

1. Realize that vocabulary improvement really means a broadening of your grasp of all the world's knowledge.
2. Be serious—a halfhearted desire will end in failure.
3. Keep your eyes and ears open for the new words that are to be seen and heard all about you.
4. Use your dictionary unsparingly.
5. Learn to glance at all the entries on a dictionary page.
6. Use the new words you learn.

When your half year is over you will find that you have done much more than just added a certain number of words to your vocabulary. You will discover that you have gained new powers of persuasion, that you can read more understandingly, that you can more fully appreciate the ideas of others, and that you have begun to tap fields of human knowledge that were once perhaps wholly unknown to you.

THREE

~~~~~~~~~~

That Bugaboo:
   Correct Pronunciation

The following pronunciation symbols are used in this section:

    ə—the obscure vowel sound of the *-a* in *sofa* (SŌ′-fə)
    ăr—as in *carriage* (KĂR′-əj)
    er—as in *very*
    o͞o—as in *moon* (MO͞ON)
    o͝o—as in *book* (BO͝OK)
    ō—as in *go* (GŌ)

ONE

~~~~~~~~~~

What Correct Pronunciation Is

POWER OVER WORDS logically entails power over correct pronunciation—but what is *correct* pronunciation?

Is it what the actors and actresses use on the Broadway stage or
the Hollywood set?

Is it what the members of the Social Register use?

Is it what the English professors at the great universities use?

Is it what the dictionaries recommend?

Is it what the political leaders of the country use?

Is it what the people use in Boston? Or in the Middle West?
Or along the Atlantic seacoast? Or in the South? Or in London,
England?

Or is it, perhaps, what your teachers taught you to use in high
school and college?

Correct pronunciation is none of these, exclusively; yet it is a
combination, in part, of all of them.

Correct pronunciation is the pronunciation used by the great majority of educated people throughout the country. This definition is agreed upon by all language scholars. It is the principle that governs the pronunciations offered in your dictionary. It is the criterion by which a skillful speaker is judged. It is the means by which our language has changed, from its Teutonic character of the sixteenth century to the modern form in which we now find it. *Correct* pronunciation, in short, is no more nor less than *current* pronunciation. The *proper* way to say a word, by this token, is simply the way educated people are saying it at the moment.

Correct pronunciation has no exclusive relationship to spelling. *Warm* and *farm* are spelled the same, but pronounced differently. *Fur* and *her* and *myrrh* are spelled differently but, except for the initial consonant, pronounced the same. In *psalm,* there is a *p* in the spelling but none in the pronunciation, while in *hiccough* (pronounced HIK'-əp) there is a *p* in the pronunciation but none in the spelling (though another spelling of this word is, of course, *hiccup*).

Correct pronunciation has no exclusive relationship to clearness. In *handkerchief, vegetable,* and *comfortable,* the correct pronunciations are those which run all the syllables together.

Correct pronunciation is not exclusively charming, or impressive, or clear, or cultured, or glamorous. It is only two things—*current and acceptable.*

The effective way to pronounce a word is the popular way. You will discover that unpopular pronunciations, no matter what authority or reasons you have for using them, are ineffective pronunciations that rob your speech of power, not add power to it.

There is no Supreme Court of Speech, no final arbiter to rule on the constitutionality or legality of a pronunciation. The dictionaries do not rule on how you must speak, nor do they make any pretense of doing so. They do no more than record how most educated people are currently speaking—and the multitudinous changes that are introduced into each new edition of a dictionary will serve to convince a skeptic that dictionaries do not try to establish trends in pronunciation, but only record those trends as accurately as they can.

This section plans, first, to discuss the popular trends in pronunciation today; second, to develop in you a keen ear for these trends among the people whom you know, and in the locality in which you live and work (for of course trends vary from group to group and from place to place); and third, to teach you to use a dictionary frequently and discriminatingly when you are in doubt about how a specific word should sound.

Once your ear and mind are trained to understand and interpret pronunciation trends you will no longer be uneasy about any of the words you use. You will *know* that your pronunciation is correct because you have discovered, at first hand, through personal experience, analytical listening, and direct contact with an authoritative dictionary that the pronunciation is the one used by most educated and skillful speakers.

T W O

~~~~~~~~~~

Three Things to Avoid

WHY DO YOU SPEAK? To relieve your feelings? To exercise your vocal chords? To impress your listeners? Or to communicate a message, a thought, an idea, an emotion? Obviously, the prime purpose of speech is communication. And, in communication, it is the word and the thought behind the word, not the form in which the word is articulated, that is of greatest importance.

Hence, when you speak, you want your listeners to be immediately and sharply aware of what you are trying to say. Unlike dress, speech should not be at all ornamental. It should be *functional* only. *Effective speech is that which expresses a thought in the simplest, most economical way.* You have gained genuine power with words when you have trained yourself to speak concisely, with no superfluous sound, with no flossiness or affectation.

Judged by this principle, that pronunciation is correct which is most effective. Effective pronunciation calls a minimum of attention to itself. The skillful speaker places his listeners under the spell of his ideas—he does not permit his pronunciation to break that spell.

He *never* pronounces a word in a way that is alien to the habits of his listeners, for he knows that such a pronunciation breaks the spell of his thoughts by distracting the minds of his listeners from the *substance* of his words to their *form*. *Form* is a sterile, useless, unfunctional quality; *substance* is a living, glowing, nourishing quality. By making your pronunciation conform as nearly as you can to the standard of the generality of educated people, you avoid drawing attention to your pronunciation; you escape the danger that the *form* of your words is detracting from their *substance*.

Three kinds of pronunciations weaken communication. They are:

1. illiterate pronunciations
2. affected or ostentatious pronunciations
3. overmeticulous pronunciations

Once you have learned to cleanse your speech of these three vitiating influences, you have taken a long step forward in gaining power with words.

I. ILLITERATE PRONUNCIATION

Effective pronunciation, to repeat, calls no attention to itself, either by design or by accident. Effective pronunciation meets a certain accepted standard of educated speech.

Exactly what that standard is in every instance is not too easy to say. It is a standard, you must bear in mind, that varies greatly from place to place, from time to time, and even from social group to social group.

This much, however, can be said with assurance: Effective pronunciation is completely free of grossly illiterate forms.

Substituting a *d* for *th* (*dis, dat, dese, de fadder of de family*, etc.) is discernible to the most untutored ear. Such a habit smacks so strongly of slovenliness in speech as to make the listener painfully aware that there is something unpleasant in the general character of what he is hearing. As it happens, elementary education is so nearly universal these days that few people in our country are addicted to the habit of *d-th* substitution. Those who are generally are completely oblivious of their fault and react with aggrieved astonishment when their mannerisms are pointed out to them.

If you feel that you yourself are sometimes guilty of a *d-th* substitution, consciously listening to your pronunciation for several days and purposefully attempting to eradicate the substitution will effect a rapid cure.

Two related habits are the dropping of the *-g* in words ending in *-ing (talkin', workin', hopin',* etc.) and, on the other extreme, clicking the final *-g* in these words. The ending *-ing* is one of the more difficult sounds in the English language; *-ing* and *th* are a pair of sounds never completely conquered by many people learning English as a foreign language.

To determine how successfully you yourself pronounce *-ing,* read the following words aloud:

> hoping
> seeing
> making
> loving

If the final syllable in these words, as you say them, is identical with the word *in,* or if you detect a sharp, clear, harsh *g* sound at the end, you do not pronounce your *-ing* words according to educated patterns. If you will train yourself to say words ending in *-ing* without closing your throat, you will have the sound conquered. A little practice here, as in the *d-th* problem, will produce speedy results.

There is a third facet of illiterate pronunciation worth discussing. A dozen and a half words, when pronounced a certain way, are usually indicative of a certain linguistic naïveté. They are thus pronounced almost solely by people with little or no experience in the language arts. Let us take a look at them:

Word	Illiterate Pronunciation	Educated Pronunciation
1. accurate	AK'-ər-ət	AK'-yə-rət
2. genuine	JEN'-yōo-wine	JEN'-yōo-ən
3. attacked	ə-TAK'-təd	ə-TAKT'
4. athletic	ATH'-ə-let-ək	ath-LET'-ək
5. elm	EL'-əm	ELM (*one syllable*)
6. film	FIL'-əm	FILM (*one syllable*)

Word	Illiterate Pronunciation	Educated Pronunciation
7. bronchial	BRON'-ə-kəl	BRONG'-kee-əl
8. mischievous	mis-CHEE'-vee-əs	MIS'-chə-vəs
9. grievous	GREE'-vee-əs	GREE'-vəs
10. faucet	FAS'-ət	FAW'-sət
11. intricate	in-TRIK'-ət	IN'-trə-kət
12. modern	MOD'-rən	MOD'-ərn
13. municipal	myōō-nə-SIP'-əl	myōō-NIS'-ə-pəl
14. deficit	də-FIS'-it	DEF'-ə-sit
15. accept	ə-SEPT'	ək-SEPT'
16. drowned	DROWN'-dəd	DROWND (*one syllable*)
17. February	FEB'-yōō-er'-ee	FEB'-rōō-er'-ee
18. wrestle	RAS'-əl	RES'-əl

Because illiterate pronunciations generally either annoy or amuse your listeners, they detract considerably from the power of your speech. Your speech must never amuse your audience, unless you consciously plan to be funny; and it must never, without qualification, annoy your audience if you wish to gain power with words. So conspicuous are the illiterate pronunciations of the eighteen words listed above that they force your listeners to focus their minds on the *form* of your speech, rather than on its *substance*. They permit your audience, if it is the average educated audience, to feel a momentary superiority over you. Nothing, as you know, so delights a listener as secretly to feel that he is superior to the person speaking; and similarly, nothing so robs your speech of power and persuasiveness as this feeling in the minds of your listeners.

II. AFFECTED, OSTENTATIOUS, OR "RITZY" PRONUNCIATION

Many people feel that a very definite and valuable kind of social prestige attaches to the pronunciation *eyether* (either). While this form is standard in some sections of New England and in parts of the South, in the rest of the country it runs the risk of sounding stagy. Many people, it is true, have been brought up on *eyether* and say it as naturally and unaffectedly as they do their own names. Others, however, have purposely and with premeditation *schooled* themselves in the use of this form because they feel it lends an air of sophistication to their speech.

The conscious, deliberate use of *eyether* illustrates two *negative* principles of effective speech:

1. Pronunciation that indicates to the listener, in however minor or momentary a form, that the speaker feels superior is *ineffective* pronunciation. Any such attitude on the part of a speaker, whether real or imagined, is met with instant hostility. Pronunciation that causes hostility is in direct conflict with the primary purpose of speech, for an unfriendly reaction thwarts communication almost as surely as if the speaker's entire language were foreign to his audience.

2. Any pronunciation that is too conspicuous is ineffective. The listener's mind should be directed *solely* toward the thought of the speaker; if he can remember later that the speaker belongs to the *eyether* school, as he usually will if the speaker uses *eyether,* then some part of his attention was occupied with the *form* rather than the *substance* of what he was hearing.

Either and *neither* are entirely neutral, colorless, inconspicuous words—as they should be, since, as conjunctions or pronouns, they contain very little thought. When pronounced *eether* and *neether,* nobody will notice them. When pronounced *eyether* and *neyether,* it is certain they will be noticed and there is at least some chance that they will cause irritation.

The late C. A. Lloyd, noted language scholar and professor of English at Biltmore College, Asheville, North Carolina, told a characteristic anecdote in this connection: [1]

"In the early days of the Far West a citizen of a small town encountered a crowd of cowboys who were dragging a man behind them, with the evident intention of lynching him.

"'Wait a minute, boys,' he said. 'What's he done?'

"'Stole a horse,' was the answer.

"'Well, that's pretty bad, boys,' said the citizen, 'but we need more law in this town. Why not turn him over to the sheriff and give him a fair trial?'

[1] *We Who Speak English,* Thomas Y. Crowell Company.

" 'Yes, pardner, but he shot the man that the horse belonged to, besides,' replied the cowboys.

" 'That's terrible, boys, but it's not your place to settle with him. Let the law do it.'

" 'Yes, but besides all that, he says "eyether" and "neyether"!'

" 'Oh, well, take him on out, boys.' "

Seven other words belong in the same category as *either* and *neither*. These are:

chauffeur	again	rather
aunt	against	avenue
vase		

They, too, can be pronounced in two ways:

The Inconspicuous, More Pop- ular, Hence Effective Way	*The Conspicuous, Less Popular, Hence Ineffective Way*
SHŌ'-fər	shō-FUR'
ant (very similar to *slant*)	ahnt
vayz *or* vays	vahz
ə-GEN'	ə-GAYN'
ə-GENST'	ə-GAYNST'
RATH'-ər (rhymes with *gather*)	RAH-thər
AV'-ən-yōō	AV'-ə-nōō

III. OVERMETICULOUS PRONUNCIATION

That a little knowledge can be a dangerous thing applies as much to pronunciation as to any other facet of human living. Thus you will often find, paradoxically, that the person who has taken a speech course or who has suddenly become interested in language or who has decided to major in English in college will begin to speak somewhat less effectively than he used to. Exactly in what respect his effectiveness has diminished may for a time elude you. But as you listen to him you are aware that his manner of ex-pressing his ideas has intangibly lost some of its smoothness, some of its casual power; that there has developed in it that slight degree of awkwardness that forces you, from time to time, to think of his speech as a series of separate words instead of a running juxtaposition of ideas.

As has so often been said before in these pages, speech that calls undue attention to the pronunciation of any of its component or individual parts is highly ineffective speech. While it is generally true that carefully enunciated speech is more to be desired than slovenly and garbled speech, extreme meticulousness in pronunciation is as much a fault, and for the same reason, as is extreme sloppiness. Sloppy speech is hard to understand and hence irritates the listener; overprecise speech is, in a certain sense, equally hard to understand, for while each word is clearly discernible, the complete pattern of the thought is obscured by the competitive prominence of every syllable that goes to make up that thought. Phrased differently, the speaker who has developed the habit of crystal-clear enunciation speaks *words* instead of phrases and sentences. As you listen to the separate words, your mind must perform a kind of gymnastics to fuse these words into understandable ideas.

The person with a rudimentary knowledge of speech principles must be careful not to become self-conscious about his speech. Self-consciousness robs speech of power. One should be word conscious, yes, but not self-conscious when using words. Word-consciousness makes for confidence in speaking, but self-consciousness, in speech as in anything else, tends to undermine confidence.

Meticulousness is manifested in three major types of pronunciation:

A. The letter *u*
B. The vowels in unemphasized syllables
C. The letter *t* in medial or final position

A. The Letter U

The correct way to pronounce *during* is, according to some speech manuals, $DY\overline{OO}'$-*ring*. By the same criterion, *new* should be $NY\overline{OO}$, *tune* should be $TY\overline{OO}N$, *stew* should be $STY\overline{OO}$, *lute* should be $LY\overline{OO}T$, *assume* should be ∂-$SY\overline{OO}M$: etc., etc.

Now let us test this principle against what we have learned about effective pronunciation.

Effective pronunciation is popular pronunciation. Except in certain parts of New England and in some areas of the South, notably Virginia, very few educated people pronounce the letter *u* in the manner indicated.

Effective pronunciation is inconspicuous pronunciation. Except in the localities previously noted, this type of pronunciation is so rare that it shouts its self-consciousness in every sentence in which it occurs.

Effective pronunciation is unobnoxious pronunciation. Again excepting those sections of the country to which it is indigenous, this overemphatic sharpening and lengthening of the letter *u* is considered affected or pedantic by most skillful speakers and down-to-earth citizens.

If you have always sharpened your *u*'s and if your friends and business associates do the same, by all means continue to pronounce words like *Tuesday, tumor, student, nuisance,* etc., as you have been accustomed to doing.

On the other hand, if you have always pronounced *tube* and *tune* as near rhymes with *boob* and *boon,* avoid schooling yourself in the meticulous pronunciation. What you are now in the habit of doing conforms to the educated standards of present-day American pronunciation.

B. The Vowels in Unemphasized Syllables

Of, as an isolated word considered out of context, is pronounced ŏv. So unimportant is this word, so completely lacking in emphasis in most sentences, that in reality it is almost always pronounced əv. For example, read these two sentences:

a. He came through the front of the house.
b. This is a government *of* the people, *by* the people, *for* the people.

You can appreciate how differently the *of* of each sentence sounds when spoken.

Meticulous pronunciation erroneously gives equal prominence

to all words in a sentence. Speakers addicted to this habit labor under the delusion that their clear and equal enunciation of every word in a sentence lends culture, tone, and impressiveness to their speech; quite the contrary, it makes their speech *pedantic, unpleasant,* and *almost meaningless.* As Margaret P. McLean points out in her excellent book *Good American Speech,*[2]

> A great many English sounds are pronounced one way when they are used alone or in a stressed position, and in different ways when combined with other words in a sentence or when used in unstressed positions. If the first, strong, pronunciation is used in place of the second, weak, it sounds very artificial and pedantic and is often called "over-correct or affected."

Speaking effectively, you will subordinate unimportant words. Note some of these:

Word	Pronunciation When Unimportant
for	fər
to	tə
of	əv
him	əm
her	ər
them	thəm
from	frəm
his	iz
was	wəz

These phonetic respellings are somewhat exaggerated in order to make the point clear. But if you will read the following sentences naturally, you will be able to listen to the exact sound that the weak, unemphatic forms possess. These sentences are quoted from *Language and Its Growth,* by Scott, Carr, and Wilkinson.[3]

> In the following list of words with illustrations of their use the first sentence or phrase illustrates the strong form and the second the weak form.

[2] E. P. Dutton and Company.
[3] Scott, Foresman and Company. Copyright, 1935.

are	Here they are. They are coming.
at	Shoot at him. Stop at the next house.
be	It can't be. He must be stupid.
could	I would stay if I could. You could do better than this.
do	There is nothing to do. What do you see?
for	What is he waiting for? He is waiting for his pay.
had	The only chance he had. He had always worked faithfully.
has	You are the only friend he has. The boat has arrived.
he	We tried but he didn't. John said he was ready.
his	The fault is his. He took his departure.
me	This letter was sent to me. The clerk gave me the wrong package.
my	Which is my seat? That is my only hope.
she	Both he and she were offended. The woman said she was tired.
should	You don't read as much as you should. How should I know?
than	"Than" is a conjunction. Braver than a lion.
was	Could you see who it was? It was only a small boy.

you   The message was for you.
         Why do you think so?

your   That was your fault, not mine.
         Get your raincoat.

The above list is by no means complete, but it serves to make clear the fact that for many words we cannot insist on a uniform pronunciation in all positions.

C. T *in Medial and Final Position*

Although *t* is generally articulated by means of a forcible expulsion of breath while the tongue hits the upper palate of the mouth just above the top of the teeth, a comparison of three words will show that in informal speech the sound of *t* undergoes certain changes. Say these words aloud:

*t*iny   be*tt*er   we*t*

In American speech the *t*'s in these three words are not identical. Only the first word contains *t* in its pure form. In *better*, the *t* begins to approximate a *d* sound, faintly. The very tip of the tongue only is used. In *wet*, the tongue is in the same position as in *tiny* but considerably less breath is used.

Meticulous speakers make the mistake of pronouncing medial *t* (as in *better, writer, hitting,* etc.) and final *t* with the tongue in the same position and with the same amount of breath required for initial *t* (*tiny, Tom, task,* etc.). Their speech as a result sounds somewhat British in flavor.

For medial and final *t* relax your mouth, take your mind off the sound, speak naturally.

THREE

~~~~~~~~~~~~~~~~~~~~

Speak Up!

A GREAT PART of your business and social life is made possible by the fact that you are able to talk. It is this ability, peculiar to
humans, that especially distinguishes you from the rest of the animal world. It is a marvelous, a phenomenal ability. And it has only
one purpose: the delivery of a message, the communication of a
thought. Consider that fact carefully. Hold on to it, for it is the
central theme of effective speech. *You speak to communicate*—and
any mannerism, any peculiarity, any poverty of vocabulary or dic-
tion that serves to frustrate communication serves also to frustrate
effective speech.

No matter how electric your sentiments, or how superbly
couched your thoughts, if your speech is indistinct, then your message is being frustrated, your ideas are not getting across.

Compare yourself to a radio. The most modern and beautifully
toned set in the world is useless if the maximum volume it can
reach is too low for comfortable listening. There you have one fault

of the indistinct speaker—his voice is so deficient in volume that it is uncomfortable to listen to.

Do you suffer from this defect? Try reading the next few paragraphs of this chapter aloud—but really *aloud*. Let the room ring with the sound of your voice, feel those vocal chords of yours vibrating! Frankly let your voice exercise and you cannot help discovering in it unplumbed depths of richness and strength.

Here is the one way to strengthen your voice: *Read aloud, a little each day*. No extra time or effort is demanded. Merely break into your silent reading, as often as you can, and read a few paragraphs to the people—or, if you are alone, to the furniture—about you. The first few times your voice may sound halting, strained, monotonous. But listen to yourself at the end of just one week of this sort of daily practice; the improvement will positively startle you. Better yet, that improvement will carry over into your normal speaking voice and begin to startle others as well. You will begin to note how much more attention your newly developed voice commands from business associates, from salespeople, and from social acquaintances.

Psychologists say that people who do not speak up, who mumble their words, whose voices are indistinct almost to the point of inaudibility, are suffering from (that much-overused word) insecurity. If this is true, as it probably is, the indistinct speaker is constantly chasing himself round the most vicious cycle in existence. Feelings of insecurity cause mumbled speech; mumbled speech, in turn, brings to the speaker's ear an awareness of his own lack of forcefulness and self-confidence, thus adding to his sense of inadequacy; this in turn makes him mumble worse than ever. This can go on without end if somewhere a break is not made in these successive links of self-destruction.

That break can most potently be accomplished by practice. The voice is capable of attaining almost divine beauty, almost perfect clarity. But these qualities of beauty and clarity do not drop from heaven if you just wish hard enough for them. No one need remind you of the grueling practice that professional singers and public speakers must undergo. Their ability is the result of hard work, not wishfulness.

Happily, learning to speak clearly and loudly is comparatively simple. Of all the things you must do to gain power with words, training your voice to make those words clear to your audience is the one thing that will show results most quickly. Does the habitual scenery of your life include people constantly saying 'What?" "How's that?" "I didn't get it!" or looking at you in that perplexed manner that shows they are trying manfully to make sense out of the jumble of sounds coming from your mouth? In a week or less you can change all this. The five-minute daily exercise of reading aloud will produce that change with such rapidity and effectiveness that you will be chagrined that you waited as long as you did before taking positive steps to eliminate your trouble.

Once you've spent your week on the elementary steps of reading aloud whatever comes into your hands, you're ready for the advanced course. For one week more, devote a little time each day to reading aloud the poetry selections on the next pages. There are seven poems, one for each day. These contain elements of difficulty that will challenge your ability. Find a time when you're alone and can expect a minimum of interference. Make yourself perfectly comfortable in your softest easy chair. First read the poem to yourself once or twice in order to capture the mood and become familiar with the poet's message. Then try it aloud. Don't recite, don't declaim. Read it naturally, meaningfully, but considerably more loudly than you are in the habit of speaking. Pretend you are facing an audience of hundreds, with all the slightly deaf people seated in the last row. Then read the poem once again, and listen to your own voice. Are the words at the end of each sentence as clear and audible as those at the beginning? (Most "mumblers" start off bravely enough with what they have to say, but falter when the period comes into view and finally peter out lamely before they reach the last words of their sentence.) Are you reading slowly enough so that even the most untutored in your audience can follow the complex thought of the poem? Keep these questions in mind as you read; read the selection over and over until you are satisfied with what you hear your voice doing.

FIRST DAY

Unwarmed by any sunset light
The gray day darkened into night,
A night made hoary with the swarm
And whirl-dance of the blinding storm,
As zigzag, wavering to and fro,
Crossed and recrossed the wingëd snow:
And ere the early bedtime came
The white drift piled the window-frame,
And through the glass the clothes-line posts
Looked in like tall and sheeted ghosts.

So all night long the storm roared on:
The morning broke without a sun;
In tiny spherule traced with lines
Of Nature's geometric signs,
In starry flake, and pellicle,
All day the hoary meteor fell;
And, when the second morning shone,
We looked upon a world unknown,
On nothing we could call our own.

JOHN GREENLEAF WHITTIER

SECOND DAY

In a dim corner of my room for longer than my fancy thinks
A beautiful and silent Sphinx has watched me through the shifting
gloom.

Inviolate and immobile she does not rise, she does not stir
For silver moons are naught to her and naught to her the suns that reel.

Red follows grey across the air, the waves of moonlight ebb and flow
But with the Dawn she does not go and in the nighttime she is there.

Dawn follows Dawn and Nights grow old and all the while this curious
cat
Lies couching on the Chinese mat with eyes of satin rimmed with gold.

OSCAR WILDE

THIRD DAY

ON FIRST LOOKING INTO CHAPMAN'S HOMER

Much have I travelled in the realms of gold,
　And many goodly states and kingdoms seen;
　Round many western islands have I been
Which bards in fealty to Apollo hold.
Oft of one wide expanse had I been told
　That deep-browed Homer ruled as his demesne:
　Yet did I never breathe its pure serene
Till I heard Chapman speak out loud and bold:

Then felt I like some watcher of the skies
　When a new planet swims into his ken;
Or like stout Cortez, when with eagle eyes
　He stared at the Pacific—and all his men
Looked at each other with a wild surmise—
　Silent, upon a peak in Darien.

JOHN KEATS

FOURTH DAY

All the world's a stage,
And all the men and women merely players:
They have their exits and their entrances,
And one man in his time plays many parts,
His acts being seven ages. At first, the infant,
Mewling and puking in his nurse's arms:
Then the whining school-boy, with his satchel
And shining morning face, creeping like snail
Unwillingly to school. And then the lover,
Sighing like furnace, with a woful ballad
Made to his mistress' eye-brow. Then a soldier,
Full of strange oaths, and bearded like the pard,
Jealous in honor, sudden and quick in quarrel,
Seeking the bubble reputation
Even in the cannon's mouth. And then, the justice,
In fair round belly, with good capon lined,
With eyes severe, and beard of formal cut,
Full of wise saws and modern instances;

And so he plays his part. The sixth age shifts
Into the lean and slippered pantaloon,
With spectacles on nose, and pouch on side;
His youthful hose well saved, a world too wide
For his shrunk shank; and his big manly voice,
Turning again towards childish treble, pipes
And whistles in his sound. Last scene of all,
That ends this strange eventful history,
Is second childishness, and mere oblivion—
Sans teeth, sans eyes, sans taste, sans everything.

WILLIAM SHAKESPEARE

FIFTH DAY

I hid my heart in a nest of roses,
　　Out of the sun's way, hidden apart;
In a softer bed than the soft white snow's is,
　　Under the roses I hid my heart.
　　Why would it sleep not? why should it start,
When never a leaf of the rose-tree stirred?
　　What made sleep flutter his wings and part?
Only the song of a secret bird.
Lie still, I said, for the wind's wing closes,
　　And mild leaves muffle the keen sun's dart;
Lie still, for the wind on the warm sea dozes,
　　And the wind is unquieter yet than thou art.
　　Does a thought in thee still as a thorn's wound smart?
Does the fang still fret thee of hope deferred?
　　What bids the lids of thy sleep dispart?
Only the song of a secret bird.

ALGERNON CHARLES SWINBURNE

SIXTH DAY

INVICTUS

Out of the night that covers me,
　　Black as the pit from pole to pole,
I thank whatever gods may be
　　For my unconquerable soul.

In the fell clutch of circumstance
　　I have not winced nor cried aloud.

Under the bludgeonings of chance
My head is bloody, but unbowed.

Beyond this place of wrath and tears
Looms but the Horror of the shade,
And yet the menace of the years
Finds and shall find me unafraid.

It matters not how strait the gate,
How charged with punishments the scroll,
I am the master of my fate:
I am the captain of my soul.

WILLIAM E. HENLEY

SEVENTH DAY

OZYMANDIAS OF EGYPT

I met a traveller from an antique land
Who said: Two vast and trunkless legs of stone
Stand in the desert. Near them on the sand,
Half sunk, a shatter'd visage lies, whose frown
And wrinkled lip and sneer of cold command
Tell that its sculptor well those passions read
Which yet survive, stamp'd on these lifeless things,
The hand that mock'd them and the heart that fed;
And on the pedestal those words appear:
"My name is Ozymandias, king of kings:
Look on my works, ye Mighty, and despair!"
Nothing beside remains. Round the decay
Of that colossal wreck, boundless and bare,
The lone and level sands stretch far away.

PERCY BYSSHE SHELLEY

If you suspect yourself of being a "mumbler," this practice cannot possibly fail to help you. In addition to getting you to speak slowly, clearly, loudly and hence distinctly, it will make you particularly conscious of your fault and in that way push you halfway along the road to eliminating it. The first step in getting rid of any bad habit is the realization that the habit affects you. The next step is to desire keenly to loosen its hold upon you. And the final step—the one in which these poetry selections can help you—is the actual escape by means of practicing the good habit that will replace the bad one.

Do not even hope to cure your habit of mumbling unless your entire being is honestly and *relentlessly* permeated with the *will* to change—not the *wish,* mind you, but the *will,* and between the two there is a world of difference. In two weeks you can change from a "mumbler" into a "talker"—but only if your will to do this is strong enough to keep you at your practice for fourteen days without exception. As Professor James L. Mursell points out in *Streamline Your Mind:* [1]

In the absence of the will to learn there will be no improvement. If one just keeps on doing something again and again—playing golf, selling insurance, directing people at their tasks, listening to music, writing the English language—without actively wanting to do it better, learning does not take place. One must feel every job, whether of work or play or social intercourse, as a challenge to learn. This is the absolutely essential condition.

If your will to improve your speaking voice is vigorous enough, you can do it. Try it—the results are wonderful!

[1] J. B. Lippincott Company.

FOUR

~~~~~~~~~~~~~~~

Recent Trends in American Pronunciation

1. "LONG" A

IN THE FOLLOWING WORDS, "long" *a* (*ay*, as in *hate*) is strongly favored by educated speakers over the so-called "short" or "flat" *a* (as in *hat*).

aviator	AY'-vee-ay-tər
radiator	RAY'-dee-ay-tər
desideratum	də-sid-ə-RAY'-təm
verbatim	vər-BAY'-təm
ultimatum	ul-tə-MAY'-təm

In some words, educated usage is divided, long *a* somewhat more popular than short *a*.

data	DAY'-tə *or* DAT'-ə
fracas	FRAY'-kəs *or* FRAK'-əs
status	STAY'-təs *or* STAT'-əs
implacable	im-PLAY'-kə-bəl *or* im-PLAK'-ə-bəl
ignoramus	ig-nə-RAY'-məs *or* ig-nə-RAM'-əs
stratum	STRAY'-təm *or* STRAT'-əm
pro rata	prō RAY'-tə *or* prō RAT'-ə
gratis	GRAY'-təs *or* GRAT'-əs
apparatus	ap-ə-RAY'-təs *or* ap-ə-RAT'-əs

2. ADJECTIVES ENDING IN -ABLE

Educated speech shows a preference for first-syllable accent in certain adjectives ending in *-able.*

am'icable	for'midable
hos'pitable	rev'ocable
lam'entable	pref'erable
ex'plicable	rep'arable
ap'plicable	rep'utable
com'parable	

In the negative form the accent is retained on the same syllable on which it fell in the positive form.

inhos'pitable	irrev'ocable
inex'plicable	irrep'arable
inap'plicable	disrep'utable
incom'parable	

Disputable is more commonly accented on the second syllable (dis-PYŌŌ'-tə-bəl), though DIS'-pyə-tə-bəl is sometimes heard; similarly the negative is in-dis-PYŌŌ'-tə-bəl or, much less often, in-DIS'-pyə-tə-bəl.

3. WORDS ENDING IN -ILE

In the following words, the American pattern is to pronounce the suffix *-ile* in such a way that it almost rhymes with *hill,* but with the vowel sound less protracted, i.e., *-əl.* The British, on the other hand, tend to rhyme the ending with *mile.* Thus, for *fertile,* we say *FUR'-təl,* Britons say *FUR'-tile.*

fertile	FUR'-təl
fragile	FRAJ'-əl
servile	SUR'-vəl
versatile	VUR'-sə-təl
imbecile	IM'-bə-səl
puerile	PYŌŌ'-ər-əl
hostile	HOS'-təl
sterile	STER'-əl
missile	MIS'-əl
juvenile	JŌŌ-və-nəl
textile	TEKS'-təl
docile	DOS'-əl
virile	VEER'-əl
mercantile	MUR'-kən-təl
domicile	DOM'-ə-səl
agile	AJ'-əl
futile	FYŌŌ-təl

In *juvenile, textile,* and *mercantile,* however, rhyming the final syllable with *mile* is equally common; and MUR'-kən-teel is also occasionally heard for *mercantile.*

In the following, *-ile* is generally pronounced as in *mile.*

infantile	bibliophile
Francophile	profile
Anglophile	exile
crocodile	reconcile
senile	turnstile

4. AMERICAN VS. BRITISH PRONUNCIATION

In a great many words, British pronunciation differs markedly from American. Some random examples:

Word	British Pronunciation	American Pronunciation
organization	awr'-gən-eye-ZAY'-shən	awr'-gən-ə-ZAY'-shən
civilization	civ'-əl-eye-ZAY'-shən	civ'-ə-lə-ZAY'-shən
docile	DŌ'-sile	DOS'-əl
missile	MIS'-ile	MIS'-əl

Word	*British Pronunciation*	*American Pronunciation*
fast	fahst	fast
laugh	lahf	laf
secretary	SEK'-rə-tree	SEK'-rə-ter'-ee
conservatory	kən-SURV'-ə-tree	kən-SURV'-ə-taw'-ree
laboratory	lə-BAWR'-ə-tree	LAB'-ə-rə-taw'-ree
miscellany	mə-SEL'-ə-nee	MIS'-ə-lay-nee
project (*n.*)	PRŌ'-jekt	PROJ'-ekt
progress (*n.*)	PRŌ'-gres	PROG'-res
process (*n.*)	PRŌ'-ses	PROS'-es
ate	et	ayt
ski	shee	skee
schedule	SHED'-yŏŏl	SKED'-yŏŏl
medicine	MED'-sən	MED'-ə-sən
circumstance	SUR'-kəm-stəns	SUR'-kəm-stance
been	bean	bin
Celtic	KEL'-tək	SEL'-tək

5. WORDS ENDING IN -AGE

In many words the ending *-age* contains the same consonant sound represented by the letter *s* in plea*s*ure. The phonetic symbol generally used to represent this sound is *zh*.

-AHZH preferable to -AHDGE

barrage	ménage
camouflage	persiflage
massage	corsage
garage	espionage

Prestige (pres-TEEZH') and *cortege* (kawr-TEZH') contain the same sound.

6. C

C is probably the most useless letter in the alphabet. Not only could we get along admirably without it, but our pronunciation and spelling would be considerably more logical and simple if it had never existed.

C is a parasite, doing nothing to earn its keep, and sponging on the letters *k* and *s*. When *c* has the sound of *k* (as in *cat*) we call it *hard;* when it has the sound of *s* (as in *citizen*), we call it *soft*. Generally (there are, of course, exceptions) this rule works:

C is soft before *e, i,* and *y;* otherwise it is hard. Note the following:

Soft C (S)

acerbity	(ə-SUR'-bə-tee)
accept	(ək-SEPT')
flaccid	(FLAK'-səd)
succinct	(sək-SINGKT')
accessory	(ək-SES'-ər-ee)
accelerator	(ək-SEL'-ə-ray-tər)
Celtic	(SEL'-tək)
ceramic	(sə-RAM'-ək)
taciturn	(TAS'-ə-turn)
viscid	(VIS'-əd)

Hard C (K)

accustom	(ə-KUS'-təm)
catastrophe	(kə-TAS'-trə-fee)
cold	(KŌLD)
cut	(KUT)
clink	(KLINK)
crawl	(KRAWL)
viscous	(VIS'-kəs)

7 . G

G follows the same principle: before *e, i,* or *y,* it is soft (*j*), as in *gem*. Otherwise, it is hard (*g*), as in *gum*. Short words of Anglo-Saxon origin are the most frequent exceptions to this rule.

Soft G (J)

orgy	(AWR'-jee)
gill	(the measure is JILL)
giblets	(JIB'-ləts)

George	(this explains the first E; without it, the word would be pronounced GAWRJ)
gesture	(JES'-chər)
gesticulate	(jes-TIK'-yə-layt)
manger	(MAYN'-jər)
gibe	(JIBE)
gibberish	(JIB'-ər-ish)
harbinger	(HAHR'-bən-jər)
longevity	(lon-JEV'-ə-tee)
turgid	(TUR'-jəd)
orgiastic	(awr-jee-AS'-tək)
gibbet	(JIB'-ət)

Hard G (G)

go
guard
game
gust
glint
grass
gill   (of a fish)
prodigal (PROD'-ə-gəl)

8. -ITIS

Diseases ending in *-itis* are generally pronounced EYE'-təs, *not* EE'-təs.

appendicitis	laryngitis
arthritis	meningitis
bronchitis	neuritis
colitis	pharyngitis
gastritis	tonsillitis

FIVE

~~~~~~~~~~~

Our Wonderful Erratic Language

IT IS NO WONDER that English is a difficult language to pronounce. Consider some of the pitfalls always present in the path of the unwary:

I. Spelling is no criterion.

a. *Warm* and *harm* are almost identical in spelling. Note how differently they are pronounced.
b. *Tough, through, though, cough, bough* all end in *-ough*. In each case this suffix has a different pronunciation.
c. Consider how perplexed a foreigner learning English would be by pairs like these:
ghost—guest
palm—thumb
plumber—hammer
hymn—dim

d. Often the spelling of a word is not even remotely connected with its pronunciation. Consider:

victuals	(VIT'-əlz)
colonel	(KUR'-nəl)
quay	(kee)
solder	(SOD'-ər)
phthisic	(TIZ'-ək)
Sioux	(sōō)

II. A tremendous part of the vocabulary of English comes from foreign languages. Every language on the face of the earth is represented: ancient languages, modern languages, dead languages, living languages. Hebrew, Latin, Greek, Sanskrit, Hawaiian, Japanese, Chinese, French, and Icelandic, to mention just a few, have contributed tens of thousands of words to our present-day dictionaries. Some of these foreign words are Anglicized when they are taken over into English; some are Anglicized years later; some always retain their foreign flavor.

For example:

a. From the French, *sachet* is still pronounced in a Gallic manner (sa-SHAY'); *valet* is sometimes Anglicized (VAL'-ət).

b. *Sotto voce,* from the Italian, has not been Anglicized (SOT'-tō vaw'-chay); *viva voce,* from the Latin, has been (VY'-və vō-see).

c. *Weltschmerz* and *wanderlust* are both from the German. The former is still Teutonic in sound (VELT'-shmairts); the latter is Anglicized (WAHN'-dər-lust).

III. Sometimes *th* is soft, as in *the* (*lithe, blithe*); sometimes hard, as in *thing* (*hearth, ether*); sometimes like *t,* as in *thyme.*

IV. Sometimes *h* is silent, as in *honor;* sometimes pronounced, as in *humor.*

V. *Oo* may be heard one way, as in *book;* another as in *moon.*

VI. *Ch* may be *tsh,* as in *chair; sh,* as in *machine; k,* as in *pachyderm;* or silent, as in *yacht.*

VII. *S* may be *sh,* as in *sugar* or *sure; s,* as in *sinecure; z,* as in *reserve;* or silent, as in *provost marshal* (PRŌ'-vō).

VIII. *-Ine* may rhyme with *wine,* as in *feline;* or sounded *-ən,* as in *genuine.*

IX. *G* may be silent in one form of a word (*phlegm, malign, diaphragm*), pronounced in a different form (*phlegmatic, malignant, diaphragmatic*).

These nine principles do not by any means exhaust the peculiarities and idiosyncrasies of English pronunciation. They are sufficient, however, to indicate the great complexity and delightful confusion of our language. An educated Frenchman, or German, or Spaniard can pronounce perfectly any word in his language with which you may wish to confront him—and this statement holds whether he's ever seen the word before or not. Pronunciation hews obediently to definite rules in these and other languages; the exceptions, if any, are infrequent and unimportant.

But, ah, English! What a language! Confusing, perplexing, without rhyme or reason, the full scale of its intricacies can scarcely be more than hinted at.

But let us see whether we can't get a little order out of the seeming chaos:

1.

In the following words, the italicized letters are usually pronounced as indicated.

sug*g*est	(sug-JEST')	govern*n*ment	(GUV'-ərn-mənt)
epitom*e*	(ə-PIT'-ə-mee)	stren*g*th	(strenkth)
canap*é*	(kan-ə-PAY')	len*g*th	(lenkth)
fla*cc*id	(FLAK'-səd)	su*cc*inct	(sək-SINGKT')
a*cc*essory	(ək-SES'-ə-ree)	*z*oological	(zō-ə-LOJ'-ə-kəl)
ag*ue*	(AY'-gyōō)		

2.

In the following, the italicized letters are silent.

indi*c*t	(in-DITE')	fore*h*ead	(FAHR'-əd *or*
mali*g*n	(mə-LINE')		FAWR'-əd)
poi*g*nant	(POY'-nənt)	so*l*der	(SOD'-ər)
piq*u*ant	(PEE'-kənt)	vi*s*count	(VY'-kount)
ches*t*nut	(CHES'-nut)	kil*n*	(KIL)
boats*wa*in	(BŌ'-sən)	*h*erb	(URB)

comptroller	(kən-TRŌ′-lər)	often	(OF′-ən)
gunwale	(GUN′-əl)	imbroglio	(im-BRŌL′-yō)
bagnio	(BAN′-yō)		

3.

Words ending in *-ine* are pronounced in one of three ways: long *i* (as in *wine*), *-ən*, or long *e* (*-een*).

-ən	*wine*	*-een*	
aquiline	alkaline	submarine	
genuine	asinine	peregrine	
heroine	canine	nectarine	
saccharine	concubine	nicotine	
gelatine	turpentine	benzine	
	leonine	gasoline	
	saturnine	cuisine	(kwə-ZEEN′)
	serpentine	guillotine	(gil-ə-TEEN′)
	feline		
	bovine		

4.

A large proportion of our two- and three-syllable words ending in *-et* have come from French, in which language the pattern is pronounced *-ay*. Some of these words retain their Gallic flavor—some have been Anglicized.

Anglicized (-et)	*Gallic (-ay)*
bayonet	sachet
cadet	sobriquet
coronet	cabaret
tourniquet	bouquet
martinet	cabriolet
	Chevrolet
	gourmet

5.

Th may be hard, as in *thing,* or soft, as in *the.* Here are the few confusing forms:

Hard (thing)	*Soft (the)*
youth	lithe
cloth	blithe
baths	thence
	youths
	bathes
	swathe

6.

Qu is sometimes pronounced as a simple *k*, sometimes as a *kw*.

K		KW
liquor		banquet
piquant	(PEE′-kənt)	quote
piqué	(pə-KAY′)	querulous
		quaint
		acquiesce
		loquacious

7.

Words from the French usually retain the Gallic pronunciation *ahn-* for the initial letters *en-*.

ennui	(AHN′-wee)	entr'acte	(ahn-TRAKT′)
en route	(ahn ROOT′)	entree	(AHN′-tray)
ensemble	(ahn-SAHM′-bəl)		

8.

H is silent in many words. In the following, however, educated usage usually pronounces it:

*h*omage
*h*umble
*h*otel
*h*uman
*h*umane
*h*umor
*h*umorous

In the following, *h* is silent:

> vehement
> prohibition
> vehicle
> herb

9.

Ch has three possible pronunciations: *tsh* as in *chair: k* as in *chaos; sh* as in *machine*. Generally, *tsh* is used in native English words; *k* in words of Greek derivation; *sh* in words of French origin.

TSH	K	SH
chair	archangel	champagne
chase	archeology	chauvinism
arch	hierarchy	chagrin
archbishop	Archimedes	chic
champion	chaos	chicanery (shə-KAY'-nə-ree)
	chasm	
	epoch	
	archaic	
	archipelago	
	chiropodist	
	chimera (kə-MEER'-ə)	

Bach (the composer) retains its German pronunciation: the *a* as in *father,* the *ch* a guttural sound.

10.

Ng is a native English sound, found, to my knowledge, in no other language (French has a similar sound, but much more nasal in character). It is for that reason that foreigners have so much trouble with this simple digraph; a speaker accustomed to a tongue other than English, or brought up in a home where some other language was spoken, tends to "click" his *ng*'s, thus: sin*gg*er, Lon*gg* *G*island, goin*gg* *g*away, etc.

Now, as a matter of fact, the *ng* click is not necessarily a foreign sound. We use it in a host of words like En*g*lish, fin*g*er, lin*g*er, an*g*er, etc. What the foreigner does is use it indiscriminately and always, even in words like *singer* and *along* and *winging*.

The native American does not need rules to know when to click and when not to. And, ironically, since no rules are necessary, a perfectly fine rule, with only four exceptions, exists. Let me give it to you if you're curious, or if you think you sometimes have difficulty with your *ng*'s.

RULE FOR PRONUNCIATION OF NG

A. *N*g at the end of a word is never clicked.
lon(*g*), *sin*(*g*), *win*(*g*), *han*(*g*).

B. When *ng* occurs in the body of a word, drop all the letters following it. If a real word is then left, do not click.

Example 1: singer; drop *-er. Sing,* a real word, remains. Do not click.
Example 2: linger; drop *-er. Ling,* a nonexistent word, remains. Click (LING'-gər).
Example 3: clanging; drop *-ing. Clang,* a real word, remains. Do not click.

And here are the exceptions. *These words are to be clicked,* though they violate the rule.

longer	younger	stronger	clangor
longest	youngest	strongest	

II.

A fairly reliable rule is that *-ate,* as a suffix in *nouns* or *adjectives,* is pronounced *-ət;* as a suffix in *verbs,* it is pronounced *-ayt.*

Verbs (-ayt)	*Adjectives or Nouns (-ət)*
graduate	graduate
aggregate	aggregate
alternate	alternate
animate	animate
appropriate	appropriate
approximate	approximate
articulate	articulate
associate	associate
aspirate	aspirate

Note these exceptions:

The following, though nouns or adjectives, are pronounced -*ayt*.

candidate	potentate
concentrate	prostrate
irate	reprobate
magnate	sedate
ornate	inmate

12.

It is a tendency of English words to shift the accent as they add or change letters from one part of speech to another. Here are a few out of a very great many examples. The italicized syllable is accented.

*dra*ma (n.)	dra*mat*ic (adj.)
*sa*tiate (v.)	sa*ti*ety (n.)
*ba*nal (adj.)	ba*nal*ity (n.)
*cred*ulous (adj.)	cre*dul*ity (n.)
*al*gebra (n.)	alge*bra*ic (adj.)
*chor*al (adj.)	cho*rale* (n.)
*mor*al (adj.)	mo*rale* (n.)
*gar*rulous (adj.)	gar*rul*ity (n.)
*the*ater (n.)	the*at*rical (adj.)

13.

Similarly, a change of part of speech may change the length of some vowels. Thus *mediocre* has a long *o; mediocrity,* a short one; *loquacious* has a long *a; loquacity,* a short one. Here are a few more examples:

tenacious	(tə-NAY'-shəs)	*tenacity*	(tə-NAS'-ə-tee)
maniac	(MAY'-nee-ak)	*maniacal*	(mə-NY'-ə-kəl)
admire	(ad-MIRE')	*admirable*	(AD'-mə-rə-bəl)
Bible	(BY'-bəl)	*Biblical*	(BIB'-lə-kəl)
saliva	(sə-LY'-və)	*salivary*	(SAL'-ə-ver'-ee)
alkali	(AL'-kə-lie)	*alkalinity*	(al-kə-LIN'-ə-tee)
analyze	(AN'-ə-lize)	*analytic*	(an-ə-LIT'-ək)
episode	(EP'-ə-sode)	*episodic*	(ep-ə-SOD'-ək)
athlete	(ATH'-leet)	*athletic*	(ath-LET'-ək)
compete	(kəm-PEET')	*competitive*	(kəm-PET'-ə-tiv)

SIX

100 *Words That Cause*
Pronunciation Problems

THIS CHAPTER IS simply a list of words: words which skillful, effective speakers pronounce a certain way. Some of them are tricky because they are "reading" rather than "speaking" words. That is, you will come across them over and over on the printed page, but perhaps say them infrequently. Hence, you may easily have blundered into mental mispronunciations and never have had the opportunity to check yourself or be checked by your listeners.

A number of words in particular are those that lend themselves all too easily to slovenly articulation. Others sound so different from the way they are spelled that mispronunciation is often too tempting to be resisted.

And still others may be in that large class of words that have two current pronunciations in educated usage, one of them, as will be indicated, somewhat more popular than the other.

The best and most helpful way to go through this chapter is to
cover the right-hand column, in which the phonetic respellings are
offered, with a blank card. Say each word in the left-hand column
aloud. Check at once with its pronunciation by shifting your card
one line. If your pronunciation and the one offered check, well and
good. If they do not, mark the word and continue. When you have
finished each list, study the words which gave you trouble.

A few have already been discussed in previous chapters; most
are offered for the first time.

I.

Is your enunciation accurate, clear, and easily understandable?
The twenty-five words in the list will provide you with a yardstick
for measuring the clarity of your speech. Keep your pencil handy,
and check for future practice any word you mispronounce.

1. government   GUV′-ərn-mənt, in which the first *n* is pronounced, is more popular in educated usage,
though GUV′-ər-mənt is also heard. GUV′-mənt
is sloppy.

2. just   JUST, *not* JIST.

3. kept   KEPT, the *t* pronounced—*not* KEP.

4. library   LY′-brer-ee *or* LY′-brə-ree, *not* LY′-ber-ee.

5. attacked   ə-TAKT′, *not* ə-TAK′-təd.

6. American   ə-MER′-ə-kən, *not* ə-MUR′-ə-kən.

7. Italian   ə-TAL′-yən, *not* eye-TAL′-yən.

8. wrestle   RES′-əl, *not* RAS′-əl.

9. elm   ELM, in one syllable, *not* EL′-əm.

10. film   Again one syllable: FILM, *not* FIL′-əm.

11. law   LAW—though in parts of New England
LAWR is often heard.

12. Cuba   KYOO′-bə, though here again, as in so many
words ending in a vowel, New England speakers add an *r* (i.e., KYOO′-bər).

13. asked   Both the *k* and the *d* are usually pronounced on
educated levels: ASKT, *not* AST.

14. potato   pə-TAY′-tō *or* pə-TAY′-tə, *not* pər-TAY′-tər.

15. window   WIN′-dō, *not* WIN′-dər.

16. accurate   AK'-yə-rət, *not* AK'-ə-rət.

17. manufacture   man-yə-FAK'-chər preferable to man-ə-FAK'-chər. man-yə-FAK'-tyo͝or is pedantic.

18. particular   pər-TIK'-yə-lər, *not* pər-TIK'-ə-lər.

19. regular   REG'-yə-lər, *not* REG'-ə-lər.

20. poem   PŌ'-əm, *not* PŌM.

21. ruin   RŌŌ'-ən, *not* RŌŌN.

22. recognize   REK'-əg-nize, *not* REK'-ə-nize.

23. question   KWES'-chən, *not* KWESH'-ən.

24. figure   FIG'-yər, *not* FIG'-ər.

25. irrelevant   i-REL'-ə-vənt, *not* i-REV'-ə-lənt.

II.

Do your pronunciation patterns conform, more or less, to educated standards in the following words? Check up on yourself.

1. bade   BAD.

2. marmalade   MAHR'-mə-layd.

3. forbade   fawr-BAD'.

4. charade   shə-RAYD'.

5. route   Generally RŌŌT, though ROWT is the common pronunciation in military and commercial use.

6. bouquet   bo͞o-KAY' has an edge, though bō-KAY' is also commonly heard.

7. brooch   BRŌCH.

8. squalid   SKWAH'-ləd.

9. nausea   NAW'-shə˙ is the more popular form, though NAW'-zee-ə, NAW'-zhə, and NAW'-zhee-ə are also heard.

10. nauseate   NAW'-shee-ayt; NAW'-zee-ayt and NAW'-zhee-ayt are also heard.

11. fjord   FYAWRD; this Norwegian import is also spelled *fiord,* but either way there is a *y* sound after the *f*.

12. finis   FY'-nis preferable; FIN'-is also heard.

13. egregious   ə-GREE'-jəs.

14. zoology   zō-OL'-ə-jee.

15. virago   və-RAY′-gō.

16. falcon   FAWL′-kən *or* FAL′-kən; the compact car is only FAL′-kən.

17. quay   KEE.

18. plebeian   plə-BEE′-ən.

19. sacrilegious   sac-ri-LEE′-jəs; also, though it does not follow the spelling, sac-re-LIJ′-əs.

20. nonpareil   non-pə-REL′.

21. flaccid   FLAK′-səd—the two *c*'s are pronounced separately.

22. decade   DEK′-ayd.

23. suave   SWAHV.

24. with   The *th* is usually voiced (i.e., as in *this*), but is also heard unvoiced (i.e., as in *thing*.)

25. comparable   KOM′-pə-rə-bəl.

III.

1. associate (*v.*)   ə-SŌ′-shee-ayt. Note that the *c* is preferably pronounced as *sh*.

2. associate (*n.*)   ə-SŌ′-shee-ət. Note the difference in the final syllable according to whether this word is a verb or a noun.

3. association   ə-sō-see-AY′-shən. Now the *c* is preferably pronounced as *s*.

4. appreciate   ə-PREE′-shee-ayt. To pronounce the third syllable -*see* is somewhat prissy and old-fashioned.

5. appreciation   ə-pree-shee-AY′-shən.

6. radiator   RAY′-dee-ay-tər. Note the sound of the first *a*.

7. illustrate   IL′-əs-trayt. Second-syllable accent is pedantic.

8. illustrative   ə-LUS′-trə-tiv. Now, however, the second syllable much more commonly *is* accented.

9. orgy   AWR′-jee. Note the soft *g* since the next letter is *y*.

10. often   OF′-ən. The *t* is usually silent, as in *soften, glisten,* and *listen,* though lately OF′-tən, following the spelling, has been widely heard in some areas of the country.

11. coupé	Strictly, kōō-PAY', following the French—but automobile salesmen, in the days when this word described a kind of car, invariably said KŌOP.
12. coupon	KŌO'-pon is better; KYŌO'-pon is largely heard on less-educated levels.
13. escalator	ES'-kə-lay-tər. Note the second syllable—the pronunciation *kya-* is considered unsophisticated.
14. percolator	PUR'-kə-lay-tər. Again note the second syllable.
15. exquisite	Either eks-KWIZ'-ət or EKS'-kwiz-ət, the former increasingly more popular.
16. pomegranate	pəm-GRAN'-ət.
17. vanilla	və-NIL'-ə; və-NEL'-ə is unsophisticated.
18. romance	Traditionally, rə-MANCE', though RŌ'-mance is becoming popular.
19. secretive	SEEK'-rə-tiv very popular when the word means *close-mouthed,* though sə-KREE'-tiv was once the "proper" form. When the word refers to secretions, only sə-KREE'-tiv.
20. dirigible	DEER'-ə-jə-bəl—note the first-syllable accent.
21. scourge	SKURJ.
22. clandestine	klan-DES'-tən better than KLAN'-də-stine.
23. posthumous	POS'-chə-məs.
24. gaol	This is the British spelling of our word *jail,* and that's how it's pronounced: JAIL.
25. saga	SAH'-gə preferable to SAG-ə, though the latter is also heard.

IV.

1. harass	HĂR'-əs is more sophisticated, though hə-RAS' is also heard.
2. traverse	trə-VURS' is almost always the pronunciation and undoubtedly how you would say it, but TRAV'-ərs was once the only "proper" form.
3. absolutely	The first syllable is accented; for emphasis, however, -LŌOT is often stressed instead. It's pedantic to say -LYŌOT.

4. positively — The same comment—first-syllable accent except for emphasis, in which case poz-ə-TIV'-lee is acceptable.

5. bicycle — BY'-sə-kəl, *not* BY'-sy-kəl.

6. isolate — EYE'-sə-layt; IS'-ə-layt is overelegant.

7. direct — də-REKT'. In some parts of the country dy-REKT' is also widely heard.

8. poniard — PON'-yərd.

9. vineyard — VIN'-yərd.

10. ignominy — IG'-nə-mə-nee. This is a bookish word and hard to say with the accent as indicated, but the easier ig-NOM'-ə-nee is considered uneducated.

11. ignominious — ig-nə-MIN'-ee-əs. In this form the accent is in a comfortable position. The uneducated ig-NOM'-ə-nəs should be avoided.

12. inexorable — in-EKS'-ər-ə-bəl. Note the accent on the second syllable.

13. impious — IM'-pee-əs. Note the first-syllable accent, as also in the next two words.

14. infamous — IN'-fə-məs.

15. impotent — IM'-pə-tənt.

16. peculiarity — pə-kyo͞o-lee-ĂR'-ə-tee. All six syllables should be there, as also in the next word.

17. familiarity — fə-mil-ee-ĂR'-ə-tee.

18. phraseology — fray-zee-OL'-ə-jee. Do not omit the second syllable.

19. era — EER'-ə. The first syllable is not the same as in *error*.

20. epoch — EP'-ək. The *ch* has a *k* sound.

21. plethora — PLETH'-ər-ə, *not* plə-THAW'-rə.

22. enigma — ə-NIG'-mə. Note the position of the accent.

23. caricature — KĂR'-ə-kə-chər. The first syllable is accented, and the prissy *-tyo͞or* for the final syllable should be avoided.

24. perfunctory — pər-FUNK'-tə-ree.

25. perfunctorily — pər-FUNK'-tə-rə-lee. Note that both adjective and adverb receive the stress on the same syllable.

SEVEN

~~~~~~~~~~~~~

How to Say It

NOTES ON THE PRONUNCIATION
OF CERTAIN INTERESTING WORDS

ABDOMEN Most of us call it *stomach,* which everyone pronounces the same despite the odd spelling. The stomach is, admittedly, the internal organ, and when we use the word we generally have in mind the *external* surface, which is properly the *abdomen,* or *belly,* only the latter sounds vulgar to those with tender ears. In any case, AB'-də-mən is now the popular pronunciation, though ab-DŌ'-mən is also heard, much less frequently.

ABSORB It's somewhat more sophisticated to "hiss" the *s* (əb-SAWRB'), though many educated speakers "buzz" it (əb-ZAWRB').

ABSURD As with *absorb,* hiss (əb-SURD') to be sophisticated, buzz (əb-ZURD') to join the rank and file.

ACCLIMATE AK'-lə-mayt is somewhat more popular, as this pattern fits in sensibly with the pronunciation of other *-ate* verbs (*aggravate, estimate, graduate,* etc.), but the traditional ə-KLY'-mət is still tenaciously holding its ground.

ADVERTISEMENT As many people say ad-vər-TIZE'-mənt as əd-VUR'-tiz-mənt or əd-VUR'-tis-mənt—take your choice.

APRICOT AP'-rə-kot is the usual pronunciation, AY'-prə-kot popularly heard only in restricted areas.

ATHLETE Two syllables only, not three, in educated speech: ATH'-leet.

AU REVOIR If you prefer this to our own less conspicuous *good-bye,* keep the French flavor: Ō' rə-VWAHR'.

AWRY ə-RYE'—the other possibility (AW'-ree) is heard usually only from people who meet the word for the first time.

BECAUSE Except in New York, almost everyone "buzzes" the *s:* bə-KAWZ'.

BONA FIDE Join the common people and say BŌ'-nə fide; the Latin scholars who add the extra syllable (BŌ'-nə FY'-dee) sound pedantic.

CHIC On less-than-educated levels you will widely hear SHIK or even CHIK, but it's usually SHEEK in sophisticated circles.

CLIQUE KLEEK is the pronunciation of choice, though CLIK is still widely heard.

COMBAT (*v.*) KOM'-bat has an edge over kəm-BAT', even though two-syllable verbs are usually accented on the second syllable.

COMBATANT The *com-* is preferably stressed (KOM'-bə-tənt), as also in *noncombatant.*

CULINARY KYŌŌ'-lə-ner'-ee is by far preferable to KUL'-ə-ner'-ee.

DEBUT Completely Anglicized to də-BYŌŌ', though the French say it differently.

DEBUTANTE The Anglicized version is the more popular (DEB'-yŏŏ-tant), though the Parisian deb-yŏŏ-TAHNT' or day-byŏŏ-TAHNT' is widely heard.

DILETTANTE Unlike the preceding word, and despite the similarity in spelling, this one is from Italian, not French, and should therefore be dil-ə-TAN'-tee, but most people, sensing a nonexistent Gallic ancestry, say dil-ə-TAHNT'.

DISHABILLE This *is* from French, but is more or less Anglicized to dis-ə-BEEL'.

DIVAN   When the word means a couch, the popular form is DY'-van.

DRAMA   DRAH'-mə more popular on educated levels, but DRAM'-ə also heard.

DRAMATIST   But DRAH'-mə-tist is an affectation—say DRAM'-ə tist.

DUTY·   DYŌŌ-tee is British, New England, or ostentatious. Most people say DŌŌ'-tee, the first syllable almost as in *doom*.

EIGHTH   Most people say AYTH—those who are very meticulous say AYT-TH, with an extra *t* sound even though there is only one *t* in the spelling.

ENVELOPE   EN'-və-lope far more popular today: AHN'-və-lope began to wane in the early 1900's and is today almost *passé*, except from older people—proving that pronunciation learned in one's youth tends to linger.

EPITOME   This is a word people read and write, but rarely say. If they do, they should pronounce it ə-PIT'-ə-mee.

ESOTERIC   Main accent is on the third syllable: es'-ə-TER'-ək.

EXILE   Equally popular are EK'-sile and EG'-zile.

EXHIBIT   Showing the delightful inconsistency of American pronunciation, the *x* in this word has a *gz* sound (əg-ZIB'-ət), but in *exhibition* a *ks* sound (ek'-sə-BISH'-ən).

EXIT   Now again usage is divided—EK'-sit and EG'-zit are equally popular.

FIANCÉE   Spelled with two *e*'s, it's a woman, and pronounced fee-ahn-SAY'; with one *e* (*fiancé*) a man, and pronounced exactly the same.

FORTUNE   Avoid the pedantic *-tyōōn* at the end—say FAWR'-chən.

GALA   GAY'-lə more sophisticated—GAL'-ə equally popular.

GENUINE   When a novelist wants a character to sound illiterate, he has him say JEN'-yōō-wine.

GRIMY   This is the adjective form of *grime,* and has nothing to do with *grim*—hence GRY'-mee.

HALF   The broad *a* here, as also in *calf, laugh, last,* etc. (HAHF, CAHF, LAHF, LAHST) is British and common in America only in parts of New England, especially Boston and its environs.

INCOGNITO   in'-kəg-NEE'-tō is the more popular pronunciation, though in-KOG'-nə-tō is more traditional and still widely heard.

INQUIRY Here again, the traditional in-KWIRE'-ee is giving ground to the folksier IN'-kwə-ree.

IMPOTENT This word, like *impious* and *infamous,* is generally accented in educated speech on the *first* syllable (IM'-pə-tənt, IM'-pee-əs, IN'-fə-məs). *Impiety,* of course, is im-PY'-ə-tee.

IODINE Most people say EYE'-ə-dine or EYE'-ə-deen; some few say EYE'-ə-dən.

IRONY Even though *iron* is EYE'-ərn, this word is EYE'-rə-nee.

KILN The *n* is preferably silent (KIL), but is heard often enough so that we can't rule it out entirely.

LICORICE The grown-up pronunciation is LIK'-ə-ris or LIK'-ris, though most of us as kids called it LIK'-rish.

LIVELONG In this form the *i* is short (LIV'-long), but in *long-lived* it's preferably long (LONG'-lyvd).

MODERN Not MOD'-rən nor MAR'-dən, except in dialectical usage —say MOD'-ərn.

NUDE NYO͞OD considered affected and dainty by most people, who say something much closer to NO͞OD, the o͞o not quite as protracted as in *noon.*

PERSPIRATION The first syllable is *pur-* not *pres-*.

POTPOURRI This French import keeps its Gallic flavor: pō'-po͝o-REE'.

PREFACE Whether noun or verb, the word is accented on the *first* syllable: PREF'-əs.

PRESCRIPTION The first syllable is *pre-,* not *pur-.* (See PERSPIRATION, above).

QUAY Proof that spelling has no seeming relevancy to sound, this is KEE.

REMONSTRATE rə-MON'-strayt, even though *demonstrate* is DEM'-ən-strayt.

RIBALD RIB'-əld, rhyming exactly with the imaginary word *dibbled.*

ROBUST A lot of people now say RŌ'-bust, but rō-BUST' is more sophisticated and has an edge in popularity.

SENILE Most commonly SEE'-nile.

SUITE Pronounced exactly the same as *sweet,* but leave the *e* off and it's so͞ot.

SUPERB sə-PURB'—syo͞o-PURB' is pedantic.

TACITURN The *c* has the sound of *s* before an *i*: TAS'-ə-turn.

THYME The *h* is silent, as it is in *Thomas:* TYME.

VAGARY və-GAIR'-ee, *not* VAY'-gə-ree.

VICTUALS Further proof that pronunciation does not necessarily conform to spelling: VIT'-əlz.

WIDTH Most educated speakers manage to pronounce, or at least hint at, the *d*.

E I G H T

~~~~~~~~~~~~~~

℞ *For Effective Pronunciation*

A RESTATEMENT OF PRINCIPLES

WE ARE AGREED THEN that ours is a tricky language, full of pitfalls for the unwary, abounding in traps for the unsuspecting. It is a language rich in inconsistencies, made up of hundreds of diverse elements, defying all attempts at logical organization.

These are not faults; on the contrary they are the very qualities which make English the most expressive, most flexible, most fascinating language on earth.

English is a beautiful and *fundamentally* simple tongue, despite its myriad apparent intricacies. This may sound like a paradox, and in a sense it is. English is paradoxical the way a jet airplane is paradoxical—maddeningly complex in details, yet boasting of an overall simplicity of design and function that is truly awesome. Modern English is a product of the machine age and is perfectly suited to carry on the business of the age that has created and refined it. You can speak English all your life without gaining perfect mastery over it. But once that mastery does come (and, believe me, it comes only as a result of hard work and conscientious endeavor) you have made an accomplishment that will aid and comfort you every moment of your life, that will augment your skill in every activity in which language plays a part.

Mastery over the pronunciation of English, to restate the principles we have discussed in this section, involves:

1. A realization that "correct" pronunciation means popular educated pronunciation.
2. An acceptance of the fact that illiterate, affected, and overmeticulous pronunciations detract strongly from effective speech.
3. The ability to speak distinctly.
4. An understanding of the few broad principles that shape our language.
5. An avoidance of those forms that are generally heard only on uneducated levels.

FOUR

*Grammar and
Correct Usage*

ONE

~~~~~~~~~~

Exactly What Is Grammar?

In considering the use of grammar as a corrective of what are called "ungrammatical" expressions, it must be borne in mind that the rules of grammar have no value except as statements of facts: whatever is in general use in a language is for that very reason grammatically correct.   HENRY SWEET, *New English Grammar*, Vol. I [1]

Most of us remember grammar as a high-school subject full of big and incomprehensible terms, and having no discernible similarity to real life. A few of us, lucky possessors of a well-developed language sense, were able to see beneath the austere labels of case, tense, voice, and mood to the underlying basis of everyday speech patterns. We were able to do that, usually, in spite of our teachers, not because of them. For until very recently grammar was almost universally taught as if it were an iron-stayed corset that held language in a relentless grip, rather than (as now handled in most

[1] Oxford University Press.

modern schools by enlightened teachers) as the science of living language, conforming, like an old and comfortable pair of shoes, to the shape of that which gives it its function and its purpose.

Those of us who were good grammar students—do we still remember the meaning and use of such terms as *predicate nominative, subject of the infinitive, appositive, direct address, noun clause, expletive?* Did we, as students, realize the value of these names as anything more than identifying symbols to be regurgitated for our teachers on examination papers? Did we realize, for even one clairvoyant moment, that grammar was as much related to life as biology, or physics, or chemistry? Did we ever manage to pull aside the befogging curtains and see the subject as an attempt to give logical explanation to one of the most miraculous phenomena of human life: communication by the proper juxtaposition of syllables? I doubt that we did. I doubt that the majority of grammar teachers in yesterday's schools did either.

Yes, grammar is an integral part of everyday living. The grammatical skill exhibited by human beings, even the most untutored of us, is simply prodigious. A person speaks, his mind only on his thoughts, and yet manages without any conscious effort to keep enough control over his tenses and subjects and predicates and phrases and clauses to make himself perfectly intelligible to those who are listening to him.

This phenomenon is the key to the purpose of grammar. Grammar in one sense is only the arbitrary system of labels given to those word relationships by means of which most of the users of a language communicate. Grammar is *not* a code of divine and unchangeable laws to which everyone must conform; on the contrary, grammar itself gradually changes as the language habits of educated people change. Grammar follows the living language of the people, not the other way around. Indeed, the only fixed grammar in existence is that of a dead language like Latin. The Latin your grandfather learned in school is identical with the Latin your grandson will learn (if he is forced to learn Latin—probably he won't be), because the only time a language becomes static is when it has died. English is far from dead. A very few out of the great number of changes in English grammar will serve to make this point clear. In the late seventeenth century, it was good grammar to say *you wasn't*. Today, of course, such an expression is heard only on illiterate levels. In Shakespeare's time, it was correct to use the double comparative or superlative ("the most unkindest cut of all") and the double negative. Today such uses are considered substandard. Fifty years ago, "It's *me*" or "*Who* are you speaking to" was considered very bad grammar. Today, as studies by that noted professor of English at Wisconsin University, the late Sterling Andrus Leonard, have proved, these expressions are considered as correct and established usages by the majority of educators in the country. (Most language scholars have completely expunged the word *whom* from their speaking vocabularies.) Once *healthy* and *healthful* and *further* and *farther* were words with clear differences of meaning. Today they are almost interchangeable in most uses; *healthful* and *farther* are beginning to disappear from the language entirely, *healthy* and *further* taking over their functions.

For you, as a student of effective English, these pages are intended to convey the following message: the simpler your grammar and the more nearly it conforms to the colloquial educated usage of the time, the more effective it will be.

What is the present status of current American grammar? That is the question with which the following pages are concerned.

T W O

Three Kinds of Grammar

THESE PAGES do not concern themselves with *formal* grammar, that is, with such academic aspects as parts of speech, tense, voice, mood, case, or the other technical verbiage of language patterns. They do concern themselves, very vitally, with the use of *accepted* and *effective* language patterns, with the *correct word* in the *correct place*. The approach which this section takes to grammar is radical rather than reactionary, current rather than traditional. Even if you have had no training whatever in grammar, the explanations that follow will be perfectly clear to you. And if you had rather intensive training a long time ago, many of the suggestions to be made may shock you, violating, as they will, some of the things you may have learned in school and college.

For living grammar is an exposition of what educated people are saying today, not what old-fashioned grammar books and eighteenth-century rhetoric principles urge them, futilely, to say.

158

Here is a fact that may startle you: *It is less effective to use overrefined, pedantic grammar than it is to use easygoing, colloquial grammar.* This is not to say that it is wise to speak and write in illiterate, semiliterate, or slovenly patterns. But it is perhaps wiser to do that than to talk like a pedant. Sloppy speech may amuse or slightly irritate your audience; stilted and overformalized speech will actively exasperate and alienate them.

There are, in the last analysis, three types of grammar:

1. illiterate or semiliterate
2. informal or colloquial
3. pedantic

The first and third are extremes; the second, the golden mean. Informal colloquial grammar is correct and established; it accurately reflects the language habits of such people as business executives, college professors, government officials, editors, lecturers, linguists. Illiterate grammar violates the language patterns used by most educated people. Pedantic grammar is meticulous, stilted, refined to the point of sterility.

Under illiterate grammar might be listed expressions like the following:

1. Lay down to sleep
2. I seen
3. That there woman
4. Them roses
5. Between you and I
6. I won't do it no more

Informal, colloquial grammar (used in everyday communication by most educated people) may contain expressions that violate formal rules of syntax, such as:

1. It is *me.*
2. *Who* are you waiting for?
3. If I *was* rich . . .
4. *Will* you see me tonight?
5. I want him *to at least try.* (the so-called "split infinitive")
6. If *anyone* objects, let *them* step forward.

And pedantic grammar makes a fetish of expressions like these:

1. It is *I*.
2. *To whom* do you refer?
3. *Shall* you answer the letter?
4. One usually obeys *one's* impulses.
5. You may invite *whomever* you like.
6. None of them *is* ready.

THREE

~~~~~~~~~~~~~~

Two Confusing Verbs

It has been my endeavor in this work to represent English Grammar not as a set of stiff dogmatic precepts, according to which some things are correct and others absolutely wrong, but as something living and developing under continual fluctuations and undulations, something that is founded on the past and prepares the way for the future, something that is not always consistent or perfect, but progressing and perfectible—in one word, human.

OTTO JESPERSEN, *A Modern English Grammar* [1]

Let us turn first to a consideration of four important areas in correct usage that are particularly troublesome. These are:

1. The verbs *lie* and *lay*.
2. Pronouns following prepositions.
3. The verb following *either* and *neither*.
4. The verb following phrases like *one of the men*.

[1] S. E. Stechert & Co.

It can safely be said that the most confusing, obstreperous, and generally devilish verbs in the entire language are *lay* and *lie*. In a more rational and less interesting language, two different verbs of such similar form and allied meaning would never be tolerated. From the sixth grade on through the senior year in high school, English teachers patiently drill their students on the subtle distinctions between these demons. Yet you will not find more than one high-school graduate out of three who can handle the verbs correctly. This is by far the hardest point in grammar to master, but, paradoxically, it is the one most indicative, when conquered, of the skilled speaker. Let us analyze the matter in detail:

To *lie* means to rest, to recline, to remain in a horizontal position, to be, or to be situated. Both persons and things or places can *lie*.

To *lay* means to place, to put.

One *lies* asleep, but *lays* (i.e., puts) his hands on the table. Note these:

A. We *lie* down for a nap.
   Europe *lies* across the ocean.
   Did you *lie* awake long?
   Democracy's power *lies* in a well-informed electorate.
B. We will not *lay* down our lives for principles we do not believe in.
   We *lay* our heads on the table and catch forty winks.
   Tyrants *lay* a heavy hand on all dissenters.

You will note that *lay* is always followed by a word indicating the *thing* or *person* that is being placed. In the sentences above, in Section B, these words are *lives, heads, hand*.

Does it seem easy enough so far? Try filling in the following sentences, using *lay, laying, lays* or *lie, lying, lies*.

1. Have you been —————— awake all night?
2. Where did you —————— the dishcloth?
3. Please —————— your baby on the table.
4. We like to —————— down for a nap after dinner.
5. Have you been —————— the goods on the shelf properly?
6. He will —————— down the law.

7. Do —————— quietly.

8. She —————— flat on the pillow. (*present tense*)

ANSWERS: 1—lying, 2—lay, 3—lay, 4—lie, 5—laying, 6—lay, 7—lie, 8—lies.

You undoubtedly got over that hurdle with no difficulty, and are possibly wondering why *lay* and *lie* are considered so confusing. The confusion starts when we get into the past tenses. Note this:

Present Tense	Past Tense
1. lie	*lay*
2. lay	*laid*

The present tense of one verb is identical with the past tense of the other!

These sentences, *all in the past tense,* will get you accustomed to the apparent contradiction:

Yesterday he *lay* asleep all day.

This morning we *laid* the blankets away in camphor.

She *lay* down, before you came, for a nap.

He *laid* the money on the table.

If you think you have control of the past tense, fill in the blanks below with *lay* (past tense of *lie*) or *laid* (past tense of *lay*).

1. Before the boat docked, we —————— on the deck sunning ourselves.

2. He —————— quietly on his back all morning.

3. She —————— the baby tenderly in its bassinet.

4. She —————— her fears to rest.

5. They —————— the body in the grave.

6. The sword —————— his face open from ear to neck.

7. The wounded man —————— patiently waiting for the ambulance to arrive.

8. The boy —————— snoozing on the sofa.

ANSWERS: 1—lay, 2—lay, 3—laid, 4—laid, 5—laid, 6—laid, 7—lay, 8—lay.

Wait—your troubles aren't over. There is a *perfect* tense for each of these verbs.

Present	Past	Perfect
lie	*lay*	has, have, or had *lain*
lay	*laid*	has, have, or had *laid*

Try these. Use any of the forms we have discussed in this chapter.

1. His genius has ——————— dormant for years.
2. His genius ——————— dormant for years. (*past tense*)
3. His genius is ———————ing dormant.
4. His genius ——————— dormant. (*present tense*)
5. Please ——————— down.
6. I have ——————— the baby in its crib.
7. Please ——————— the baby down.
8. Have you ——————— away your woolens?
9. We have ——————— in hiding all month.
10. ———————ing on its side, the child was able to breathe better.
11. Yesterday, she ——————— asleep for several hours.
12. Did you ——————— awake all night?

> lie—lay—lain
> lay—laid—laid

ANSWERS: 1—lain, 2—lay, 3—lying, 4—lies, 5—lie, 6—laid, 7—lay, 8—laid,
9—lain, 10—Lying, 11—lay, 12—lie.

FOUR

Pronouns and Prepositions

. . . Grammar is seen to be not something final and static but merely the organized description or codification of the actual speech habits of educated men. If these habits change, grammar itself changes, and textbooks must follow suit. To preserve in our textbooks requirements no longer followed by the best current speakers is not grammatical but ungrammatical. It makes of grammar not a science but a dogma.

STERLING A. LEONARD, in Marckwart and Walcott, *Facts about Current English Usage* [1]

Between you and I, fairly common on unsophisticated levels of speech, is in opposition to a venerable grammatical principle that a preposition (*between*) is followed by the objective form of a pronoun (*me*). Thus we say, *Give it to* (preposition) *me* (objective), and *We work for* (preposition) *him* (objective).

Let's present it graphically.

[1] National Council of Teachers of English.

| | *Objective Pronouns Follow* |
Prepositions	*a Preposition*
between	me
to	you
for	him
with	her
against	us
before	them
after	
except	
but (when it means *except*)	
like (when it means *similar to*)	
of	

Of course, looking at grammar from a scientific, rather than a traditional, point of view, the rule itself is no criterion of what should be used. But the rule, in this instance, describes educated usage, and so the effective speaker will in all cases follow a *preposition* with an objective pronoun. For example:

Between you and *me,* he is an incorrigible liar.
Everyone *but him* has filled out a questionnaire.
It was sent *for* Margery and *me.*
All *but him* have fled.

The famous line of poetry "Whence all *but he* had fled" may come to mind. This arresting violation of traditional and popular usage will have to be put down to poetic license; to the poet's ear *he* simply sounded better than *him.*

Try these sentences, checking the correct pronoun in each case:

1. That is a matter to be settled between the insurance company and (we, us).
2. Between you and (I, me) I don't think he's telling the truth.
3. Do it for your mother and (I, me).
4. Would you like to take a walk with John and (I, me)?
5. Go in before (her, she).
6. They're all here except (he, him).

7. Everyone but (he, him) is willing.
8. Try to be more like (we, us).

ANSWERS: 1—us, 2—me, 3—me, 4—me, 5—her, 6—him, 7—him, 8—us.

Pronouns to be used after prepositions:
me, you, him, her, us, them.

FIVE

~~~~~~~~~~

How to Manage Either *and* Neither

Not one of the classic writers of English measures up to the grammarian's standard in his writing. It is pitifully easy to catch Milton
nodding, or to find the Great Panjandrum out. Not a single one of
the great authors of English literature chose to make, or perhaps
was able to make, his language free from errors in grammar.

JANET RANKIN AIKEN, *Commonsense Grammar* [1]

Either and *neither,* as pronouns (i.e., *either of the boys, neither
of your parents*), are usually followed by a *singular* verb in educated
speech and writing. In the constructions mentioned, *either* means
either one, neither means *neither one*—they are therefore clearly
singular and, as you know, the natural pattern of the language

[1] Thomas Y. Crowell Company.

is for singular nouns and pronouns to take singular verbs, plural nouns and pronouns to take plural verbs.

That is, when the nouns and pronouns are singular or plural in *meaning and flavor*—form is of much less importance.

Consider, for example:

> A *lot* of people *are* here today. (*A lot* is singular in form, but its obvious meaning in this sentence is *many*—hence the plural verb *are*.)
>
> This *lot* of books *was* sold at a high price. (Now we're talking about *one lot,* as a single unit—hence the singular verb *was*.)
>
> The *family is* a more or less stable unit in human society. (We mean *family* as a *single* type of grouping.)
>
> The *family are* all gathered round the table. (Here we're thinking of *family* as a number of individuals.)
>
> *None* of my friends *were* present. (That is, *not any*.)
>
> *None* of the work *was* done right. (That is, *no part*.)

So, to return to *either* and *neither* as pronouns:

Since they are *singular* in meaning and flavor, they are usually followed by *singular* verbs:

> Neither of these girls (i.e., neither one) *is* very pretty.
>
> *Does* either of your children (i.e., either one of the two) have red hair?
>
> Neither of my brothers (i.e., neither one of the two) *is* rich.
>
> *Has* either of your parents (i.e., either one) returned yet?

Try this test:

1. (Has, have) either of the bottles been emptied?
2. Neither of your reasons (is, are) true.
3. If either of the notes (falls, fall) due this month, pay (it, them).
4. Neither of my sisters (were, was) very cordial to him.
5. Neither of these books (are, is) of any use to me.
6. Neither of us (is, are) very happy with the situation.

ANSWERS: 1—has, 2—is, 3—falls, it, 4—was, 5—is, 6—is.

When *either* and *neither* are conjunctions (i.e., *either . . . or, neither . . . nor*), the nouns or pronouns that are joined govern the verb.

These nouns or pronouns may both be *singular,* in which case the verb will be *singular.*

Neither *John* nor *Mary was* on time.
Either your *mother* or your *father was* to have come in to see me.
Neither *money* nor *fame is* what he's looking for.
Either *milk* or *cream is* delicious with this cereal.
Neither *snow* nor *rain is* able to stop him.

On the other hand, if the nouns or pronouns are both *plural,* the verb is *plural.*

Neither *Democrats* nor *Republicans are* working hard enough in this campaign.
If either the *roses* or the *chrysanthemums look* wilted, throw them out.
Neither *we* nor *they are* very happy with the situation.

Now try this test, choosing carefully between singular and plural verbs:

1. Either Mr. Jones or his wife (is, are) always in the store.
2. Either the doctor or his nurse (is, are) sure to be in the office tomorrow.
3. Neither my wife nor my daughter (was, were) home.
4. Neither the Browns nor the Smiths (were, was) invited.
5. Neither his house nor his car (was, were) paid for yet.

ANSWERS: 1—is, 2—is, 3—was, 4—were, 5—was.

Let us consider, finally, one remaining possibility with *either . . . or* and *neither . . . nor.*

Suppose one of the nouns or pronouns is *singular,* the other *plural?* Then we have a dilemma, which we can solve by the arbitrary rule of *making the verb agree in number with the noun or pronoun closer to the verb.*

Thus:

Either John or *the girls have* taken care of it.
Neither the men nor *my wife has* arrived.
Has either *George* or my cousins come in?
Neither you nor *I am* capable of finishing this work.

This solution may not appeal to you, however, since the awkwardness of these sentences is apparent. What else can you do? Avoid the dilemma by rephrasing your thought:

Either John has taken care of it, or the girls have.
The men have not arrived, nor has my wife.
Has George come in? How about my cousins?
I am not capable of finishing this work, and you're not either.

S I X

~~~~~~~

One of . . .

HOW ABOUT SENTENCES like these—would *you* use a plural verb?

>One of us *are* coming.
>Each of us *have* a duty to perform.
>One of the men *were* present.
>One of my sisters *are* married.

The person who follows this kind of pattern in speech or writing is making an honest and understandable mistake. He feels that the noun nearest the verb should govern the number (i.e., singular or plural) of that verb.

us (we) are
us (we) have
men were
sisters are

But there is a more logical, reasonable, and, on educated levels, more popular way of analyzing these sentences.

To wit:

One ~~of us~~ is coming.

Each ~~of us~~ has a duty to perform.

One ~~of the men~~ was present.

One ~~of my sisters~~ is married.

What principle, then, operates in educated language patterns?

The singular pronouns *one* and *each,* even though followed by a prepositional phrase containing a plural (*of us, of the men, of my sisters*), still take a singular verb.

Try these:

1. One of those boys (is, are) my brother.
2. Every one of the men (is, are) satisfied.
3. Each of your pencils (has, have) a broken point.
4. One of the books (has, have) fallen down.
5. One of the characters (enters, enter) the scene.

ANSWERS: 1—is, 2—is, 3—has, 4—has, 5—enters.

Do not let the rule for *one of . . .* and *each of . . .* influence your thinking about *none of . . . .*

You will recall from the previous chapter that the pronoun *none* takes a singular or plural verb depending on whether it has a singular or plural meaning and flavor, i.e., whether it stands for *not any* or *no part.*

Contrast these two groups of sentences:

A (*not any*)	B (*no part*)
None of the men *are* working.	None of the work *is* finished.
None of the pages *have* been checked.	None of the butter *has* melted.
None of your answers *were* correct.	None of my help *was* appreciated.

SEVEN

~~~~~~~~~~~~~

Test Your Grammar

HERE ARE TWO yardsticks by which you can measure your own grammatical patterns. In the elementary test, a score of 90 percent or better will indicate to you that your speech is free of the type of error that is a hallmark of illiterate usage. In the advanced test, a score of 80 percent or more will signify a better-than-average grasp of the fundamentals of good speech. In checking your choices in both tests, *be guided solely by what you generally say or would be inclined to say,* not by what you believe to be "correct."

ELEMENTARY TEST

(Credit 3% for each correct choice)

1. You (was, were) not present at last night's meeting.
2. (Them, Those) hats are very becoming.
3. I (seen, saw) an interesting sight yesterday.
4. She gave Mary and (I, me) some candy.

174

5. Crazy people speak to (themselves, theirselves).
6. We (can, can't) hardly hear him.
7. We won't go there (any, no) more.
8. He must (of, have) walked around the block ten times.
9. Have you (et, eaten) all the watermelon?
10. I (stood, stayed) at the farm all summer.
11. He took my best pencil (off of, from) me.
12. We (done, did) all we had to.
13. (Leave, Let) me do it for you.
14. (This here, This) book is the one I need.
15. He (don't, doesn't) do anything I ask him to.
16. We work (good, well) together.
17. Did you (learn, teach) him how to skate?
18. We want you and (she, her) to go.
19. All his money was (robbed, stole, stolen).
20. We (began, begun) early and finished early.
21. Give it to (us, we) girls.
22. (We, Us) boys are going out tonight.
23. (Him and me, Him and I, He and I) had a terrible fight last night.
24. The dog licked (its, it's) chops.
25. He is (happier, more happier) because of what happened.
26. Have you (drank, drunk) your milk?
27. (Set, Sit) down for a few minutes.
28. The sun has (rose, risen).
29. He (ain't, isn't) my friend any more.
30. Don't (ever, never) do that to me.
31. Have you (wrote, written) the letter yet?
32. The man (drowned, drownded) before we could save him.
33. I'll do it (irregardless, regardless) of what you say.
34. Did you get an (invite, invitation) to her party?
35. We (did, done) the work and went home.

ANSWERS: 1—were, 2—Those, 3—saw, 4—me, 5—themselves, 6—can, 7—any, 8—have, 9—eaten, 10—stayed, 11—from, 12—did, 13—Let, 14—This, 15—doesn't, 16—well, 17—teach, 18—her, 19—stolen, 20—began, 21—us, 22—We, 23—He and I, 24—its, 25—happier, 26—drunk, 27—Sit, 28—risen, 29—isn't, 30—ever, 31—written, 32—drowned, 33—regardless, 34—invitation, 35—did.

ADVANCED TEST

(Credit 4% for each correct choice)

1. He (lay, laid) asleep for an hour.
2. Please (lay, lie) your hand on mine.
3. John is (lying, laying) down.
4. Have you (laid, lain) on the grass this morning?
5. How (is, are) your mother and father today?
6. What kind (of, of a) man did she marry?
7. Everything he (prophesied, prophecized, prophesized, prophecied) came true.
8. How has the war (affected, effected) your business?
9. The (principal, principle) street of most towns is called Main Street.
10. (Beside, Besides) your interest, I also want your help.
11. Is this the man (who, whom) you claim defrauded you?
12. Everyone but (he, him) is accounted for.
13. All except (she, her) have turned in their papers.
14. Neither of the girls (are, is) here.
15. (Has, Have) either of the men returned?
16. George as well as John (is, are) on our side.
17. One of us (is, are) always here.
18. The captain or the lieutenant (is, are) always on hand.
19. He's a lot older than (I, me).
20. I am (uninterested, disinterested) in lectures on ancient civilizations.
21. The memoranda (is, are) on your desk.
22. The murderer was (hanged, hung) at daybreak.
23. Do it (as, like) you were instructed.
24. So that's (who, whom) you thought it was!
25. (Your, You're) going to get the surprise of your life.

ANSWERS: 1—lay, 2—lay, 3—lying, 4—lain, 5—are, 6—of, 7—prophesied, 8—affected, 9—principal, 10—Besides, 11—who, 12—him, 13—her, 14—is, 15—Has, 16—is, 17—is, 18—is, 19—I, 20—uninterested, 21—are, 22—hanged, 23—as, 24—who, 25—You're.

EIGHT

Words Misused and Confused

1. PRINCIPLE-PRINCIPAL

A PRINCIPLE is a rule, a law, or a doctrine. Life operates by natural *principles*. A man of *principle* fears no criticism.

Principal, as an adjective, means "chief, main, or leading." The *principal* means of winning a war is by offensive action. Coffee is one of the *principal* products of Brazil. New York is the *principal* city on the East Coast.

Principal as a noun refers to the main or leading person, as the *principal* of a school, in a divorce action, or in a drama. The money on which interest is paid is also spelled *principal:* He tries to earn at least 6 percent on his *principal.*

TEST

1. We drove down the ———— street of the city.
2. I do not understand the ———— of gravity.

3. What is your _____ objection to my plan?

4. A meeting of the _____ stockholders was called.

5. The _____ on which the store was founded has not changed in fifty years.

6. He has been receiving a 5 percent return on his _____ for the last three years.

7. When I sell my house I want to deal with _____s only—no agents.

8. This is a little-understood _____ of English grammar.

ANSWERS: 1—principal, 2—principle, 3—principal, 4—principal, 5—principle, 6—principal, 7—principal, 8—principle.

2. EFFECT-AFFECT

Effect is mainly a *noun* and usually means "result." What *effects* are you looking for? That was an unexpected *effect*.

As a verb, *effect* means "to bring about, cause, produce, or create." She wants to *effect* a change in her friend's attitude. We must *effect* better international relations if peace is to be secure.

Affect in general use is a verb, and usually means "to change, influence, or pretend." How does the weather *affect* you? His grief *affected* you deeply, didn't it? Why do you *affect* interest when you're really bored?

(*Affect* has a special, technical use as a noun in psychology meaning *emotion,* or *feeling tone.*)

TEST

1. Has the weather _____ed your business?

2. What is the _____ of sudden fear on the heart?

3. One _____ of high prices is to cut down demand.

4. We shall try to _____ a more rapid completion of our tasks.

5. Lack of parental love can _____ a child's complete life; this _____ is usually an adverse one.

ANSWERS: 1—affected, 2—effect, 3—effect, 4—effect, 5—affect, effect.

3. CREDULOUS-CREDIBLE

A person who is too ready to believe is *credulous*. A fact or account that can be believed is *credible*. The negatives are *incredulous* (unwilling to believe) and *incredible* (unbelievable).

TEST

1. You are too —————; can you not distinguish fact from fancy?
2. I believe that is the truth; at least, it's a perfectly ————— story.
3. He stared —————ly at the strange sight, refusing to believe his eyes.
4. He told an ————— story of his night's adventures.
5. The climate at the Equator is —————ly hot.

ANSWERS: 1—credulous, 2—credible, 3—incredulously, 4—incredible, 5—incredibly.

4. LUXURIOUS-LUXURIANT

Anything man-made and expensive is *luxurious*. Something in nature (hair, vegetation, etc.) that grows richly or lushly is *luxuriant*.

TEST

1. The tropics contain ————— vegetation.
2. Her ————— black hair is the most beautiful I have ever seen.
3. He owns a ————— yacht.
4. Coral grows —————ly on that reef.

ANSWERS: 1—luxuriant, 2—luxuriant, 3—luxurious, 4—luxuriantly.

5. UNINTERESTED-DISINTERESTED

In general, though some people use *disinterested* interchangeably with *uninterested,* the following distinction is observed:

Uninterested means "bored, indifferent, lacking interest."

Disinterested means "unbiased, impartial, unprejudiced, not personally involved." You tell a salesman that you are *uninterested* in what he is selling; an apathetic child is *uninterested* in what's going on around him. You hope that your case will be tried before a *disinterested,* not an *uninterested,* judge; in a controversy you seek the opinion of a *disinterested* person, i.e., one who will render a fair and objective judgment since he has no personal interest, or stake, in the matter. The noun is *disinterest.*

TEST

1. As you are a (an) ———— party, we will let you settle our dispute.
2. Don't look so ————; the play is not as boring as you seem to think.
3. Try to arrive at a ———— conclusion after hearing both sides.
4. Why is he always ———— in how his wife spends her time?
5. I doubt your ———— in the case. Don't you have something to gain from the outcome?

ANSWERS: 1—disinterested, 2—uninterested, 3—disinterested, 4—uninterested, 5—disinterest.

6. ALTERNATIVE-CHOICE

An *alternative* is one of *two* things, or possibilities, either of which must be chosen. A *choice* is one of two or more things, or possibilities, with freedom to take one or none implied.

TEST

1. I must accept his offer; I have no ————.
2. I have three courses of action and cannot decide which ———— to make.
3. We have, finally, only two ————s: live or die.

ANSWERS: 1—alternative, 2—choice, 3—alternatives.

7. BARBARIC-BARBAROUS

Something is *barbaric* which refers, pertains to, or describes uncivilized or savage people or cultures. Something is *barbarous* that is done by a civilized person in a savage, uncivilized, or cruel manner.

TEST

1. The third degree is a ——————— police practice frowned upon by the courts.
2. In some remote parts of the world certain ——————— customs can still be observed.
3. Voodoo, totem poles, and animal worship are ——————— in character.
4. Torture is a ——————— act.

ANSWERS: 1—barbarous, 2—barbaric, 3—barbaric, 4—barbarous.

8. BESIDE-BESIDES

Beside means *next to*. *Besides* means *in addition to, also,* or *furthermore.*

TEST

1. Sit ——————— me.
2. He sat ——————— the river.
3. ———————, he is a notorious liar.
4. ——————— Jack, Roy also works for us.

ANSWERS: 1—beside, 2—beside, 3—Besides, 4—Besides.

9. CAPITAL-CAPITOL

The *capitol,* or legislative building, is situated in the *capital* of a state or nation. Most such buildings are topped by a *dome;*

the shape of a dome, as well as the *o* in its spelling, will remind you of the crucial letter in *capitol,* which by the way is spelled with a capital *c* when it refers to the building in which Congress sits in Washington.

TEST

1. Washington is the ——— of the United States.
2. The Senator met his wife on the steps of the ———.
3. When was the cornerstone of the ——— laid?

ANSWERS: 1—capital, 2—Capitol, 3—capitol.

10. DESIRABLE-DESIROUS

That which one wants is *desirable.* A person who desires something is *desirous.*

TEST

1. Money is usually ———.
2. Men have always been ——— of money.
3. Good food is ——— for building health.
4. Men are ——— of improving their station in life.

ANSWERS: 1—desirable, 2—desirous, 3—desirable, 4—desirous.

11. CONTEMPTIBLE-CONTEMPTUOUS

You feel *contemptuous* of *contemptible* people or things.

TEST

1. Do not act so ———ly or no one will have any faith in you.
2. He spoke ———ly of his less fortunate friends.
3. Tom acted ———ly toward his brother (i.e., as if he thought very little of him).
4. Tom acted ———ly toward his brother (and as a result, we thought very little of *Tom*).

5. Don't be ———— of ignorance, for ignorance is not ————.

ANSWERS: 1—contemptibly, 2—contemptuously, 3—contemptuously, 4—contemptibly, 5—contemptuous, contemptible.

12. ELDEST-OLDEST

The *eldest* in a family is the firstborn. The *oldest* is the one who has attained the most advanced age. Thus, the *eldest* may also be the *oldest,* but the *oldest* need not be the *eldest,* for the *eldest* may have died.

13. HANGED-HUNG

People or objects which are suspended are *hung.* Pictures are *hung,* ropes are *hung* from trees, and John *hung* from the tree until we rescued him. Idiomatically, we say that a painter is or has been *hung* when his pictures appear in a gallery. A criminal who is put to death by hanging is *hanged.* We *hung* the picture; we *hanged* the murderer.

TEST

1. They ———— the criminal at dawn.
2. At one time in our history, horse thieves were ————.
3. The mob ———— the prisoner.
4. We ———— your coat in the hall.
5. Sam ———— from the roof in order to reach the open window.

ANSWERS: 1—hanged, 2—hanged, 3—hanged, 4—hung, 5—hung.

14. IMMORAL-UNMORAL

When we call a person *immoral,* we imply that he violates our morals with a full realization of what he is doing. When we call someone *unmoral,* we imply that he has no moral judgment and cannot distinguish right from wrong.

15. IMPLY-INFER

To *imply* is to hint or express indirectly. Only a person speaking, writing, or acting can *imply* anything.

To *infer* is to draw a conclusion. Only a listener, reader, or watcher can *infer* anything.

The nouns are *implication* and *inference*—we make an *implication* and draw an *inference*.

TEST

1. Your words —————— that I am a liar.
2. Do you —————— from what he said that he dislikes you?
3. His actions —————— that he does not know what he is doing.
4. What —————— can we draw from the facts he has presented to us?
5. I think you're making an —————— that I cheated you.
6. It is unfortunate that you have drawn the —————— that I mistrust you.

ANSWERS: 1—imply, 2—infer, 3—imply, 4—inference, 5—implication, 6—inference.

16. INGENIOUS-INGENUOUS

Ingenious means "skillful, adroit, clever." The noun is *ingenuity*. *Ingenuous* means "innocent, naïve, unsophisticated." The noun is *ingenuousness*.

TEST

1. Edison was an —————— man.
2. You are simply too —————— if you believe he really has etchings to show you.
3. It takes great —————— to escape from Alcatraz.

4. You show such ———— that people cannot resist the temptation to deceive you.

ANSWERS: 1—ingenious, 2—ingenuous, 3—ingenuity, 4—ingenuousness.

TEST YOURSELF

This quiz will show you how successfully you have mastered
the contents of the chapter.

1. New York is one of the (principle, principal) ports of the
   United States.
2. What (affect, effect) did his refusal have on you?
3. He (effected, affected) a rapid change of plan.
4. He stared (incredibly, incredulously) at the strange animal.
5. You are too (credulous, credible) for your own good; why do
   you believe everything your wife tells you?
6. Flowers will grow (luxuriously, luxuriantly) in this rich soil.
7. Let us submit our controversy to a (an) (uninterested, disinterested) person.
8. You have three (alternatives, choices): medicine, law, or teach-
   ing.
9. When anthropologists study primitive cultures at first hand,
   they live the same (barbarous, barbaric) life as the natives.
10. Stand (beside, besides) that chair.
11. The dome on top of the (capital, capitol) is being painted black
    for the duration.
12. That is a most (desirous, desirable) location.
13. His actions are (contemptuous, contemptible); they are be-
    neath the consideration of honorable people.
14. Have they (hung, hanged) the murderer?
15. Your (unmoral, immoral) acts will be punished; this you knew
    before you committed them.
16. Do you (imply, infer) from what he wrote that he will return
    the money to you?
17. Your words (imply, infer) that you do not expect to see her
    again.

18. That is an (ingenious, ingenuous) method of attack; your opponent is certain to be deceived by it.

19. It is hard to believe that a person of your age can show such childish (ingenuity, ingenuousness).

20. Albany is the (capitol, capital) of New York State.

Excellent Score: 18–20 right
Creditable Score: 15–17 right
Poor Score: fewer than 10 right

ANSWERS: 1—principal, 2—effect, 3—effected, 4—incredulously, 5—credulous, 6—luxuriantly, 7—disinterested, 8—choices, 9—barbaric, 10—beside, 11—capitol, 12—desirable, 13—contemptible, 14—hanged, 15—immoral, 16—infer, 17—imply, 18—ingenious, 19—ingenuousness, 20—capital.

NINE

~~~~~~~~

℞ *For Good Grammar*

WHICH IS CORRECT:

Walk *further* or *farther?*
Try *and* do it, or try *to* do it?
I've *got* to go, or I *have* to go?
I have *drank* or I have *drunk?*

To answer these questions, we must first define our criterion of "correctness." Is it the body of restrictive, eighteenth-century rules derived by scholars of that period from Latin? (But English in its structure is a derivative of Anglo-Saxon, a Teutonic tongue, not an offshoot of Latin, despite the thousands of words we've taken from that classical language.)

Or is our criterion the actual language patterns of the educated users of English?

Modern linguistic philosophy points out that good grammar is synonymous with educated usage at any given time. Usage changes, and grammatical principles, if they are to be valid and in accordance with reality, must change also, for scientifically the grammar of a language describes how that language operates today, not how it ought to operate or how it operated centuries ago.

So, to decide whether an expression is right or wrong, we have to examine its occurrence or nonoccurrence in the speech and writing of educated people.

Some years before his recent death, Dr. Sterling Andrus Leonard, professor of English at the University of Wisconsin, did this very thing.

Under the sponsorship of the National Council of Teachers of English, he set about obtaining what he called a "consensus of expert opinion" about controversial questions of grammatical usage. Selecting 230 expressions "of whose standing there might be some question," he mailed a questionnaire to 231 judges. These judges were:

    30 linguistic specialists
    30 well-known editors
    22 established authors
    19 business executives
    50 college teachers of English
    50 high-school teachers of English
    30 speech teachers

These experts, who represented a diverse and educated cross-section of American life, were asked to indicate what, to their minds, was the standing of each of the controversial expressions. "Score, please," they were told, "according to your observation of what is actual usage rather than your opinion of what usage should be."

Here, then, was a wonderful test of American usage—a true laboratory test to be freed, theoretically, of subjective reactions and ethical considerations. Obviously, Dr. Leonard was totally uninterested in what grammar books preached about correct usage or what the judges thought *ought* to be correct usage. His one concern was to discover what the majority of educated American speakers and writers were actually doing with their language.

No one except the purists and precisians (and these gentle-men have been losing considerable caste since as far back as 1925) would argue with Dr. Leonard's philosophy, to wit, that what most of the sophisticated users of the language say, is good usage, contrary or not to ancient and academic rules of grammar.

The results of this questionnaire are most interesting. Thirty-eight of the 230 items were almost unanimously rated as illiterate usages. Among these were such expressions as: [1]

> I have*n't hardly* any money.
> The kitten mews whenever it *wants in.*
> All came except *she.*
> My Uncle John, *he* told me a story.
> I must go and *lay* down.
> I *have drank* all my milk.
> *That there* rooster is a fighter.
> You *was* mistaken about that, John.
> Just *set* down and rest awhile.

This was much to be expected. Your average high-school fresh-man will tell you that such expressions are "bad" grammar. The revolutionary aspects of the Leonard study concerns those expres-sions that a majority of the judges considered established, correct, and fully acceptable English. One hundred five, or close to 50 percent of the test items, were so rated. Let us glance at a random sampling of them:

1. Invite *whoever* you like to the party. (Outmoded restriction: *whomever.*)
2. I felt I could walk no *further.* (Outmoded restriction: *farther.*)
3. We will *try and get* it.
4. I've absolutely *got* to go.
5. We can expect the commission *to at least protect* our interests. (The split infinitive.)
6. You'd better go *slow.*
7. There are some *nice* people around here. (Purists claim *nice* means only one thing—*exact.*)
8. *Will* you be at the Browns' this evening? (By strict and out-

---

[1] *Facts about Current English Usage,* National Council of Teachers of English.

moded grammatical rules, *Shall* is the "proper" word in this construction, because "shall" would be used in the answer, i.e., I *shall* be at the Browns' this evening.)

9. If it *wasn't* for football, school life would be dull. (The "subjunctive" is largely ignored in everyday informal English.)

10. We *only* had one left. (Purists insist on "We had *only* one left.")

11. This room is *awfully* cold.

12. It's *me*.

13. *Who* are you looking for? (Language scholars agree that *whom* will eventually disappear from the spoken language.)

14. *Can* I be excused from class?

15. *Everyone* was here, but *they* all went home early. (Grammar says *everyone* is singular; logic claims it implies plurality in a construction like this one. Why not be logical?)

What are some other expressions once tabooed by the unrealistic "rules" of restrictive grammar, but now freely used by educated people and thoroughly established, therefore, not only as correct and permissible, but even, at times, preferable in informal conversation and writing?

1. He *got sick*. (Outmoded restriction: He *became ill*.)

2. Don't *get mad* if I tell the truth. (Outmoded restriction: Don't *become angry*.)

3. I'll come *providing* you let me. (Outmoded restriction: *provided*.)

4. The reason I love you is *because* you are so pretty. (Outmoded restriction: *that*.)

5. That dress is different *than* mine. (Outmoded restriction: *from*.)

6. He is not *as* tall as he looks. (Outmoded restriction: After a negative verb, use *so*.)

7. She was most *aggravated*. (Outmoded restriction: *exasperated*.)

8. It's *liable* to rain. (Outmoded restriction: *likely*.)

9. The *above* remarks . . . (Outmoded restriction: *Above* is only an adverb.)

10. Have you *got* my book? (Outmoded restriction: *Have* you my book?)

11. *Due to* the telephone strike . . . (Outmoded restriction: *Owing to* or *because of*.)

12. Everybody stood up and shouted at the top of *their* lungs. (Outmoded restriction: *his* lungs.)

13. I *will* write to him tonight. (Outmoded restriction: I *shall* write.)
14. I *would* like to see you tonight. (Outmoded restriction: I *should* like.)
15. He had an *awful* cold. (Outmoded restriction: a *severe* cold.)
16. I feel *badly* about his death. (Outmoded restriction: I feel *bad*.)

The restrictions listed are unrealistic. The grammar of any language is founded upon the current and reputable use of that language by its educated speakers. And if you will keep your ears wide open you will hear educated people saying *mad* (meaning *angry*); *nice* (meaning *pleasant*); *awful* (meaning *severe*); and *aggravating* (meaning *exasperating*). You will hear them saying *different than* and *have you got*. And you will see, in reputable books, magazines, and newspapers, *liable* for *likely*, *above* as an adjective, *further* for *farther*, *due to* as a preposition, and similar "errors" in the very type of sentence patterns railed against by restrictive grammar.

Our inescapable conclusion, then, is that good grammar, like good pronunciation, should be unostentatious—neither painfully pedantic nor conspicuously illiterate. Effective speech and writing steers a midcourse between two equally bad extremes—it is informal and casual, yet cultivated without being meticulous or stilted.

For example, on educated levels you will rarely, if ever, encounter the following:

1. Double negatives. (*Don't eat no more*, etc.)
2. Double comparatives. (*More happier*, etc.)
3. Misuse of *lay* and *lie*.
4. *This here, that there, them there*, etc. preceding a noun.
5. Incorrect tenses. (He *growed*, he *seen*, he *et*, he *brung*, etc.)
6. *You was* and *you wasn't*.
7. Between you and *I*. (Or other nominative pronouns after *between*.)
8. Plural verbs with *either* and *neither* as pronouns. (Neither of the men *are* here, etc.)
9. Plural verbs with *one of*. (One of the boys *are* absent.)
10. Negative with *hardly*. (He *hasn't hardly* any money.)
11. *But, except, like*, and other prepositions with *I, we, she, he,*

they. (But *we,* except *she,* give it to *we* girls, send it for Mary and *I,* etc.)

12. Use of *leave* for *let.* (*Leave* me do it.)

On the other hand, it is the rare educated person who speaks like a pedant, unless he is one and wishes to impress that doubtful fact on all and sundry.

Don't let your grammar go high hat. Don't scare people with a well-aimed *whom* [2] or a devastating *"It's I."* Don't ever try to impress people with your linguistic accomplishments by speaking with so-called impeccable or perfect grammar, by using the longest words in the dictionary, or by affected or oversophisticated pronunciations. You do not gain power with words by striking awe in the hearts of your listeners.

Bear in mind that there are two kinds of grammar: *traditional* or *prescriptive,* which aims at the perpetuation of usages that conform to Latin syntax and to those principles of word patterns set by eighteenth-century scholars; and *descriptive* or *scientific,* which examines language as it actually exists, which adopts the experimental approach and considers correct all usages that are currently found in the speech and writing of educated people.

The traditional concept views language as unchanging—what pleased the ears of our great-grandfathers must not be deviated from, not one jot, by speakers of our modern day. If it was good enough for Caesar and Cicero (for most of our syntax is based on Latin grammar), then any attempt to improve or simplify is heresy of the most dangerous sort.

On the contrary, say our modern language scholars, there is only *one* criterion of good English: Do most educated people use an expression? If they do, that expression is accepted, established, and correct English; and if rules are violated, then the rules, not the speakers, are wrong.

This modern philosophy is tersely summarized by the eminent linguist H. C. Wyld, in his *Elementary Lessons in English Grammar,*[3] as follows:

---

[2] Generations ago, George Ade, commenting in jaundiced humor on Hoosier culture, wrote this classic and unforgettable line: " 'Whom are you,' said he, for he had been to night school."

[3] S. E. Stechert & Co.

A grammar book does not attempt to teach people how they ought to speak, but on the contrary, unless it is a very bad or a very old work, it merely states how, as a matter of fact, certain people do speak at the time at which it is written.

The same thought is phrased in different words by the scholars Grattan and Gurrey in their excellent volume *Our Living Language:* [4]

The grammar of a language is not a list of rules imposed upon its speakers by scholastic authorities, but is a scientific record of the actual phenomena of that language, written and spoken. If any community habitually uses certain forms of speech, these forms are part of the grammar of the speech of that community.

There is no other sensible standard by which to judge correct grammar, and if it is feared that such a radical and revolutionary philosophy will result in the scuttling of all those musty grammar manuals that you and I struggled so patiently with in school, then—and this attitude is echoed by every modern grammarian—the quicker the manuals are scuttled the better it will be for everyone concerned.

[4] Thomas Nelson and Sons.

FIVE

~~~~~~~~~~

How to Become
a Skillful Reader

ONE

~~~~~~~~~~

So You Think You Can Read?

AMERICA IS ONE of the most literate nations on the face of the earth. In few other countries does the printed word reach so great a number, or have so marked an effect.

But that does not mean that all Americans are *skillful* readers. Skill in reading is a highly refined quality that involves many complex abilities. A skillful reader is a rapid reader. His eyes skim over a page with great speed; his mind grasps immediately and retains for long periods the facts and ideas in front of him. The skillful reader quickly reacts to the mood and atmosphere that an author creates. For him a page of print does not contain individual words and sentences and paragraphs, but rather thoughts, information, pictures, which his mind, like a dry sponge, sops up without conscious effort.

Are you a skillful reader? Would you like to find out? The tests that follow offer you a yardstick by which to measure your ability, a mirror to reflect your competence (or lack of it, perhaps) in three different kinds of reading.

TEST I. DOES YOUR MIND REACT QUICKLY TO A SIMPLE THOUGHT?

This is the easiest of the tests and one on which a reader of average efficiency should make a high score. Read each question quickly, *and once only,* then check Yes or No. Your reaction should be immediate, as no question in the lot is at all controversial.

1. Do children generally love their parents?   Yes No
2. Do all people have the same degree of intelligence?   Yes No
3. Do most people prefer life to death?   Yes No
4. Does public opinion ever influence government leaders?   Yes No
5. Is friendliness usually met with hostility?   Yes No
6. Is it always possible to be sure of what the future holds in store?   Yes No
7. Can a debate always be relied on to settle an issue?   Yes No
8. Do natural resources contribute to the wealth of a nation?   Yes No
9. Can all laws be enforced with equal facility?   Yes No
10. Does freedom of the press generally undermine the liberty of a nation?   Yes No
11. Do editorials generally reflect some type of opinion?   Yes No
12. Do immoral women commonly have unsavory reputations?   Yes No
13. Will poor health probably militate against an athlete's success?   Yes No
14. Are Supreme Court justices infallible?   Yes No
15. Is it possible to reason with infants?   Yes No

ANSWERS: 1—yes, 2—no, 3—yes, 4—yes, 5—no, 6—no, 7—no, 8—yes, 9—no, 10—no, 11—yes, 12—yes, 13—yes, 14—no, 15—no.

Great skill is indicated only by a perfect score—fifteen correct. Twelve to fourteen right shows average ability to understand the printed word. A lower score is a danger signal of inefficiency in reading.

TEST II. DOES YOUR MIND ABSORB
AND RETAIN DETAILS?

In the following test, which is of a much more demanding character, you are offered an item from *The New York Times*. Read it through *once only,* at your usual speed, concentrating carefully on all facts. When you have finished, cover the selection and mark each of the ten statements that follow it either *True* or *False*. This test is valid only if you refrain from consulting the selection while taking the test.

FREEZING METHOD IN ULCERS QUERIED

Surgeons Voice Reservation
on Widely Used System

By Robert K. Plumb

SAN FRANCISCO, Oct. 28—The nation's top surgeons, gathered here in the 50th anniversary year of the American College of Surgeons, took a second questioning look today at a new therapy for ulcers that has been widely accepted throughout the United States.

The treatment is the so-called stomach "freeze." It was first introduced about two years ago by Dr. Owen H. Wangensteen and associates of the University of Minnesota Medical School.

Since that time some 5,000 commercially produced machines to freeze stomachs have been purchased by physicians across the nation. Each stomach freeze takes about an hour. The procedure can be done in a doctor's office or in a hospital.

Skeptics now maintain that too many freezes are being done by too many persons unskilled in the technique.

They also question the fees, usually upwards of $100. Surgeons here think the fees are too high compared with those surgeons receive for more complicated operations.

In the stomach freeze, the patient swallows a tube to the end of which is attached a balloon shaped like the stomach. When the balloon is in place cold alcohol is pumped through the tube.

It was originally believed that the stomach was frozen solid in 45 minutes to an hour. It was also believed that the freezing shut off the flow of acids and helped duodenal ulcers.

Many patients have had stomach pain return in a few months after the freezing treatment. Usually, after stomachs were refrozen, the pain again disappeared.

At the session here, all agreed that the technique does stop ulcer pain often, if not in every case. The new question regards the possible harmful effects of the procedure.

Today, for instance, a University of Oregon team reported that it is impossible to freeze a stomach solid by the technique as it is now widely used. The flow of warm blood, said Dr. E. Douglas McSweeney, Jr. and Dr. Stanley W. Jacobs, keeps the stomach from freezing.

Effect Questioned

Moreover, the treatment when tried in dogs does not appear to reduce the amount of acid in the stomach, Dr. McSweeney and Dr. Jacobs said. Whatever the effects of freezing, whether psychological or physiological, they do not come from lowering the stomach acids, the two reported.

Others on the program agreed.

A report from the University of Mississippi School of Medicine maintained that the procedure is not so benign as had been originally believed.

Dr. John B. McFarland, Dr. C. Thomas Fitts, and Dr. Curtis P. Artz looked at the stomachs of a series of patients after they had been "frozen."

They used a flexible glass fiber device that passes through the throat to the stomach. They found in many of the patients evidence of damage to the lining of the stomach. They also saw bleeding in the stomach and ulcers induced by the freezing. Four patients out of one series of 108 required blood transfusions for bleeding after the treatment. One patient died of a perforation of a gastric ulcer after freezing.

"We want to give a word of warning," Dr. McFarland said. "This treatment does dramatically alleviate ulcer symptoms. But we think it has been overplayed. It should not be used by everybody. We should continue to investigate it."

It is not known why gastric freezing should relieve pain.

TEST

1. The doctors meeting in San Francisco are stomach specialists.   True   False
2. The so-called stomach "freeze" was introduced about ten years ago.   True   False
3. Doctors have bought over 20,000 machines to freeze stomachs since that time.   True   False
4. The usual fee for a stomach "freeze" is upwards of $100.   True   False
5. As a result of the technique, the stomach is frozen solid within five minutes after cold alcohol is pumped through the tube.   True   False
6. In many patients, stomach pain returned a few months after the treatment.   True   False
7. Upon retreatment the pain usually disappeared again.   True   False
8. Experimentation on dogs has shown that "freezing" reduces the amount of acid in the stomach.   True   False
9. In some patients, the treatment damaged the lining of the stomach.   True   False
10. One patient died after the "freezing" treatment.   True   False

ANSWERS: 1—false, 2—false, 3—false, 4—true, 5—false, 6—true, 7—true, 8—false, 9—true, 10—true.

In this test eight correct choices shows a better than average ability to absorb and retain. A score of nine or ten indicates reading skill of the highest order.

SECTION III. CAN YOU READ POETRY?

Most difficult of all types of reading is poetry. A rare and consummate skill is required for a thorough and immediate under-

standing of the language of a poem. Robert Browning's famous
"Prospice" is here used to test your ability. Read the poem as slowly
and as often as you wish, but do not look at the test below it until
you have finished.

Get into the mood of the poem. Shut everything else out of
your mind. Try to *feel* Browning's thoughts, *see* the images he draws
for you. Throw yourself wholeheartedly into what you read. When
you feel that you have mastered the selection, turn to the test. *Do
not, under any circumstances, refer again to the poem.*

PROSPICE

> Fear death?—to feel the fog in my throat,
>   The mist in my face,
> When the snows begin, and the blasts denote
>   I am nearing the place,
> The power of the night, the press of the storm,
>   The post of the foe;
> Where he stands, the Arch Fear in a visible form,
>   Yet the strong man must go:
> For the journey is done and the summit attained,
>   And the barriers fall,
> Though a battle's to fight ere the guerdon be gained,
>   The reward of it all.
> I was ever a fighter, so—one fight more,
>   The best and the last!
> I would hate that death bandaged my eyes, and forbore,
>   And bade me creep past.
> No! let me taste the whole of it, fare like my peers
>   The heroes of old,
> Bear the brunt, in a minute pay glad life's arrears
>   Of pain, darkness and cold.
> For sudden the worst turns the best to the brave,
>   The black minute's at end,
> And the elements' rage, the fiend-voices that rave,
>   Shall dwindle, shall blend,
> Shall change, shall become first a peace out of pain,
>   Then a light, then thy breast,
> O thou soul of my soul! I shall clasp thee again,
>   And with God be the rest!

TEST

1. The poet fears death.   True False
2. If he must die, he would like to do so quickly.   True False
3. He would like death to creep up on him secretly, so that he need not realize what is happening.   True False
4. If people have courage the most frightful things are quite tolerable.   True False
5. Death is a complete black end to everything.   True False

ANSWERS: 1—false, 2—true, 3—false, 4—true, 5—false.

You may be very very proud of your ability if you have chosen correctly in four or five instances. Even for the skilled reader of prose, poetry is often a hard nut to crack, and a score as low as two should not be discouraging.

Do you think your reading can be improved? Here are some suggestions that should be helpful:

1. Try for more rapid reading than that to which you are generally accustomed. The more quickly you can read, the more skillfully you are likely to read.

2. Try to absorb a greater number of words with each eye span. Have someone watch you as you read a page. How often do your eyes move? A skillful reader can absorb an average line in three or four eye spans, a poor reader needs six or more.

3. Try for greater concentration. Is your mind 100 percent involved in what you read? Does your attention ever wander? Are other things crowding out of your mind the facts on the page before you? Check up on yourself.

4. Never, never, move your lips as you read. If you are a "lip reader," consciously clamping your mouth shut while you read will eventually help you to overcome this unfortunate habit.

5. Never read isolated words, but take in phrases, thoughts, ideas.

6. Start your improvement program on easy reading (children's

books if necessary), gradually advancing to more difficult forms—nonfiction, semitechnical reading, poetry.

Reading can be improved. Three things are necessary: desire, determination, and loads and loads of practice.

These points will be covered in detail in the chapters to follow.

T W O

~~~~~~~~~~

Speed Up!

IT MAY POSSIBLY sound paradoxical that the speediest readers are the most skillful readers. Slowness, care, and thoroughness
have always been considered the highest of virtues, and we have all
admired the tenacious, plodding tortoise who got there ahead of the
speedy hare. On the other hand, it is logical to assume that what one
can do well one can also do quickly. Scientific testing has established
that those readers who can sprint through a selection absorb far more
from what they read than those who struggle and plod.

The mediocre adult reader has a rate of about 250 words per
minute. Professor Robert M. Bear, director of the Reading Clinic at
Dartmouth College, points out that "after a brief period of self-
training," the average person "should be able to read between 400
and 600 words a minute." Dr. Bear continues:

> In the ten years that we have been helping Dartmouth students im-
> prove their reading, I have seen few freshmen who read nearly as
> rapidly or efficiently as they should—and could after a little train-

ing. Year after year, our reading classes start off at an average of around 230 words a minute, and finish up a few weeks later at around 500 words a minute.

The chapters that follow aim to give you that period of self-training which will permit you, if you are a slow reader, to increase your present rate by 25–50 percent or more.

First, let us discover what that rate is. Provide yourself with a watch or clock that has a second hand. When you come to the black arrow, note down the exact time to the *second* on the blank provided for that purpose. Then continue reading, at your usual rate, until you reach the second black arrow. Again record the exact time.

Time at Starting:

———————

→ The history of the United States is replete with the names of famous pioneers and pathfinders who are credited with blazing the old trails of the old West. Yet few of them blazed a trail that had not been traveled for countless generations. It is probable that most of the more important western trails had been worn deep long before the first human foot was planted on the North American continent.

Some sixty million years ago, the western portion of the North American continent lay beneath the sea, and southern Arizona was a tropical swamp. Then the Sierra Nevada and Cascade Mountains were heaved up, forming a great peninsula and leaving a shallow inland sea to the eastward. The sea was roughly four hundred miles wide and a thousand long, stretching from the Gulf of California to southern Idaho. When the mountains rose they blocked the course of rain clouds blown in from the Pacific, and the inland sea evaporated until its only remaining vestige is Great Salt Lake. During millions of years the evaporating moisture was blown eastward in rain clouds, watering lush forests and grasslands that covered the high plateaus of Arizona, New Mexico, eastern Utah, and western Colorado. When the evaporation was completed Nevada, western Utah, southeastern California, and western Arizona were left desolate salt-impregnated deserts, and the high plateaus became arid wastelands.

Long before the rising of the Sierra Nevada, the Rocky Mountains had formed a solid bulwark, robbing rain clouds borne by the prevailing westerly winds, and leaving the high, rolling plains that stretched five hundred miles to the eastward a semiarid wilderness. Thus, for millions of years before there was human habitation, the western half of what is now the United States was arid or semiarid, except for the mountainous regions. But in the high altitudes snow fell deep in winter and the summer rains were abundant.←

The Old Trails West by Ralph Moody (Thomas Y. Crowell Company), copyright © 1963 by Ralph Moody, reprinted by permission.

Time at Finish:

_____

Now, to determine your rate, subtract your starting time from your finishing time. Record the difference: Sec. —————. Calculate your rate from this table:

Time (in seconds)	Rate (words per minute)
15	1,252
20	939
25	756
30	626
35	540
40	471
45	420
50	378
55	348
60	313
65	288
70	270

Time (in seconds)	Rate (words per minute)
75	252
80	234
90	210
100	189
110	174

The chances are very remote that you will find your rate either at the top or bottom of the scale. It is the rare athlete who can read at the rate of 1,250 words per minute and few people are as slow as 175 words per minute. Doubtless you will find your rate between 234 and 626 words per minute. From the following table, deduce your skill:

Words per Minute	Skill
626 or more	Superior
471–625	Excellent
313–470	Good
234–312	Average
225 or less	Poor

Whatever your rate of reading at the present time, it can be materially increased before you have turned the last page of this section.

Your first step is to determine to read more rapidly. Dr. Bear suggests:

The fundamental rule for increasing reading speed is simply this: *For five minutes every day for a month, force yourself to read a little faster than is comfortable.* Don't worry if occasionally you miss the exact meaning of a phrase, sentence, or even a paragraph. Just keep plowing ahead, grasping the main theme and letting the niceties of expression go hang.

The next exercise will give you an opportunity of putting Dr. Bear's suggestion into practice. Again I offer you an excerpt, of about the same length as the first one, from *The Old Trails West*. Read it quickly—push yourself ahead a little faster than is completely comfortable. Keep alert for the main ideas, for the total picture, so to speak. If you do this exercise properly you will find your time cut by 10 to 20 percent. As before, note your starting time at the first arrow, and again at the second one.

Time at Starting:

→ California well might be called the fabled land, since its name and the discovery of the portion now lying within the United States were due to the Spanish propensity for accepting fiction as fact. In 1510 the Spanish author Ordóñez de Montalvo invented California, an island lying east of the Indies and inhabited by a race of Amazons. He let his imagination run wild, and wrote: "Their island was the strongest in all the world, with its steep cliffs and rocky shores. Their arms were of gold, and so was the harness of the wild beasts they tamed to ride: for in the whole island there was no metal but gold." The tale so caught the fancy of the Spaniards that when, in 1533, a mountainous peninsula lying to the west of the Mexican mainland was discovered, it was named California. Settlements and missions were hastily established on the lower end of the peninsula and expeditions sent into the mountains to locate the gold, but the colonies failed when no rich deposits were discovered.

The second fable was of the Strait of Anián. From the time of Columbus's second voyage, a notion had persisted in Europe that the Pacific could be reached by a watercourse through the North American continent. To the French and British this imaginary watercourse became known as the Northwest Passage, and to the Spanish as the Strait of Anián. It was believed that whichever nation first discovered such a passage would be made wealthy through trade with India and the Orient.

Magellan, on his world-circling voyage of 1521, had discovered the Philippine Islands, and New Spain opened a highly profitable trade with them in 1542, sending out a great seven-hundred-ton galleon from Navidad, a little Pacific port straight west from Mexico City. But the Spanish Crown was extremely anxious for a direct trade route between Spain and the Philippines. In 1542, Juan Cabrillo, an expert sailor and explorer, was sent northward along the Pacific coast of Lower California with only a small frigate and an open boat to discover the Strait of Anián. Mapping the shore line carefully as he fought his way against the prevailing winds, he discovered San Diego Bay, and continued charting the coast for another four hundred miles. ←

> *The Old Trails West* by Ralph Moody (Thomas Y. Crowell Company), copyright © 1963 by Ralph Moody, reprinted by permission.

Time at Finish:

_____

Number of seconds required:

_____

Now calculate your new rate from the following table.

Time (in seconds)	Rate (words per minute)
15	1,500
20	1,125
25	900
30	750
35	648
40	564
45	500
50	450
55	408
60	375
65	348
70	324
75	300
80	282
90	250
100	225
110	204
120	188

You have undoubtedly found that your rate is materially faster. Your comfort, just as likely, was materially less. With enough practice, however, this new rate will eventually be fully comfortable, and when that happens you'll be ready to push on to still greater accomplishment.

THREE

~~~~~~~~~~~

Practice in Speed Reading

LEARNING TO READ quickly requires no particular aptitude. Perhaps not everybody can be a poet, or a skillful surgeon, or a star athlete; *anybody,* with a little practice, can become a rapid and skillful reader.

When you begin consciously to increase your speed, you will find, doubtless to your dismay, that you are losing some of the meaning of what you read. That is perfectly normal; it is to be expected—for a short while. Gradually you will discover that your mind is grasping more and more of the meaning of a selection, without any sacrifice of speed. If you will practice faithfully, you will be delighted to realize, after not too long a time, that because of your improved rate the meaning comes to you more quickly and with less effort.

Let's begin our practice at once. Below are reprinted, with permission, ten short selections from *The New Yorker* magazine. Read each one a little faster than is completely comfortable, then try to answer the questions that follow it. You will, possibly, do very poorly at first. Do not be discouraged if you fail on many of the answers in the first five tries. As you turn into the home stretch, however, you will notice that the questions seem to be somewhat easier. You will not have decreased your speed any, but, with practice, your comprehension will have adjusted to your new rate. To derive the most benefit from these exercises, keep pushing yourself along, even though the temptation to relax and read at the old, slow, comfortable pace will be very great.

I.

Last Sunday at dusk, three people were strolling along Rockefeller Plaza—a knowledgeable New York lady and a pair of country cousins, apparently. As they approached the Time and Life Building, famed Lucedifice, the well-informed lady said, "They call this the Time of Life Building—I don't know why."

    1. The day was: *a.* Monday *b.* Saturday *c.* Sunday

    2. How many people were involved? *a.* 2 *b.* 3 *c.* 4

    3. What time of day was it? *a.* morning *b.* afternoon *c.* evening

II.

Lady stopped in at her favorite Madison Avenue hat shop and ordered a couple of dashing little numbers. "Now, be sure you get the address right," she told the girl. "Last time I bought a hat here you sent it to the wrong address, and it was several days before I got it." "You'll positively get these hats tomorrow," the girl said. "The saleslady that makes the mistakes is out sick."

    1. Articles being bought were: *a.* hats *b.* dresses *c.* shoes

    2. One of the salesgirls: *a.* was dead *b.* was sick *c.* had been fired

III.

A physician we know, making his leisurely way up to the Presbyterian Hospital by Fifth Avenue bus, became interested in the conversation of two young ladies ahead of him. "I simply can't understand why the Army hasn't snapped him up long before this," one of them said. "As I understand it, it's his eyes," said the other. She went on to retail such amazing symptoms of eye abnormality that our friend was tempted to interrupt her with some questions of his own. It's as well he didn't, because it developed a moment later that they were talking about Superman.

1. The doctor was traveling by: *a.* bus *b.* taxi *c.* subway

2. Superman was rejected because of his: *a.* citizenship *b.* heart *c.* eyes

IV.

A flighty matron we know got embroiled with Macy's over an article which she returned, unused, with a request for a refund. Macy's said sorry, the ten-day period during which refunds are permitted had elapsed, and the best they could do was issue a credit slip entitling her to purchase something else that cost the same amount. She gamely carried the battle all the way to the office of somebody who was, obviously, a rather important executive. He stood firm on the credit-slip dictum. "Well, look," she said. "Suppose I take a credit slip and buy something else with it. I could return it immediately and ask for a cash refund, couldn't I?" "You couldn't," he told her, "but even if you could it wouldn't be cricket."

1. Refunds are permitted during a period of: *a.* five days *b.* ten days *c.* two weeks

V.

A woman friend of ours who has a garden apartment also had ants a while back. She got on the telephone, and presently an exterminator man appeared briskly with a flashlight and an ominous little black bag. The two of them looked for the ants, but they had gone. "I'm sorry," said the lady, and was surprised at the chagrin in her voice. "They *were* here. There were really millions of them." "That's all right, Ma'am," the exterminator man answered in a resigned fashion. "That's the way ants are— very undependable."

1. The insects in question were: *a*. Japanese beetles *b*. ants *c*. bees

2. How many were there? *a*. hundreds *b*. thousands *c*. millions

VI.

Three British naval officers whose ship had just put in at the Brooklyn Navy Yard hailed a taxi and asked to be taken over to Times Square. They further requested, since they were complete strangers to the city, that the driver point out any interesting or significant landmarks. "O.K.," the driver said. However, they drove in silence, so far as the driver was concerned, until they had crossed the river and headed uptown. Then the cabman pointed with a flourish at a large building and said, "Gentlemen, the Tombs!" He drove them around the Tombs, and then took them up to Times Square, again in silence.

1. The officers were: *a*. American *b*. British *c*. Chinese

2. The taxi driver pointed out: *a*. Grant's Tomb *b*. the Tombs *c*. Times Square

VII.

A friend of ours, fresh from the opening game of the World Series, rushed to a phone to tell us breathlessly of a shiny Cadillac sedan parked outside the Yankee Stadium. We were totally unimpressed until our correspondent explained that a regulation hot-dog pushcart, complete with orange umbrella and steaming sauerkraut containers, was attached to the Cadillac and was doing business as usual.

1. The sedan was a: *a*. Chevrolet *b*. Lincoln *c*. Cadillac

2. The car was parked outside: *a*. the Polo Grounds *b*. the Yankee Stadium *c*. Carnegie Hall

VIII.

When a young mother of our acquaintance took her turn as chauffeur for six eight- and nine-year-olds whose parents belong to a school car pool, she asked her passengers, in order to keep the conversation going, what lunches they preferred above all others. "Hamburgers," said five of them. "Beef Stroganoff," said the sixth.

1. The children were: *a.* six to nine years old *b.* six to ten years old *c.* eight and nine years old
2. Most of the youngsters preferred: *a.* Beef Stroganoff *b.* hamburgers *c.* hot dogs
3. How many children were there? *a.* eight *b.* nine *c.* six

IX.

The other day, we saw a pretty lady all dressed in blue lose her hat to some vagrant airs prowling about Sixth Avenue and Forty-second Street. Taxicabs maneuvered around the object, and even private cars swerved to avoid it. Finally, an enormous trailer truck, with enough licenses to clear it to the moon, stopped cold. The driver of the behemoth got out, picked up the hat, dusted it off with care, and handed it to the lady. As he headed back to his vehicle, his day's good deed done, the cop on the corner handed him a ticket for blocking traffic.

1. The lady was dressed in: *a.* blue *b.* red *c.* white
2. The episode occurred at: *a.* Seventh Avenue *b.* Sixth Avenue and Forty-second Street *c.* Sixth Avenue and Forty-third street
3. The hat was rescued by a: *a.* truck driver *b.* pedestrian *c.* cop

X.

Fifteen minutes later, where should we be but in the Gold Room of the Sheraton-East, deep in a Sake Tasting Party, which was being given by the Officers of the Japan Sake Central Association? *"Sake* is to the Japanese what champagne is to the French and vodka is to the Russians," Mr. Jiro Tokuyama, director of public affairs of the Japan Trade Center, told us. "You can drink it warm, in little cups, in the traditional Japanese fashion, or you can have it in the Westernized versions of 'on the rocks' or in a *sake* Martini, with a base of gin and a dash of orange bitters."

1. What was served at the party: *a.* champagne *b.* vodka *c.* sake

2. The party was given by: *a*. Russians *b*. Frenchmen
c. Japanese

3. The party was held in the: *a*. Gold Room *b*. Blue Room
c. Red Room

ANSWERS: I. 1—c, 2—b, 3—c.
    II. 1—a, 2—b.
   III. 1—a, 2—c.
   IV. 1—b.
    V. 1—b, 2—c.
   VI. 1—b, 2—b.
  VII. 1—c, 2—b.
VIII. 1—c, 2—b, 3—c.
   IX. 1—a, 2—b, 3—a.
    X. 1—c, 2—c, 3—a.

Reading at a slightly-faster-than-comfortable rate you attempted to grasp the details of ten short paragraphs. If you answered correctly fifteen or more of the twenty-three questions, consider that you did very well—you have learned that you can absorb material with greater speed than you are completely used to.

With more practice (and this will be provided in the chapters to come), you will adjust to a more rapid rate and your comprehension will shortly be as good as, or, quite likely, better than, it was before.

FOUR

~~~~~~~~~~~~~~~

Your Eyes and How to Use Them

ONE OF THE chief obstacles to skillful reading is an inability to use the eyes properly. You've doubtless been reading for years and years and no longer realize what a complexity of habits is required for reading.

Let us examine the matter clinically. As your eyes travel over a page of print, the following phenomena occur:

1. Your eyes shift several times on a single line. In between shifts the actual reading is accomplished. These periods of rest, or *fixations,* to use the technical term, are extremely short—so short, indeed, that they are measurable in hundredths of a second. The skillful reader uses fewer shifts, and hence fewer fixations, in covering a line of type. A very good reader uses no more than three or four fixations to a line, a poor reader as many as six or seven, or even more.

2. At the end of each line, your eyes travel from right to left to start the new line. This is called the "return sweep."

3. Under normal circumstances your eyes should always travel in a continuous left to right direction, except in the return sweep. Occasionally, however, as a thought eludes you, or as you fail to appreciate the meaning or implication of a word or phrase, your eyes will return to a previously read portion of a line. This return is called a "regression." Obviously, the more skill a reader possesses, the fewer regressions he makes; the less skill, the greater number of regressions.

4. Actual reading, as has been said, occurs in those minute periods of time which we have called "fixations." During a fixation a certain number of words are read. The space these words occupy on a line is called the "eye span." The better you read, the larger your eye span; the less skillfully you read, the smaller the span. An illustration will show the value of long eye spans. Take the line:

Mary had a little lamb; its fleece was white as snow.

A phenomenally skillful reader will absorb it in two spans, as follows:

Mary had a little lamb│ ;│its fleece was white as snow.

Note that each span covered a meaningful phrase and that the thought therefore could be absorbed instantaneously. Let us now watch a phenomenally poor reader:

Mary ha│d a lit│tle lamb│ ;│its fle│ece was wh│ite a│s snow.
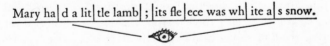

Seven separate eye spans were required to complete the line, as against two for the highly trained reader. Most of these spans brought to the mind of the poor reader meaningless patterns:

Mary ha
d a lit
tle lamb;
its fle

ece was **wh**
ite a
s snow

d a lit, its fle, ece was wh, and other such combinations frustrate the poor reader's attempts to absorb the thought, and hence numerous regressions are necessary. Under such circumstances, reading becomes an unpleasant chore, and it is no wonder that he feels mentally winded after struggling through several hundred words.

5. A good reader achieves a certain "rhythm" in his reading. "Rhythm" refers to a uniform number of fixations in each line, plus a certain uniformity in the "angle" of the return sweeps. Let us again spy on a good reader, to observe the possession of rhythm.

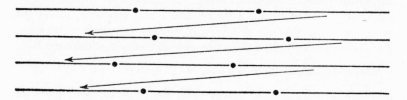

While the spans themselves were of different lengths, there were three in each line, and the angle of the return sweep was fairly uniform.

You can discover, with little trouble, how many eye spans you yourself use in covering a line of type. Sit at a desk and place a hand mirror on the left-hand page of this book. Have someone stand behind you and adjust the mirror so that he can follow your eyes in it. Start reading the right-hand page. The person helping you can, after a little practice, count the number of fixations you use for each line. If only three or four fixations are counted on each line, your reading ability is in fine shape. If five or more fixations are counted, there is room for improvement.

Now hand him the book and let him query you on the content of the page. Can you report on the material accurately?

You have three goals:

1. Lengthen eye spans.
2. Reduce the number of fixations per line.
3. Avoid regressions.

These goals can be reached by practice. Let us start at once.

Follow the lines carefully, suiting your eye spans and fixations to the rhythm indicated: Attempt to see both *x*'s each time you glance at a line.

• x _____ x • x _____ x • x _____ x •
• x _____ x • x _____ x • x _____ x •
• x _____ x • x _____ x • x _____ x •
• x _____ x • x _____ x • x _____ x •
• x _____ x • x _____ x • x _____ x •
• x _____ x • x _____ x • x _____ x •
• x _____ x • x _____ x • x _____ x •
• x _____ x • x _____ x • x _____ x •
• x _____ x • x _____ x • x _____ x •
• x _____ x • x _____ x • x _____ x •
• x _____ x • x _____ x • x _____ x •
• x _____ x • x _____ x • x _____ x •
• x _____ x • x _____ x • x _____ x •
• x _____ x • x _____ x • x _____ x •
• x _____ x • x _____ x • x _____ x •
• x _____ x • x _____ x • x _____ x •
• x _____ x • x _____ x • x _____ x •
• x _____ x • x _____ x • x _____ x •
• x _____ x • x _____ x • x _____ x •
• x _____ x • x _____ x • x _____ x •
• x _____ x • x _____ x • x _____ x •
• x _____ x • x _____ x • x _____ x •
• x _____ x • x _____ x • x _____ x •
• x _____ x • x _____ x • x _____ x •
• x _____ x • x _____ x • x _____ x •

Go over this material several times until you can breeze through the page easily. Then apply the same technique in the following exercise, in which you attempt to see complete phrases in a single glance, making no more than three fixations to the line. Again we'll use material from *The New Yorker*'s Talk of the Town:

- We sometimes fear • that visitors • to New York •
- find the city • a cold, • inhospitable place, •
- but a recent • dispatch from • one of our •
- United Nations correspondents • has put • our mind •
- at rest • at least temporarily. • It seems •
- that one of • the popular dishes • of Indonesia •
- is made with carp, • and that carp, • like lobster, •
- should be kept alive • until the moment • it's cooked. •
- Unable to find • live carp • at their •
- neighborhood • fish stores, • the wives of •
- a number of • Indonesian diplomats • made inquiries, •
- and finally heard about • a stream • on Long Island •
- that contains • whole schools of • the gold and black •
- varieties of carp, • both of which • are considered •
- merely nuisance fish • by uncosmopolitan • anglers. •
- On a recent • Sunday morning, • a committee of •
- the ladies • set forth • with fishing poles, •
- nets, • baskets, • and pails, •
- and, after a subway ride, • a bus trip, • and a short walk •
- to the stream, • hauled out • a good catch •
- which they • managed to • bring back alive. •
- Their husbands • were so pleased • with the •
- culinary results • that the ladies • now plan •
- to repeat • the expedition • at regular intervals. •

Go over this material as many times as necessary until you feel complete comfort, increased speed, and full comprehension.

Let us try the same technique, next, with a news item from *The New York Times*. Again suit your rhythm and fixations to the phrases within the black dots.

- The use • of personality tests • in deciding •
- college admission • involves • "very serious risks" •
- at the present time, • the College Entrance • Examination Board •
- has warned • its membership. • The board •
- of trustees • of the college board, • in a statement •
- distributed at • its annual meeting • here, •
- pointed out • that no • personality test •
- known to the board • seemed to • have been •

• sufficiently studied • to warrant • the acceptance •
• of those risks. • Many colleges, • faced with •
• growing enrollments • and more • qualified applicants •
• than they • can accommodate • have been looking •
• to tests • of such characteristics • as "creativity," •
• "independence," • "motivation," • and "need achievement" •
• for help • in selecting students. • The college board •
• itself has made • substantial grants • to further research •
• in these areas • and many • independent efforts •
• have also • developed tests • for such traits, •
• the trustees noted. • They expressed hope • that within •
• a few years • these measures • might become part •
• of the advisory process, • if not • of selection. •
• The board • expressed concern, • however, •
• that "some authors • and supporters • of these •
• new instruments • seem, • quite understandably •
• but nonetheless • unfortunately, • to be urging •
• actual use • of these instruments • in college admissions •
• before the full • consequences • of such use •
• has been • satisfactorily explored." • The trustees •
• said • that schools, • students, •
• and parents • tended to regard • any test requirement •
• as a representation • of a college's policy. • Ethical and •
• moral problems • are also raised • by tests, •
• the trustees said. • When students report, • rather than exhibit, •
• their behavior, • they often must • "make hard choices •
• between lying • and informing • upon themselves •
• to their own disadvantage." • The tests • also put •
• personal and • private information, • into the hands •
• of school authorities • who probably • do not •
• understand completely • what the measurements • mean, •
• the trustees said. • There is no • adequate information •
• on the sensitivity • of personality tests • to faking •
• and coaching, • nor is it likely • that genuinely new •
• but parallel forms • can be produced • continuously •
• to prevent • the contents • from becoming known •
• to students • in advance, • the trustees said. •
• They continued that, • although the tests •
• were generally designed • to measure •
• non-intellectual qualities, • there was no assurance •
• that the results • would not be used • in an attempt •

• to improve accuracy • in predicting grades. • "Even if this purpose •
• is accepted, • the gains in • simple predictive power •
• shown thus far • by personality tests • are modest," •
• the trustees said. •

Read this passage as often as required until you can sail right along, with no confusion or discomfort, making the fixations indicated.

So far, we have realized that the following goals must be attained if reading is to be improved:

1. Conscious increase of speed, even though temporarily uncomfortable.
2. Reduction of the number of fixations per line.
3. Increase of the length of eye spans.
4. Elimination of regressions.

Our next concern is with "vocalization."

FIVE

Are You a Vocalizer?

THE MIND CAN understand a page of print *four times as rapidly* as the vocal organs can pronounce the words that make up that page.

Such being the case, readers who "vocalize" cut their speed to as little as 25 percent of the rate they're capable of.

"Vocalization," which is the complete or partial pronunciation of words during the process of silent reading, is a bad habit usually built up over the years, but fairly easy to eradicate once the reader is made aware of what he is doing.

Do you vocalize? To find out, read this paragraph aloud, at the same time placing your forefinger on your throat, just below the Adam's apple, to locate your vocal chords. You'll know your finger is in the right place as soon as you feel a vibration. When you have discovered your vocal chords, continue reading silently. Do you feel any further vibration, even of the slightest sort? If you do, you are vocalizing; and if you vocalize to any extent, you are, as I have said, reading much more slowly than you're able to—you may be cutting your rate by as much as 75 percent.

The most flagrant vocalizers are the "lip readers." Not only their vocal chords, but all other parts of their vocal mechanisms are intent on forming the words in front of them. As a result, much of their attention is concentrated on the actual sounds of the words; and that energy which should be directed toward understanding and appreciating the content of what they are reading is wasted in articulating syllables.

If you are a lip reader or a vocalizer, you cannot hope to improve your reading until you eliminate your failing. Every time you find yourself sounding the words in your throat or with your lips, every time you realize that your thoughts are concentrated on the *sound* of what you are reading, *stop reading*. Go back over the paragraph you just finished and *drink in the ideas,* attempting to lose all consciousness of the words as *individual* units.

(And doing all your reading at a rate that is slightly uncomfortable will act to impede any impulse to form the words with any part of your vocal apparatus.)

Here is another surefire method, as suggested in *The Improvement of Reading* [1] by Luella Cole: *put your finger in your mouth!*

Sounds childish, doesn't it? But it's effective—if you insert your forefinger between your teeth and over your tongue, you cannot vocalize without becoming aware of what you're doing.

A clean piece of wood or a pencil held between your teeth will serve as well, but, as Miss Cole suggests, you always have your finger with you, ready for use when necessary. Miss Cole in her book cites an interesting case:

> John was a loud vocalizer. Whatever else might be wrong with him, it was evident at once to the teacher of the remedial class that something must be done to stop the noise John made, if the other children were to get their work done. Without waiting to make any analysis, Miss A. promptly recommended the finger-in-the-mouth technique. There ensued a silence—but almost no comprehension of the reading matter. John seemed unable to recognize even the simplest words unless he could pronounce them. In order to find something that

[1] Farrar and Rinehart.

John could read without vocalizing, it was necessary to use a second-grade book. During the first week John had his doubts about the value of this method but agreed to give it a fair trial. Before the end of the second week he had begun to feel that his reading was much less labored than ever before. Instead of being work, the simple book he was using became play. At about this time the boy appeared one morning with a neatly whittled and sandpapered piece of wood, all wrapped up in a clean handkerchief. During the following six weeks John kept the piece of wood between his teeth whenever he was reading. No other treatment was used for this boy. Yet in two months' time he improved nearly three years in speed and over a year in comprehension. Moreover, he reported a great increase in the ease with which he read. After leaving the class, John continued to carry the wood around with him, but he used it less and less. At the end of the year he was reading without any artificial aid to keep him from vocalizing.

As an adult, your vocalizing is not likely to be as great as John's was—hence, it will take you less time to overcome it. After a little practice you will stop pronouncing the words you see on a page of print.

As a matter of fact, the skillful reader not only does not pronounce the words he sees—not only doesn't fully see *individual* words—but indeed is almost unaware of certain unimportant words. A skillful reader will see the following when he reads: [2]

Fraud

This one's about little chap eight who recently went Boston visit Grandmother, train journey alone travelling, shortage Pullman chairs, day coach. Arrived, reported Grandmother trip uneventful, except strange encounter sailor. Seems Mother had put train, and then nice lady had sat down beside him. He and lady talked long time, then train stopped lots and lots sailors got on. (This would have been New London, we figure.) So then they rode and rode long time, train stopped nice lady got off. (Providence, undoubtedly.) "And then," the child told Grandmother, bewilderment voice, "one sailors acted real mad. He came over said, 'Listen, you little weasel, you might have told us that babe wasn't your mother.' "

[2] This selection, like many of the others, is from the incomparable *New Yorker*.

Prepositions, articles, and other small words that do not definitely add to the sense of the piece have a barely momentary recognition in the skillful reader's mind. Now here is the piece as it originally appeared. Read it yourself, as rapidly as you can, skimming over the unimportant words.

Fraud

This one's about a little chap of eight who recently went up to Boston to visit Grandmother, making the train journey all alone and travelling, because of the shortage of Pullman chairs, in a day coach. When he arrived, he reported to Grandmother that the trip had been uneventful, except for a strange encounter with a sailor. It seems that Mother had put him on the train, and then a nice lady had sat down beside him. He and the lady talked for a long time, and then the train stopped and lots and lots of sailors got on. (This would have been New London, we figure.) So then they rode and rode for a long time, and then the train stopped and the nice lady got off. (Providence, undoubtedly.) "And then," the child told Grandmother, bewilderment in his voice, "one of the sailors acted real mad. He came over and said to me, 'Listen, you little weasel, you might have told us that babe wasn't your mother.'"

To recapitulate, there are three main objections to vocalization:

1. It interferes with absorption of meaning, for the unit of vocalization is a syllable, while the unit of meaning is a word or phrase.
2. It slows the rate, as the eye can travel four times as fast as the voice can articulate.
3. As the eye constantly gets ahead of the voice, the habit of excessive regressions is developed.

SIX

~~~~~~~~~~

℞ *For Improved Reading*

WITH A FEW weeks of intensive self-training, you can materially increase your reading rate, considerably improve your reading skill. Is it worth doing? Well, much of your intellectual sustenance comes from books, newspapers, and magazines. Double your reading speed (a goal quite easy to reach if you are a poor or average reader, i.e., if your rate is 175-275 W.P.M.) and, without spending any more time or energy on your reading, you double the amount of pleasure and information you derive from the time you usually give to reading.

Keep in mind some simple rules whenever you read:

1. Always read a bit faster than is completely comfortable. Comprehension may suffer at first, but gradually you will adjust to the new rate you set for yourself.
2. Above all else, force yourself to avoid vocalization and lip movements.

3. Read by phrases, not word by word.
4. Concentrate on the author's ideas and thinking, never on his individual words.
5. Stop yourself from making regressions. Resist any impulse to go back over parts of a line already covered. If you feel you have missed, or misunderstood, something important, start the paragraph again. In this way you will develop and reinforce the habit of sailing smoothly through a page of print.

SIX

How to Be a Good Speller

O N E

~~~~~~~~

Anyone Can Spell

THE ONLY PERSON who cannot learn to spell is one who has no "visual memory." You do not belong to that class. If you did, you could never have learned to read, and you would never have got this far in this book.

Now it is true that some people have better visual memories than others. Let us test yours. Study the following box for fifteen seconds, then cover it with your hand or a blank card.

Can you reproduce what you have seen? Try it.

The degree of success you attained in reproducing the meaningless symbols which you studied will tell you how keen your visual memory is. The test was a difficult one, as the symbols were unusually complicated. If you were able to approximate the five symbols in their relative positions, your visual memory is far above average, and therefore you should be a better than average speller.

233

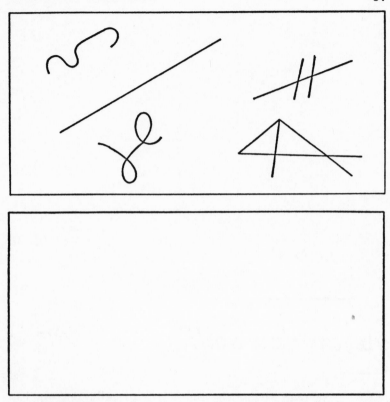

If you did not come through too successfully, try this simpler test, proceeding as before:

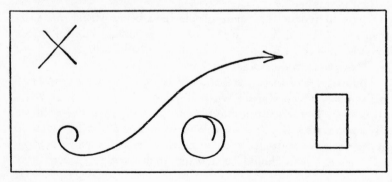

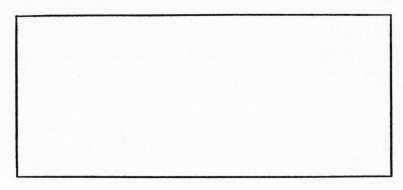

If this test did not trouble you, your visual memory is adequate, and spelling should not be one of your weak spots.

If you feel, however, that there is some room for improvement in your general spelling ability, two things can help you:

1. A knowledge of certain useful spelling rules.
2. A familiarity with certain spelling "demons." (A "demon" is a word that most people misspell.)

SPELLING PROBLEMS AND THEIR SOLUTIONS

Problem I

In a word like *occur,* shall we double the *r* before adding a suffix? Should it be spelled *occurence* or *occurrence?*

Solution

As the accent falls on the final syllable (*oc-cur'*), the terminal consonant is doubled (*occurrence*). The same rule applies to *control', controlling; re-pel', repelling; pre-fer', preferring;* etc. The key is the position of the accent—*double the final consonant only if the accent falls on the final syllable.*

Problem II

What about *prefer, preference; refer, reference;* and other such combinations?

Solution

Since the accent shifts in these words (*pre-fer', pref'-er-ence; re-fer', ref'-er-ence*) the final consonant *is not doubled.* In *referred, referring* and *preferred, preferring,* a doubled consonant is required because the accent has *not* shifted.

Problem III

Why is the final consonant of words like *marvel, conquer,* and *travel* not doubled when a suffix is added?

Solution

In these and similar words, the accent has not fallen on the final syllable: *mar'-vel, con'-quer, trav'-el,* etc. Thus, any longer form contains a single consonant:

conqueror	traveling	marveling
conquered	traveled	marvelous
conquering	traveler	marveled

Other words that belong in the same category are:

profit	jewel
cancel	peril
combat	shovel
chisel	shrivel
equal	libel

TEST

Write each of the words above with an *-ing* ending.

1. ————   3. ————

2. ————   4. ————

5. ———————   8. ———————
6. ———————   9. ———————
7. ———————   10. ———————

ANSWERS: 1—profiting, 2—canceling, 3—combating, 4—chiseling, 5—equaling, 6—jeweling, 7—periling, 8—shoveling, 9—shriveling, 10—libeling.

Problem IV

Shall we double the *t* when a suffix is added to *hit?* Is it *hiting* or *hitting?*

Solution

Words of *one* syllable which end in a *single* consonant (in this case *t*), preceded by a single vowel (in this case *i*), double the consonant before adding a suffix. Examine these:

hit	bat	hop
hitting	batting	hopping
hitter	batted	hopped

Now in *fail,* since a double vowel (*ai*) precedes the final consonant, no doubling is necessary.

fail	seal	kneel
failed	sealed	kneeled
failing	sealing	kneeling

TEST

Write forms ending in *-ed* and *-ing* for the following:

	-ed	*-ing*
swap	———————	———————
sail	———————	———————
rap	———————	———————
man	———————	———————
pin	———————	———————

ANSWERS: swapped, swapping; sailed, sailing; rapped, rapping; manned, manning; pinned, pinning.

Problem V

How can one remember whether to write *ei* or *ie?*

Solution

There is the justly famous story about the man who always wrote words containing an *ie* or *ei* so that both vowels looked identical; then he placed a dot right in the middle:

That, however, is evading the issue. A practical rule, with some notable exceptions, applies:

Rule: *i* before *e* except after *c.*

yield	grieve
believe	chief
field	siege
wield	achieve
relieve	niece

But:

receive	conceive
deceive	conceit
receipt	perceive
deceit	

Here are the exceptions:

1. Words in which the pronunciation is *ay.*

weigh	neigh	inveigh
feign	freight	sleigh

2. The following special words, frequently misspelled, in which *ei* is the correct pattern even though there is no immediately preceding *c*.

s*ei*ze	l*ei*sure
counterf*ei*t	n*ei*ther
for*ei*gn	*ei*ther
forf*ei*t	w*ei*rd

TEST

Fill in the blanks with either *ei* or *ie,* according to which is required:

1. s————ge
2. gr————ve
3. f————gn
4. for————gn
5. h————ght
6. l————sure
7. rec————ve
8. dec————ve
9. bel————ve
10. ch————f

11. f————ld
12. n————ce
13. p————ce
14. w————ld
15. y————ld
16. counterf————t
17. w————rd
18. s————ze
19. n————ghbor
20. w————gh

ANSWERS: 1—siege, 2—grieve, 3—feign, 4—foreign, 5—height, 6—leisure, 7—receive, 8—deceive, 9—believe, 10—chief, 11—field, 12—niece, 13—piece, 14—wield, 15—yield, 16—counterfeit, 17—weird, 18—seize, 19—neighbor, 20—weigh.

Problem VI

Which is correct, *noticable* or *noticeable?*

Solution

After *c* and after *g* the *e* is retained before *-able* or *-ous,* thus:

notic*e*able	trac*e*able
replac*e*able	marriag*e*able

chang*e*able	peac*e*able
charg*e*able	courag*e*ous
enforc*e*able	outrag*e*ous
servic*e*able	advantag*e*ous

The retention of the *e* keeps the *g* and *c* soft (like *j* and *s*, respectively). However, this rule applies *only* before *-able* and *-ous,* not before *-ing.* The reason: while *a* and *o* are "hardening" vowels (i.e., they make a *c* or *g* hard), *i* is a "softening" vowel (i.e., it keeps the *g* or *c* soft).

noticing	servicing
changing	charging
replacing	tracing

After other letters than *c* or *g, e* is dropped before *-able* or *-ous.*

blame—blamable
deplore—deplorable
live—livable
admire—admirable
desire—desirable

Note: Because *d* preceding *g* has the same "softening" influence as a following *e,* no *e* is necessary in:

lo*d*gment	abri*d*gment
ju*d*gment	acknowle*d*gment

Problem VII

Is it *honor* or *honour?*

Solution

-Our is a British ending. It is found in American spelling only in the word *glamour.* The derived form, however, is *glamorous.*

hon*o*r,	*not*	hono*u*r
neighb*o*r,	*not*	neighbo*u*r
hum*o*r,	*not*	humo*u*r
harb*o*r,	*not*	harbo*u*r

Problem VIII

How can one know whether a word ends in *-ence* or *-ance*, *-ent* or *-ant?*

Solution

Only visual memory will help in such instances, as there is no reliable rule to guide the speller. The following words are those most frequently misspelled:

abund*ance*	abund*ant*
resist*ance*	resist*ant*
persever*ance*	
appear*ance*	
repent*ance*	repent*ant*
	descend*ant*
occurr*ence*	
superintend*ence*	superintend*ent*
insist*ence*	insist*ent*
persist*ence*	persist*ent*
depend*ence*	depend*ent*
inadvert*ence*	inadvert*ent*
exist*ence*	exist*ent*
confid*ence*	confid*ent*
compet*ence*	compet*ent*
differ*ence*	differ*ent*
intermitt*ence*	intermitt*ent*

When a misspelling does occur, it is more likely that *-ance* has been incorrectly substituted for *-ence* than the other way around. If seriously in doubt about a word, then, you're probably safe in choosing *-ence* or *-ent* in preference to *-ance* or *-ant.*

Problem IX

How about *-able* or *-ible?*

Solution

Again no rule is really satisfactory, though it often helps to think of a derived form:

access*ible*—access*ion*
aud*ible*—aud*i*tion
corrupt*ible*—corrupt*ion*
permiss*ible*—permiss*ion*
admiss*ible*—admiss*ion*
comprehens*ible*—comprehens*ion*

inviol*able*—viol*a*tion
limit*able*—limit*a*tion
inimit*able*—imit*a*tion
irrit*able*—irrit*a*tion

Problem X

Which is correct, *panicy* or *panicky?*

Solution

As we know, *c* may be pronounced "soft" (as in *cent*) or "hard" (as in *came*). Before the vowels *e, i,* and *y* (*y* is a consonant only when it has the sound heard in *yes* or *you*), we must therefore insert a *k* to keep the *c* "hard." *Panicky* is the correct pattern, as *panicy* would be pronounced *panissy*. Note the following, in which the same principle operates:

colic*k*y,   *not* colicy
frolic*k*ing, *not* frolicing
picnic*k*ing, *not* picnicing
picnic*k*er,   *not* picnicer
traffic*k*er,   *not* trafficer
traffic*k*ing, *not* trafficing
mimic*k*ing, *not* mimicing

Problem XI

How can you tell whether a word should end in -*ize*, -*ise*, or -*yze*?

Solution

Only two common words in the language end in -*yze*:—*analyze* and *paralyze*. Otherwise, most words end in -*ize*. Just a few important ones end in -*ise*, namely:

advertise	rise
advise	despise
arise	surmise
chastise	disguise
comprise	enterprise
compromise	exercise
devise	improvise
likewise	sidewise
otherwise	supervise
revise	

If in doubt, use -*ize*.

This has been a rather difficult chapter, full of important details. If you can conquer the eleven problems discussed in these pages, you have gone far toward improving your spelling. Look over the problems once more. When you feel that you are master of the problems and their solutions, take this test.

TEST

In the following list, exactly twenty words are misspelled. When you detect what you consider an error, rewrite the word correctly in the indicated blank. If you feel that a word contains precisely the right letters in their proper order, place a check in the appropriate blank.

1. occurrence	———	21. deplorable	———
2. referrence	———	22. desireable	———
3. controling	———	23. judgement	———
4. travelling	———	24. acknowledgment	———
5. conquerring	———	25. glamour	———
6. marveling	———	26. labour	———
7. perilous	———	27. glamourous	———
8. begining	———	28. resistance	———
9. receive	———	29. confidance	———
10. beleive	———	30. audable	———
11. siege	———	31. comprehensible	———
12. weird	———	32. irritable	———
13. leisure	———	33. inimitible	———
14. conceive	———	34. irresistible	———
15. sieze	———	35. panicky	———
16. feign	———	36. frolicing	———
17. neice	———	37. picnicker	———
18. noticeable	———	38. analyze	———
19. couragous	———	39. paralize	———
20. servicable	———	40. advertize	———

ANSWERS: 1—√, 2—reference, 3—controlling, 4—traveling, 5—conquering, 6—√, 7—√, 8—beginning, 9—√, 10—believe, 11—√, 12—√, 13—√, 14—√, 15—seize, 16—√, 17—niece, 18—√, 19—courageous, 20—serviceable, 21—√, 22—desirable, 23—judgment, 24—√, 25—√, 26—labor, 27—glamorous, 28—√, 29—confidence, 30—audible, 31—√, 32—√, 33—inimitable, 34—√, 35—√, 36—frolicking, 37—√, 38—√, 39—paralyze, 40—advertise.

T W O

Fifty Spelling "Demons"

THE FIFTY WORDS that comprise this chapter are among the most frequently misspelled in the language.

You can conquer these "demons" in less than an hour in three simple steps. Taking one group of ten at a time:

1. Look at each word carefully. Really look at it, noting especially the capitalized letters, for these are the ones most people have trouble with. Read also the hint in parentheses in order to fix the proper combination of letters securely in your mind.

2. Now cover the word with your hand or any slip of paper or card, and write it in the blank next to it. Check your learning immediately, making any necessary corrections.

3. Then take the short test following each group. If your learning has been successful, you should not only make a perfect score but be able to do so without the slightest doubt, hesitation, or confusion.

Group I

1. aLL right _____
   (Two words, two *l*'s, no matter how used. Think of its opposite, *aLL wrong.*)
2. accidentALLy _____
   (The adjective *accidental* plus the adverbial ending *-ly*—hence the double *l.*)
3. arGUMent _____
   (The *e* of *argue* is, illogically, dropped before *-ment.*)
4. trULy _____
   (The *e* of *true,* again illogically, is dropped before *-ly.*)
5. abSence _____
   (No *c* immediately following the *s*. Think of the adjective *absent.*)
6. abSCess _____
   (Here, however, a *c* does follow the *s.*)
7. aNoint _____
   (One *n* only following the *a.*)
8. iNoculate _____
   (Again one *n*—think of the synonym *inject,* which also has only one *n.*)
9. aSSaSSin _____
   (Two pairs of double *s*'s.)
10. aSSiStant _____
    (One double *s,* followed by a single *s.*)

TEST I

Every word below is misspelled. Can you rewrite it correctly?

1. alright _____
2. accidently _____
3. arguement _____
4. truely _____
5. abscence _____
6. abcess _____
7. annoint _____
8. innoculate _____

9. asassin _____

10. assisstant _____

ANSWERS: 1—all right, 2—accidentally, 3—argument, 4—truly, 5—absence, 6—abscess, 7—anoint, 8—inoculate, 9—assassin, 10—assistant.

Group II

11. benEfit _____
     (Note the crucial *e*, not *i*.)
12. baLLoon _____
     (Round, usually, like a *ball*.)
13. coMMiTTee _____
     (Double *m*, double *t*.)
14. cooLLy _____
     (*Cool* plus *-ly*, hence the double *l*.)
15. comparAtive _____
     (Watch that *a*, even though *comparison* has an *i* in the same place.)
16. coNNoiSSeur _____
     (Double *n*, double *s*.)
17. diSaPPear _____
     (*Appear* plus the prefix *dis-*, hence one *s*, two *p*'s.)
18. diSaPPoint _____
     (Same construction, same problem, same solution—*appoint* plus *dis-*.)
19. drunkeNNess _____
     (*Drunken,* the adjective, plus the suffix *-ness*—hence two *n*'s.)
20. diSSIPate _____
     (That *ssip* combination fools the most erudite writers!)

TEST II

Every word below is misspelled. Can you rewrite it correctly?

11. benifit _____

12. baloon _____

13. comittee _____

14. cooly _____

15. comparitive _____

16. conoiseur   _____
17. dissapear   _____
18. dissapoint   _____
19. drunkeness   _____
20. disapate   _____

ANSWERS: 11—benefit, 12—balloon, 13—committee, 14—coolly, 15—comparative, 16—connoisseur, 17—disappear, 18—disappoint, 19—drunkenness, 20—dissipate.

Group III

21. embaRRaSSment _____
    (Double *r*, double *s*.)
22. ecstaSy _____
    (-*Sy*, not -*cy*.)
23. exCEED _____
    (This word, and the next two, are the only ones in English ending in -*ceed*.)
24. proCEED _____
25. sucCEED _____
26. frIEnd _____
    (Note *ie*, not *ei*.)
27. grammAR _____
    (Not -*er*.)
28. mathEmatics _____
    (Not *a*.)
29. miSSpell _____
    (*Spell* plus the prefix *mis-*, hence double *s*.)
30. miSShapen _____
    (-*Shapen* plus *mis-*, hence again double *s*.)

TEST III

Every word below is misspelled. Can you rewrite it correctly?

21. embarassment   _____
22. ecstacy   _____
23. excede   _____
24. procede   _____
25. succede   _____

26. freind _____
27. grammer _____
28. mathamatics _____
29. mispell _____
30. mishapen _____

ANSWERS: 21—embarrassment, 22—ecstasy, 23—exceed, 24—proceed, 25—succeed, 26—friend, 27—grammar, 28—mathematics, 29—misspell, 30—misshapen.

Group IV

31. newSStand _____
    (*News* plus *stand*, hence double *s*.)
32. booKKeeper _____
    (*Book* plus *keeper*, hence double *k*.)
33. privIlEge _____
    (note two *i*'s followed by two *e*'s.)
34. paraLLel _____
    (The double *l* comes first.)
35. preCEDE _____
    (Unlike *proceed*, this word ends in *-cede*.)
36. superSEDE _____
    (But this one, absolutely unique, ends in *-sede*.)
37. poSSeSSion _____
    (Double *s*'s, just as in *assassin*.)
38. proNUNciation _____
    (Even though the verb is spelled *pronounce*.)
39. reCoMMend _____
    (The verb *commend*, plus the prefix *re-*.)
40. sacrIlEgious _____
    (Note the similarity in the order of the vowels to *privilege*.)

TEST IV

Every word below is misspelled. Can you rewrite it correctly?

31. newstand _____
32. bookeeper _____
33. priveledge _____
34. paralell _____

35. preceed _____
36. supercede _____
37. posession _____
38. pronounciation _____
39. reccomend _____
40. sacreligious _____

ANSWERS: 31—newsstand, 32—bookkeeper, 33—privilege, 34—parallel, 35—precede, 36—supersede, 37—possession, 38—pronunciation, 39—recommend, 40—sacrilegious.

Group V

41. sepArate _____
    (Means *apart*, hence *p* is followed by *a*, not *e*.)
42. stationAry _____
    (Use *a* meaning *standing still*—the *a* in *stand* is your guide.)
43. stationERy _____
    (This is *paper*—note the *er* in both words.)
44. sincerEly _____
    (*Sincere* plus -*ly;* do not omit the crucial *e*.)
45. suRpriSe _____
    (Most people forget that first *r*, others use the incorrect -*ize* ending.)
46. ukUlele _____
    (That second *u* is a complete surprise to most spellers.)
47. you'RE _____
    (Meaning *you are; your* shows possession.)
48. indispensAble _____
    (Note the -*able* ending even though *defensible, comprehensible,* and *reprehensible* end in -*ible*.)
49. definItely _____
    (Not *definately,* the common misspelling.)
50. irrEsistIble _____
    (Common misspellings are *irrisistable, irrisistible*.)

TEST V

Every word below is misspelled. Can you rewrite it correctly?

41. seperate _____
42. stationery (objects) _____

43. stationary (for writing) _____
44. sincerly _____
45. supprize _____
46. ukelele _____
47. your (i.e., you are) _____
48. indispensible _____
49. definately _____
50. irrisistable _____

ANSWERS: 41—separate, 42—stationary, 43—stationery, 44—sincerely, 45—surprise, 46—ukulele, 47—you're, 48—indispensable, 49—definitely, 50—irresistible.

By now you should be complete master of these difficult words. Just to be sure, take this final test of your learning.

FINAL TEST

Of the following thirty words selected from the preceding groups, exactly half have deliberately been misspelled. Can you find the fifteen incorrect patterns? If a word is spelled right, merely check the line following it; if wrong, rewrite it correctly.

1. alright _____
2. accidently _____
3. argument _____
4. truly _____
5. anoint _____
6. innoculate _____
7. benifit _____
8. coolly _____
9. dissapoint _____
10. drunkeness _____
11. dissipate _____
12. embarassment _____
13. ecstasy _____
14. procede _____
15. mathematics _____
16. mishapen _____
17. newsstand _____

18. priviledge   _____
19. parallel   _____
20. supercede   _____
21. posession   _____
22. reccomend   _____
23. sacrilegious   _____
24. separate   _____
25. sincerly   _____
26. surprise   _____
27. ukulele   _____
28. indispensible   _____
29. definitely   _____
30. irresistible   _____

ANSWERS: 1—all right, 2—accidentally, 3—√, 4—√, 5—√, 6—inoculate, 7—benefit, 8—√, 9—disappoint, 10—drunkenness, 11—√, 12—embarrassment, 13—√, 14—proceed, 15—√, 16—misshapen, 17—√, 18—privilege, 19—√, 20—supersede, 21—possession, 22—recommend, 23—√, 24—√, 25—sincerely, 26—√, 27—√, 28—indispensable, 29—√, 30—√.

THREE

~~~~~~~~~~~~~~~

℞ *For Perfect Spelling*

THERE IS NO such thing as a word spelled pretty well, or almost right; it is either absolutely perfect, or it is all wrong. You are judged as much by your spelling as by your speech. People being the miserable mortals that they are, nothing gives them keener pleasure than to find someone napping. Write a letter, file a report, jot down a message in which there is even one misspelled word, and you can bet your bottom dollar that someone is going to seize the opportunity of snickering at you. It's sad—but that's life.

If you've mastered all the words in Chapters I and II in this section, you are hardly likely, under ordinary circumstances, to misspell everyday words.

You can improve your spelling of other specific words about which you're in doubt by looking them up in the dictionary at the time you have to write them—and looking at them so carefully at that time that you will not be likely to misspell them in the future.

Note especially any surprising combination of letters—get so indelible an impression of the acceptable pattern that any other violates your mental image of the word. Then write the word two or three times, no more, concentrating particularly on the letters you were in doubt about.

Remember this: there is no such thing as a constitutionally poor speller. If you generally have trouble, a little study and patience, and some extra training of your visual memory when you look up the spelling of a word, will bring improvement.

SEVEN

How to Learn Over 200 New Words in Just One Week

Phonetic respellings to indicate pronunciations used in this section are as follows:

> ə—the very brief vowel sound heard as the first syllable of *about* (ə-BOWT′) or the last syllable of *sofa* (SŌ′-fə).
> er—the sound of the first syllable of *very* (VER′-ee).
> ō—the vowel sound of *go* (GŌ)
> ŏŏ—the vowel sound of *book* (BŎŎK)
> ōō—the vowel sound of *moon* (MŌŌN)
> zh—the sound of the *s* in *pleasure* (PLEZH′-ər)

Accent is indicated by a stress mark (′) on a capitalized syllable; secondary accent is shown by a stress mark on a lower-case syllable. For example: *metamorphosis* is met′-ə-MAWR′-fə-sis.

Your One-Week Vocabulary Builder

A GREAT DEAL has been said, in the early pages of this book, about the value of a large and increasing vocabulary, and a number of practical plans have been suggested that will keep your vocabulary growing every day.

Let me demonstrate, in this final section, how easy and exciting it is to map out a simple, continuous program for yourself and within one week—no more—get on such good, in fact intimate, terms with over two hundred vital, expressive words that you will have a whole new supply of fresh, vigorous terms in which to express your ideas.

Most of the words in the pages that follow are discussed in depth. How is each word used? What kind of sentence pattern does it fit into? What are its implications, its emotional flavor, its sidelights? What does a speaker or writer really intend when he uses it? What is its derivation (or etymology), and what other words are built on the same Greek or Latin root?

I offer you a seven-day syllabus, some twenty to forty words each day, and at the end of each day's stint a three-part test that will reinforce your learning, test your understanding, and clear away any misconceptions you may have.

How is it possible to study so many words in a single day without running the risk of utter confusion? *The trick is to work on groups of words that are related in some way.*

They may be related by being different forms or parts of speech, such as *nepotist, nepotism,* and *nepotic.*

Or they may revolve around a central core of meaning, such as *misanthrope, misogynist,* and *misogamist.*

Or they may derive from a common parent root, such as *mellifluous, flux, influx, efflux,* and *affluent.*

Or they may be somewhat synonymous, as *penurious* and *parsimonious*, or *acerb* and *acrimonious*. Or antonymous, as *aphrodisiac* and *anaphrodisiac, equivocal* and *unequivocal*.

It's the relationship that makes them simple to understand, easy to remember. By learning words in related groups you can acquire twenty, thirty, forty new ones at a time without the slightest trouble or confusion.

How should you go about working with these words, and about how long will each day's study take?

You will notice, once you start, that a day's syllabus is divided into a number of sections, and that each section is headed by the phonetic pronunciations of the words to be discussed. Pronounce the words *aloud,* several times, as a means of making your first important contact with them. Then copy each word on a separate index card, or slip of paper, or a new page of a notebook. You have now *seen* the word, *said* the word, *written* the word. (Bear in mind that the more varied your activities with a word, the more meaningful and alive that word is for you, the tighter and more lasting your control over it.)

Now read the section carefully, understanding every point thoroughly. Soon each word will seem like an old friend; you will almost feel it viscerally as well as respond to it intellectually.

Next write a brief, simple phrase or sentence containing each word; in this way you will really nail the word home, gain complete mastery over it, give it a permanent, active place in your thinking, speaking, and writing vocabulary.

And then go on to the next section. *In no more than an hour* you will have thoroughly assimilated the twenty to forty words prescribed for the day, and will be ready to check your learning by taking the tests that follow each day's work.

Hard? No—surprisingly easy, immensely rewarding, as you will discover as soon as you begin.

Does it require application, self-discipline, and concentration? Yes—as what does not that is worth achieving?

And total conquest of the two hundred or so words in this section is well worth achieving. For they are words that belong in every growing vocabulary, that particularly mark the educated person, that will add immeasurably to your verbal skill and self-assurance.

CHECK LIST OF WORDS
THAT BELONG IN THE
GROWING VOCABULARY

(The number after each word is a *section reference,* not a page reference.)

abortive, 14
abominable, 11
abominate, 11
abstruse, 22
abstemious, 17
acerb, 23
acerbity, 23
acquiesce, 25
acquiescence, 25
acquiescent, 25
acrimonious, 23
acrimony, 23
acumen, 23
acute, 23
adamant, 34, 47
advert, 16
affable, 42
affluent, 36
aggregate, 12
altruism, 31
altruist, 31
altruistic, 31
amorphous, 1
anachronism, 27
anachronistic, 27
anachronous, 27
anaphrodisiac, 38

anathema, 29
anodyne, 35
anthropology, 28
antipathetic, 30
antipathy, 30
aphrodisiac, 38
apocryphal, 40
asinine, 58
attrition, 56
austere, 45
austerity, 45
avert, 16
badinage, 46
banal, 49
banality, 49
bigamy, 28
bovine, 50
bromide, 39
bromidic, 39
cadaver, 18
cadaverous, 18
carnivorous, 4
cavil, 43
chauvinism, 44
chauvinist, 44
chauvinistic, 44
choleric, 9

FIRST DAY

1. No Shape

metamorphosis (met'-ə-MAWR'-fə-sis)
morphology (mawr-FOL'-ə-jee)
Morpheus (MAWR'-fee-əs)
amorphous (ə-MAWR'-fəs)

Morphe, in Greek, means form or shape—thus, *metamorphosis* is a complete change of form; *morphology* is the biological science of form and structure; and *Morpheus* is the mythological god of dreams, i.e., forms and shapes seen during sleep. (And, from Morpheus, *morphine* was so named because it was originally used to induce sleep.)

The prefix *a-* in words of Greek derivation is negative, usually denoting *without*—hence *amorphous,* on the face of it, means without shape or form.

We call something *amorphous* when we can recognize no definite shape, form, or pattern, whether we are speaking literally or, as more often happens, figuratively. If a political party is *amorphous,* no clear outlines of its aims can be seen, or its adherents have no common characteristics, or its method of operation is changeable and varied. *Amorphous* feelings, attitudes, fears, etc. have no perceptible shape; they are vague, formless.

On the other hand, a fat girl cannot, except humorously, be labeled *amorphous*—she's shapeless, to be sure, but only in not having the soft and prominent curves so highly regarded by present-day culture.

2. Up to No Good

clandestine (klan-DES'-tən)

A person may do many things in secret, often out of perfectly creditable motives. He might make secret arrangements to give someone a surprise party (if it were found out, all the fun would be spoiled), or to capture enough votes to be elected president of a company (why let the opposition know what he's up to?); but he makes *clandestine* arrangements to rob a bank, assassinate a political figure, hold an underground meeting in a Fascist country, sell stolen goods, or give a "tea" party (i.e., the kind of "tea" that means marijuana).

And what distinguishes these latter activities? They are obviously either illegal, illicit, or dangerous; discovery or exposure will result in disgrace, arrest, death, or something equally dire.

So if you plan to do something that violates morals, laws, or the prohibitions of those in tyrannical power, you had best do it as quietly and inconspicuously as possible—in short, *clandestinely*.

3. No Humility

pompous (POM'-pəs)
pomposity (pom-POS'-ə-tee)

No matter how important a man is, we like him to be, or at least seem, modest. And most truly great men *are* modest—the respect, the deference, the attention, the admiration they get from us we give them voluntarily, not because they demand it.

But then there are others whose importance is solely in their own minds. They are so solemnly puffed up with a sense of self-importance, so grandiosely aware of their imagined magnificence, so ostentatious in flaunting their status, and so insistent on the pomp and ceremony they believe due their position, that they end up, for the most part, appearing only ridiculous. Such people we call—with a certain smug contempt, for of course *we* never act that way—*pompous*. Phrases like *pompous ass* or *pompous little man* clearly show the flavor of the word.

Pompous also describes language or style of writing that is pretentious, grandiose, unnecessarily solemn, or excessively and hence laughably dignified or lofty. The noun is *pompousness* or *pomposity*.

4. Watch Out, There It Goes Again!

ubiquitous (yōō-BIK'-wə-təs)	omnivorous (om-NIV'-ər-əs)
omnipresent (om'-nə-PREZ'-ənt)	omnibus (OM'-nə-bəs)
omnipotent (om-NIP'-ə-tənt)	carnivorous (kahr-NIV'-ər-əs)
omniscient (om-NISH'-ənt)	herbivorous (hur-BIV'-ər-əs)

There is an adverb in Latin, *ubique,* everywhere, that gives us a charming word—*ubiquitous.* The Good Humor man in the New York and New England area, or the ice-cream vendor under whatever name in other parts of the country, is *ubiquitous*—come spring and summer, at various times of the day and evening you hear his tinkling bells no matter where you may be. And then there is the *ubiquitous* little red wagon that seems to follow airplanes around to refuel them (of course, it might just *not* be the very same wagon at every airport). Not to mention the *ubiquitous* teen-agers at every pizza parlor, the *ubiquitous* beggars that infest Greenwich Village and the Bowery in New York, the *ubiquitous* oil wells along the coast of southern California, the *ubiquitous* peddlers of gimcracks at the U.S. border in Tia Juana, Mexico. In short, then, *ubiquitous* (the noun is *ubiquity*) means apparently present everywhere—no matter where you look, there it is again.

A somewhat more dignified adjective that expresses the same idea is *omnipresent,* built on Latin *omnis,* all—hence present in all places or at all times. We may speak, thus, of *omnipresent* fear, danger, unemployment, etc. or the *omnipresent* revulsion (sadness, shock, etc.) that gripped the nation when John F. Kennedy was assassinated. *Ubiquitous,* despite its identity of meaning, is too light a word to use in such contexts.

Latin *omnis,* all, is the source also of *omnipotent,* all-powerful; *omniscient,* all-knowing; and *omnivorous,* all-devouring. An *omnibus* may be a vehicle for all people, and is then usually shortened to *bus;* or a volume containing all the writings of a particular author, or on a particular subject, as a John Galsworthy or Shakespeare *omnibus,* or a Civil War or crime *omnibus.*

We might go back for a moment to *omnivorous.* Lions, tigers, etc. are *carnivorous*—they devour (Latin, *voro*) only meat or flesh (Latin, *carnis*). Deer, cows, etc. are *herbivorous*—they eat only grains and vegetation (Latin, *herbis*). But man (and, strangely, also rats), is *omnivorous*—he devours everything: meat, grains, vegetation, pâté de foie gras, chocolate mousse, Lobster Cantonese, raw oysters, fried ants, pigs' feet, and so on without foreseeable end. An *omnivorous* reader figuratively devours everything in print that he can lay his eyes on, an *omnivorous* theatergoer attends every play that opens within a radius of one hundred miles.

5. Separating the Men from the Boys

puerile (PY$\overline{OO}$′-ər-əl)
puerility (py$\overline{oo}$′-ər-IL′-ə-tee)

"Boys will be boys" according to an old saying, and no doubt it's equally fair to conclude that girls will be girls.

Just so. We excuse certain acts and attitudes of immaturity—prankishness, destructive high spirits, ebullient, ear-splitting noisiness or obstreperousness, occasional unfeeling callowness, insensitivity to the needs of others, sudden petulance or moodiness, rambunctiousness, etc.—in the very young, both male and female (though girls of any age are constantly exhorted by our culture to be "ladylike"), because we know that eventually they will grow up, exercise greater self-control, and develop at least a degree of wisdom and maturity.

We expect more from adults. And when someone who chronologically has passed adolescence still exhibits the unpleasant characteristics of juvenility, or still acts or talks like some of our less bearable teen-agers, we call him *puerile*. And quite rightly, for the word is built on Latin *puer,* young boy. (Girls, reacting to the demands of society, somehow manage to grow up a lot faster.) What such a person does, how he acts, or the things he says, may also be labeled *puerile*.

Despite the derivation of the term, women as well as men may be accused of *puerility,* but it appears, at least to this observer, that adult males more frequently than females deserve the accusation.

6. Death and Burial

posthumous (POS′-chə-məs)   inter (in-TUR′)
humus (HY$\overline{OO}$′-məs)   exhume (eks-HY$\overline{OO}$M′)
inhume (in-HY$\overline{OO}$M′)   disinter (dis′-in-TUR′)

The Latin words *post,* after, and *humus,* ground or earth, combine to form the English adjective *posthumous*. That is *posthumous* which is born, brought to public notice, or continues to have an effect after (*post*) its creator has been buried in the ground (*humus*).

Thus a *posthumous* child is born after its father has died; a *posthumous* book is published after the death of the author; a *posthumous* symphony is discovered, or perhaps given its first public performance, after the death of the composer; a *posthumous* bronze is unveiled after the death of the sculptor; a *posthumous* decoration or medal is awarded after the recipient has died; and so on. John F. Kennedy, to use the word somewhat differently, will *posthumously* influence politics and world history for many years; his ideas will have a *posthumous* effect on humanity.

The decomposed, organic matter in soil that we call *humus* comes directly from the Latin word; also, less directly, *humble* and *humility,* since whoever is lowly and small is close to the ground. To bury (a corpse) in the earth is to *inhume,* a verb less often used than *inter,* the latter built on another Latin word for earth, *terra.* *Exhume* and *disinter* are to dig up or unbury (a corpse). *Exhume* and *disinter* are also used figuratively, in the sense of bringing to light information or facts that were hidden or buried.

FIRST DAY'S TESTS

I. Match words and definitions.

A	B
1. amorphous	*a.* found all over
2. clandestine	*b.* devouring everything
3. pompous	*c.* vegetarian
4. ubiquitous	*d.* meat-eating
5. omniscient	*e.* after-death
6. omnivorous	*f.* childish, immature
7. carnivorous	*g.* secret
8. herbivorous	*h.* all-knowing
9. puerile	*i.* formless
10. posthumous	*j.* self-important

II. Write the word, starting as indicated, that fits the definition.

1. A volume containing all the works of a particular author   o———————
2. To dig up a corpse   d———————
3. Science of structure and form   m———————

4. Existing everywhere   o_____
5. To bury (a corpse, etc.)   i_____
6. To bring to light (something hidden)   e_____
7. Organic constituent of soil   h_____
8. God of dreams   M_____
9. Complete transformation   m_____

III. What is the English meaning of each root?

1. Greek *morphe*   _____
2. Latin *omnis*   _____
3. Greek *a-*   _____
4. Latin *ubique*   _____
5. Latin *vor-*   _____
6. Latin *humus*   _____
7. Latin *terra*   _____

ANSWERS:

I. 1—i, 2—g, 3—j, 4—a, 5—h, 6—b, 7—d, 8—c, 9—f, 10—e.
II. 1—omnibus, 2—disinter, 3—morphology, 4—omnipresent, 5—inter, 6—exhume, 7—humus, 8—Morpheus, 9—metamorphosis.
III. 1—shape, form; 2—all; 3—without; 4—everywhere; 5—devour; 6—ground, earth; 7—earth.

SECOND DAY

7. *The Age of Guilt*

punctilious (punk-TIL'-ee-əs)
compunction (kəm-PUNK'-shən)

In Latin there is the verb *pungere,* to prick, stick, or pierce, the past participle of which is *punctus*. When *punctus* is a noun it quite logically means a *point*. Thus a *puncture* is a piercing, or a hole made by a sharp point; *punctual* designates being right on the *point* (of time); and *punctilious* describes one who scrupulously or obsessively observes the strictest *points* of form, ceremony, or behavior.

Compunction, from this same verb, is also a kind of piercing with a sharp point, in this instance of the conscience. Having had one's conscience pricked, one is left with an uneasy (but temporary) feeling of guilt over some real or imagined wrongdoing. Generally *compunction* results from minor sins or transgressions, but then you know how easily guilt is aroused in this age of psychiatry.

If you can do something without *compunction* (even though you realize it's not quite proper or ethical), then your conscience is too tough to be pierced by the garden variety of sharp points— you are that rare person whose guilt is not readily stirred up.

8. *Piercing*

poignant (POYN'-ənt)
poignancy (POYN'-ən-see)
pungent (PUN'-jənt)
pungency (PUN'-jən-see)
expunge (eks-PUNJ')
expunction (eks-PUNK'-shən)

Latin *pungere* is also the derivation, though indirectly through Old French and Middle English, of *poignant*. Something *poignant* pierces one's heart (as a *poignant* account of unrequited love, the *poignant* cry of a lost child, the *poignant* desperation of those who have been out of work for years, etc.), and thus arouses all one's tenderest feelings: sorrow, sympathy, pity. One empathizes with the sufferer, feels his pain as if it were one's own, is, at least momentarily, as emotionally distressed as he is. *Poignant* memories, words, experiences, etc. hit one in the guts, produce a visceral rather than a purely intellectual reaction. The noun is *poignancy.*

More directly from *pungere* comes *pungent,* which describes something that is piercing, sharp, stinging in taste or odor (food, drink, perfume, chemicals, gases, air, etc.)—either pleasantly or unpleasantly so, depending on the context. This adjective may also be used figuratively to describe language that is piercing, penetrating, biting, or sharp, or that pricks one's attention because of its cleverness or expressiveness. We may refer, for example, to *pungent* wit, satire, style, use of words, etc. The noun is *pungency.*

Now imagine yourself with a sharp-edged instrument that can prick or pierce; imagine using this instrument to cut out every vestige of something you wish to be rid of. You *expunge* it, i.e., you eliminate it completely, cut away every drop and bit of it. For example, one may (and often does) *expunge* all conscious memory of a traumatic experience; the governor's refusal of a pardon *expunged* the prisoner's last hope of avoiding execution.

The noun is *expunction.*

9. This Little "Humor" Went to Market

phlegmatic (fleg-MAT'-ik)   choleric (KOL'-ər-ik)
sanguine (SANG'-gwin)   melancholy (MEL'-ən-kol'-ee)

What were little girls made of, hundreds of years ago? Not sugar and spice, apparently. Nor were little boys made of snips and snails and puppy dogs' tails, as our modern nursery rhyme has it.

Back in the second century A.D., Claudius Galen, court physician to Emperor Marcus Aurelius and the final medical authority of the time, propounded the doctrine that human bodies contain four cardinal "humors," or fluids—phlegm, blood, yellow bile, and black bile. And the relative proportion of these body fluids, said Galen, determines one's personality and disposition. (Here was one doctor, apparently, who would have paid very little attention to the theories of Sigmund Freud.)

Was phlegm the dominant humor? Then one was dull, sluggish, hard to rouse to action or feeling.

But perhaps, of the four fluids, it was blood that predominated?

Then one was warm and cheerful, possessed bouncing good health, and had a high, ruddy complexion.

Was it yellow bile? Then one was temperamentally irritable, hard to get along with, generally angry.

Black bile? One was gloomy by disposition, usually depressed, cheerless, pessimistic.

Needless to say, there isn't a word of truth in all of this, though medieval physiology followed Galen's doctrine for centuries. (The sugar-and-spice, snips-and-snails theory is perhaps equally without foundation in fact, but at least it rhymes fetchingly, which is more than can be said of Galen's pronouncements.)

In any case, though the doctrine of "humors" is long since dead and buried, the four words that derive from the Latin or Greek names for the fluids remain very much alive and in active use in English.

From Latin *phlegma,* the clammy humor of the body, we get *phlegmatic,* which describes one who is by temperament emotionally dull, sluggish, torpid—it is impossible to rouse in him any strong responses. In circumstances to which most of us would react with a blaze of feeling—passion, anger, delight, ecstasy, or whatever—he is maddeningly calm, passive, practically inert.

From Latin *sanguis,* blood, we get *sanguine,* which describes someone who is cheerful, confident, optimistic. From Greek *chole,* yellow bile, we get *choleric* to describe someone who is testy, irritable, hot-tempered, quickly and easily aroused to anger. And from Greek *melanos chole,* the black bile that Galen thought came from the spleen or kidneys, we get of course *melancholy.*

So which are you—emotionless (*phlegmatic*), optimistic (*sanguine*), irritable (*choleric*), or gloomy (*melancholy*)? It all depends on the fluid that is coursing most strongly through your body.

10. Seeing and Thinking

perspicacious (pur'-spə-KAY'-shəs)
perspicacity (pur'-spə-KAS'-ə-tee)
perspicuous (pər-SPIK'-yōo-əs)
perspicuity (pur'-spə-KYOO'-ə-tee)

Perspicio, in Latin, means to look or see through—and so, by etymology, one who is *perspicacious* can see through things easily and quickly. Not *literally* see through, by means of X-ray vision that renders opaque objects transparent. But rather *figuratively,* by means of keen mental perception and understanding that can see right through to the heart of a problem or other abstraction, that can immediately and successfully penetrate the meaning of events, circumstances, relationships, etc., no matter how hidden or obscure to a less-discerning intellect. The noun is *perspicacity.*

Perspicuous, from the same Latin verb, describes things that can easily be seen through. Again, not literally, but only in reference to language, phrasing, style, verbal presentation of ideas, etc., so that what is *perspicuous* is so clear and understandable, so free of obscurity or confusion, that it can immediately be penetrated by the mind's eye. (Even a blind person unselfconsciously says, "I *see* what you mean.") If, then, you admire the *perspicuity* of someone's analysis of a situation, you indicate that you grasp at once and without difficulty the meaning of what he is saying. In general, no doubt, the man with a *perspicacious* mind writes and talks *perspicuously,* but the two words are not synonymous. *Perspicacious* describes the *process* of thinking, while *perspicuous* describes the verbal *product* of thought.

The root *spic-,* to look or see, is found also in *conspicuous,* easy to see; and in *despicable,* able to be looked down on, that is, despised. *Despise* itself comes from Latin *despicere,* but was changed somewhat in spelling before it reached us through French and Middle English.

11. Bad Omens

abominable (ə-BOM′-ə-nə-bəl)
abominate (ə-BOM′-ə-nate′)

Imagine something unpleasant. But extremely, almost indescribably, unpleasant. In fact, you can scarcely stand it. It's nasty, vile, repulsive, disgusting, detestable—and these are all strong adjectives because we're describing feelings of dislike that are strong to the point of revulsion and hatred. *Hatred* is the key word— anything so bad that our reflexive reaction is hate may be called *abominable,* a word which, on one level, literally means able to evoke hatred (from the verb *abominate,* to hate, detest, loathe, abhor), and, on another level, indicates etymologically that all the signs are inauspicious (from Latin *ab,* away from, and *omen,* sign, portent). And so you will find the term in such combinations as *abominable* taste, *abominable* viciousness, *abominable* arrogance, *abominable* sneakiness, etc., not to mention (allowing for normal human exaggeration) an *abominable* cold, an *abominable* sense of humor, and the *abominable* snowman.

12. Out of the Herd

egregious (ə-GREE′-jəs)
gregarious (grə-GAIR′-ee-əs)
congregate (KONG′-grə-gate′)
congregation (kong′-grə-GAY′-shən)
segregate (SEG′-rə-gate′)
aggregate, n. (AG′-rə-gət)

Consider a whole flock or herd of crimes (the reason for using such odd group nouns as "flock" or "herd" will be clear in a moment): shoplifting, fraud, burglary, arson, embezzlement, murder, etc. Since they're crimes, they're all bad—but certain ones are so terrible, so heinous, so unspeakable that they stand out from all the rest; they make the others pale by comparison. What crimes come at once to mind? The kidnaping and murder of the Lindbergh baby, the Leopold-Loeb murder, the assassinations of Lincoln and Kennedy, for quick examples. Precisely because they're outstanding, because they're incomparably worse than most others, they're called *egregious.*

And why "herd" or "flock"? The Latin root *greg-* refers to a herd of animals, a flock of sheep; *e-* is the shortened form of *ex-,* out. Anything so bad that it stands out from the rest of the "herd" of bad things is *egregious.* Thus we may speak of *egregious* crimes, lies, accusations, blunders, errors, immorality, sinfulness, treachery, etc.

The same root *greg-* is found also in *gregarious,* fond of being with people, i.e., liking to be part of the herd; *congregate,* to flock together; *congregation,* a religious flock; *segregate,* to remove from the herd, for whatever reason; and *aggregate,* a whole "herd," mass, or total.

13. Man Is a Social Animal

gregarious (grə-GAIR'-ee-əs)
convivial (kən-VIV'-ee-əl)
conviviality (kən-viv'-ee-AL'-ə-tee)

Gregarious, then, comes from the Latin root *greg-,* herd or flock.

The *gregarious* person, I have said, enjoys being part of the herd—he is most comfortable when he is with others, rather than alone. He prefers group activity to solitary endeavor, and tends to seek others out because of the warmth and security he derives from being surrounded by people. (Most of us have such needs—hence clubs, cities, political parties, social gatherings, religious affiliations, and crowds watching a parade. So when one says, as one often does, "I am by nature *gregarious,*" he could as easily substitute the adjective *human.* Certain other creatures are also *gregarious*—ants, bees, the social wasps, sheep obviously, seals, etc.)

A *gregarious* person is of course friendly, but friendliness is not the quality emphasized in the word—far more important is the power of the herd instinct, the need to find and be with other people.

Convivial also implies friendliness, but again marginally. The *convivial* person enjoys the warmth and joviality of the table and cocktail lounge—he likes to eat and drink with others in a spirit of good-fellowship. A *convivial* atmosphere is one in which there is a holiday-like mood of expansiveness and gaiety, the food is heaped high and the liquor flows, so that stiffness and inhibitions melt away. The noun is *conviviality.*

14. Never Gets off the Ground

abortive (ə-BAWR'-tiv)

If a fetus is aborted, whether by natural processes or through outside interference, the infant is never born and the child that was to be is nothing—it dies before it has even got well started. And so anything *abortive*—as an *abortive* attempt to gain one's ends, an *abortive* coup in a Latin American country, etc.—ends in total failure from the very beginning, is entirely fruitless almost from the moment it is conceived. Etymologically we might say that it never gets off the ground—the word is built on Latin *ab-*, which in this instance is negative in meaning, and *oriri,* to rise.

15. How to Cry Poor

parsimonious (pahr'sə-MŌ'nee-əs)
parsimony (PAHR'-sə-mō-nee)
penurious (pən-YŌŌR'ee-əs *or* pə-NŌŌR'-ee-əs)
penury (PEN'-yə-ree)

Words are tricky.

Let us say that you and I exercise great prudence in financial matters. We are, then, frugal, thrifty, or economical—we hate extravagance and waste.

But what about the other fellow who has similar attitudes to his money? He, of course, is tight-fisted, penny-pinching, niggardly, stingy, or, at best, *parsimonious*—he hasn't a generous bone in his body.

Note how easily words that are basically synonymous can have utterly different connotations. We think of ourselves in one set of terms, all complimentary—but when we meet someone else who has the same intense need to hold fast to his wealth and possessions we have no trouble finding a disparaging or derogatory label to pin on him.

So *parsimony* never describes ourselves, only the other person; it suggests *excessive* carefulness in one's spending, economy which to us (since we're using the word) is either unreasonable or extreme to the point of miserliness or stinginess. Frugality, thrift, economy are considered virtues, and therefore praiseworthy; *parsimony* oversteps the boundary of necessity and, like all qualities in immoderation, becomes a vice.

Penurious, a close synonym of *parsimonious,* indicates an even greater degree of miserliness or niggardliness, so great as to make one seem absolutely destitute (whether one actually is or not, however, is open to question), totally without funds or resources. The noun *penury,* on the other hand, is true financial poverty, complete destitution to the point where one is no longer able to live a dignified or self-respecting existence. In America there are still millions of poor people, despite the general affluence of the times—their total family earnings fall short of an amount necessary to live a decently comfortable life. And there are many in *penury,* hardly subsisting, unable to afford enough food to maintain basic health, dwelling in rudimentary, inadequate, and unsanitary shelters, and possessing only the shabbiest and most threadbare of clothing.

SECOND DAY'S TESTS

I. Match words and definitions.

A	*B*
1. punctilious	*a.* emotionally sluggish
2. poignant	*b.* irritable, testy
3. phlegmatic	*c.* mentally keen
4. sanguine	*d.* touching, moving
5. choleric	*e.* clear, understandable
6. melancholy	*f.* very bad, nasty, horrible
7. perspicacious	*g.* enjoying companionship
8. perspicuous	*h.* gloomy
9. abominable	*i.* optimistic, cheerful
10. gregarious	*j.* meticulously formal

II. Write the word, starting as indicated, that fits the definition.

1. Conscience pang   c———
2. Dire want; utter destitution   p———
3. Complete elimination   e———
4. Combined total   a———
5. Stingy, close-fisted   p———
6. Outstandingly bad   e———
7. Failing from the outset   a———
8. Good-fellowship, especially combined with eating and drinking   c———
9. To hate, loathe   a———
10. To gather in groups   c———
11. To remove, separate, set apart   s———

III. What is the English meaning of each root?

1. Latin *pungere*   ———————
2. Latin *sanguis*   ———————
3. Latin *spic-*   ———————
4. Latin *greg-*   ———————
5. Latin *punctus*   ———————

ANSWERS:

I. 1—j, 2—d, 3—a, 4—i, 5—b, 6—h, 7—c, 8—e, 9—f, 10—g.

II. 1—compunction, 2—penury, 3—expunction, 4—aggregate, 5—parsimonious *or* penurious, 6—egregious, 7—abortive, 8—conviviality, 9—abominate, 10—congregate, 11—segregate.

III. 1—pierce, stick, prick; 2—blood; 3—see, look; 4—herd, flock; 5—point.

16. All About Turning

introvert (IN'-trə-vurt')	avert (ə-VURT')
extrovert (EK'-strə-vurt')	divert (də-VURT')
vertigo (VUR'-tə-gō)	advert (ad-VURT')
revert (rə-VURT')	inadvertent (in'-ad-VUR'tənt)
invert (in-VURT')	inadvertence (in'-ad-VUR'-tənce)

Verto, the Latin verb *to turn,* is used as the base of many English words. An *introvert* turns his attention inward, more interested in his own thoughts, fantasies, and feelings than in the environment; he is often a creative person, an artist, poet, composer, or writer, and seems moody, withdrawn, hard to know. An *extrovert* turns *his* psychic energy outward, relating well to the outside world and to people; he is talkative, friendly, expansive. *Vertigo* is the medical term for dizziness, the feeling that everything about one is turning or whirling. To *revert* is to turn back, *invert* to turn in or inside out, *avert* to turn aside, *divert* to turn away.

To *advert* is to turn (one's mind) toward something, hence to refer or call attention to it. And *inadvertent* describes an action showing that one's mind or attention is not turned toward what one is doing. So an *inadvertent* omission, error, misstatement, discourtesy, etc. arises out of absent-mindedness, woolgathering, heedlessness, lack of concentration—it is not a bit deliberate or intentional.

If, for example, someone claims that he failed to invite you to a gathering through sheer *inadvertence,* he means that he had no desire whatever to slight you or keep you away—he was simply so busy or involved with other things that your name never entered his mind.

Advertise, by the way, comes from the same root. Etymologically, it is to turn people's minds toward something, i.e., call their attention to it, make them notice it.

17. No Self-indulgence

abstemious (ab-STEE'-mee-əs)

Temetum is the Latin word for strong drink, i.e., hard liquor. The prefix *ab-* in this instance means *away from* (an *s* is often added for purposes of euphony between a *b* and a *t*), so, etymologically, one who leads an *abstemious* life stays away from alcoholic beverages. But since nondrinkers are perhaps experts at resisting temptation, the adjective also applies to those who avoid rich foods, whose diet, in short, is neither interesting nor fattening.

18. Death Warmed Over

cadaver (kə-DAV'-ər *or* kə-DAY'-vər)
cadaverous (kə-DAV'-ər-əs)

It is rare that we refer to a person who has died as a *corpse* or even a *dead body*. These direct, unvarnished terms, since they violate the taboos most people have about death, are likely to offend. Usually, for our own comfort as well as the other person's, we employ such euphemisms as *the deceased, the departed, the remains,* or *the body*. (Slang, on the other hand, which takes delight in shocking, uses *stiff,* or *carcass,* the latter word properly designating a dead animal.)

In medical usage, where tender feelings need not be taken into account, a corpse used for dissection is called a *cadaver,* a word that comes quite inoffensively from Latin *cadere,* to fall. Imagining, then, if you have never engaged in medical dissection, the appearance of a *cadaver,* you can appreciate how a live person looks to us when we describe him as *cadaverous:* his body is gaunt, emaciated, even wasted—the skeletal structure almost seems visible; his skin is deathly pale; his face is pinched, his eyes lifeless. In short, one who looks *cadaverous* seems as if he isn't long for this world. With all these rich (though gruesome) connotations, *cadaverous* is as strong a term as exists in the language (somehow even more graphic than its synonym *corpselike*) for one who has lost the glow of health and the flesh that results from a robust appetite for food and for life.

19. Why Does Everyone Pick on Me?

paranoia (păr'-ə-NOY'-ə)
paranoiac (păr'-ə-NOY'-ak)
paranoid (PĂR'-ə-noyd)

Paranoia is a psychosis. The victim of this form of mental illness, the *paranoiac,* believes the world is against him, that people are constantly talking about him and laughing at him in a hostile or malicious manner. Sometimes he hallucinates voices telling him to kill his supposed enemies. He has, in short, delusions of persecution.

The adjective *paranoid* is often used today in a loose, non-psychiatric, way to describe a more or less healthy person who, on little or no evidence, sees hostility where in fact none exists. We call someone *paranoid* who too easily believes others are out to get him, that much of the world is organized only to contrive his downfall, and that people around him act mainly to wound, humiliate, or thwart him. He does not realize that we all have our own troubles, and cannot devote either the time or the energy to devise elaborate schemes for making his life miserable.

20. Early Times

incipient (in-SIP'-ee-ənt)
inception (in-SEP'-shən)

Anything just starting, so that now it is in its first or earliest stage, may be called *incipient.* (The derivation is, logically enough, the Latin verb *incipere,* to begin.)

In medical parlance, *incipient* tuberculosis or an *incipient* tumor, for random example, has just recently come into existence. The symptoms are for the first time evident to the victim, or the signs have just become noticeable to the physician. If we speak of *incipient* life on earth, we again refer to the very beginnings, that phase when the most primitive living organisms first appeared. And usually, if something is called *incipient,* the implication is that a flowering out or strengthening is expected later.

Inception, from the same Latin verb, means the beginning, but almost always of a business, undertaking, activity, institution, etc., as the *inception* of a professional career, of the Catholic Church, of the Extension Division of U.C.L.A., of General Motors, of the Democratic (or Republican) party, etc.

21. Slavish Following

obsequious (əb-SEE'-kwee-əs)   consequent (KON'-sə-kwənt)
sequel (SEE'-kwəl)   sequence (SEE'-kwənce)
subsequent (SUB'-sə-kwənt)

Who follows you around worshipfully, eager to cater to, or preferably anticipate, your every wish, intent only on pleasing you? Who fawns on you, licks your hand, makes it plain that in his book you can do no wrong, that you are master and God and sun and moon all wrapped in one? Who is constantly there at your beck and call, like a puppy? Who, of course, but your own dog?

But people aren't dogs, and when a person almost acts like one, when he is excessively deferential and compliant, fawning, overly submissive and obedient, servilely ingratiating, saccharinely polite and attentive, then we call him, somewhat contemptuously, *obsequious,* a word ultimately derived from Latin *sequor,* to follow.

And what manner of man is usually *obsequious?* One who feels, or out of fear or hope of reward pretends to feel, inferior to someone he works for or waits on or wishes to get a favor from—a waiter, doorman, salesman, servant, etc. Note, please that in our democratic and highly mobile society few waiters, doormen, etc. *are* obsequious—the refreshing air of equality shown by workers in such jobs is what most impresses visitors from abroad. And note, also, that *obsequiousness* is an extreme, and not to be confused with the courtesy and respect normally offered even in a democracy to a president, governor, mayor, judge, teacher, employer, or customer. *Obsequiousness* is self-effacing, composed of bootlicking and kowtowing—an attitude as unpleasant to the recipient as it should be to the giver.

Sequor, to follow, is the root found also in such common English words as *sequel,* something (often a story) that follows; *subsequent,* following at a later time; *consequent,* following as a result; and *sequence,* things that follow in a series, or one after the other.

22. Can't Understand It? Push It Away!

intrude (in-TROOD')   intrusion (in-TROO'-zhən)
protrude (prō-TROOD')   protrusion (prō-TROO'-zhən)
extrude (eks-TROOD')   extrusion (eks-TROO'-zhən)
abstruse (ab-STROOS')

Abstruse and *intrude* are, illogical as it may seem on the face of it, etymologically related.

When you *intrude*, you push or thrust yourself in where you're not wanted. Similarly, something that *protrudes* pushes or thrusts forward from the main part, and to *extrude* is to push or force out. *Intrude, protrude, extrude* come from Latin *trudere*, to push or thrust; another form of this verb, *trusus*, accounts for the spelling of the nouns *intrusion, protrusion,* and *extrusion,* and also for the adjective *abstruse,* which by etymology means pushed or thrust away. Anything *abstruse* is pushed away from ready understanding, hence is deep, difficult to comprehend, so complex, abstract, or profound as to be beyond the grasp or experience of the average man in the street. Thus Einstein's Theory of Relativity is *abstruse,* as are also atomic fission, the principles of Zen Buddhism, the psychology of women, Yoga, and the workings of the stock market. Words, ideas, philosophies, concepts, subjects, etc. can all be *abstruse.*

THIRD DAY'S TESTS

I. Match words and definitions.

A	B
1. inadvertent	*a.* deluded by a feeling that the world is hostile
2. abstemious	*b.* overly and insincerely self-ingratiating
3. cadaverous	*c.* coming as a result
4. paranoid	*d.* next; following
5. incipient	*e.* difficult to understand
6. obsequious	*f.* self-denying
7. subsequent	*g.* self-absorbed
8. consequent	*h.* just beginning

9. abstruse   *i.* absent-minded
10. introverted   *j.* gaunt

II. Write the word, starting as indicated, that fits the definition.

1. A series; things that follow in order   s————
2. Mental illness in which the victim has delusions of persecution   p————
3. The very beginning   i————
4. One whose psychic interests are turned outward to other people and the world of things   e————
5. To turn back   r————
6. To push or force out   e————
7. To refer, or call attention (to)   a————
8. That which follows   s————
9. A corpse used for dissection   c————
10. Dizziness   v————

III. What is the English meaning of each root?

1. Latin *vert-*   ————
2. Latin *incipere*   ————
3. Latin *sequor*   ————
4. Latin *trudere*   ————

ANSWERS:
I. 1—i, 2—f, 3—j, 4—a, 5—h, 6—b, 7—d, 8—c, 9—e, 10—g.
II. 1—sequence, 2—paranoia, 3—inception, 4—extrovert, 5—revert,
    6—extrude, 7—advert, 8—sequel, 9—cadaver, 10—vertigo.
III. 1—turn; 2—begin; 3—follow; 4—push, thrust.

FOURTH DAY

23. Sharpness

acerb (ə-SURB′)
acerbity (ə-SUR′-bə-tee)
acrimony (AK′-rə-mō′-nee)

acrimonious (ak′-rə-MŌ′-nee-əs)
acumen (ə-KYOO′-mən)
acute (ə-KYOOT′)

An *acerb* remark shows a number of related feelings: irritation, resentment, anger, crabbedness—some or all of these with a strong lacing of sourness of disposition. *Acerb* language, then, is sharp, snappish, hostile; *acerbity* of temper indicates (how else may one indicate the dark opposite of gentleness, affection, warmth, and sunshine?) liverishness, waspishness, spleen, irascibility. People noted for their *acerbity* are not popular—they have a serpent's tongue and a caustic attitude that makes them a pleasure not to have around.

Acerbity is from Latin *acer,* sharp, a root found also in *acrimony. Acrimony* is the stronger of the two words; it implies ill-will or maliciousness combined with bitterness so thick you can feel it hanging heavy in the air. An *acrimonious* person dedicates himself to inflicting wounds—he stings, he blisters, he lashes out. In an *acrimonious* argument between husband and wife, for example, each partner knows, by long experience, the especially tender and vulnerable areas of the other; and these he (or, of course, she) concentrates on sadistically—where else can the most damage be done? A heated debate shows high feeling on both sides; an *acrimonious* debate indicates an impulse to verbal assassination.

Like *acerbity* and *acrimony, acumen* also involves sharpness (it derives from Latin *acuere,* to sharpen), but sharpness of the mind rather than of language or feelings. One who has business *acumen* possesses the sound judgment, keen thinking, and logical mind that usually result in commercial success; one who has psychological *acumen* has a keen understanding of human motivation; one who has mathematical *acumen* is comfortably at home in the world of figures.

Acute, which comes from the same Latin verb, means sharp in any of its various senses; we may talk of an *acute* mind, *acute* perception, *acute* pain, an *acute* crisis in world affairs, *acute* shortages in housing, an exquisitely *acute* sense of timing, etc.

24. *Kindly Uncles and How to Make the Most of Them*

nepotism (NEP'-ə-tiz-əm)
nepotist (NEP'-ə-tist)
nepotic (nə-POT'-ik)

If you're a senator, congressman, or other public official with lucrative jobs at your disposal, should you put your relatives on the payroll regardless of their qualifications for the work? If you're a high executive in a large corporation, should you favor members of your family over more capable people when you hire or promote employees?

Ethically, of course, the answer is *No.* Much as we may objectively and theoretically frown upon such favoritism, however, we know that the practice is widespread, and so of course there is a word for it—*nepotism,* from the Latin *nepos,* nephew. (And how nice to have a rich or influential uncle who is sufficiently loyal to family ties to see that one gets ahead in life without too much competition!)

The "uncle" who treats his "nephews," etc. so generously and helpfully at the expense of others is a *nepotist;* the practice is referred to as *nepotic.*

25. *Passive Acceptance*

acquiesce (ak'-wee-ES')
acquiescence (ak'-wee-ES'-ənce)
acquiescent (ak'-wee-ES'-ənt)

The same Latin root from which we derive *quiet* is also the source of the verb *acquiesce.* When you *acquiesce,* you accept quietly. You take no steps to oppose, but on the other hand you show by your quietness a conspicuous lack of enthusiasm. You're not crazy about the idea, you may even have great reservations, but you remain still nevertheless, and let it go, as it were, by default.

Acquiescence, then, is a passive idea. When you are *acquiescent* you are saying, in effect, "I won't get in your way, or protest, or do anything to stop you, but don't look to me for any help."

These words, by the way, are properly followed by the preposition *in*—you *acquiesce in* someone's proposal, you show mere *acquiescence in* his plan, etc.

26. Insubstantial as a Cloud

nebula (NEB'-yə-lə)
nebulous (NEB'-yə-ləs)

The Latin for cloud is *nebula,* a word we have taken into English to describe a cloudlike, luminous patch or mass that can sometimes be seen in the sky at night. A *nebula* (plural: *nebulae,* pronounced NEB'-yə-lee) is composed either of gaseous matter or stars far outside our solar system.

From Latin *nebula* we have also derived the adjective *nebulous,* used either to describe something (a liquid, for example) as cloudy in appearance; or, more commonly, to characterize certain abstractions as so vague, hazy, unclear, or indistinct that they seem like wispy, insubstantial clouds floating far up in the heavens.

Thus we may speak of *nebulous* plans for the future, *nebulous* recollections of early childhood, *nebulous* ideas, etc.—it is as impossible to describe them clearly, accurately, and concretely as it is to catch a cloud in your hand.

27. A Question of Time and Timing

anachronism (ə-NAK'-rə-niz'-əm)
anachronous (ə-NAK'-rə-nəs)
anachronistic (ə-NAK'-rə-nis'-tik)

If we call something (or, in rare instances, someone) an *anachronism,* we are suggesting a defect in timing.

Thus the horse-drawn carriages that take tourists for a spin through Central Park, in New York, are *anachronous*—such vehicles belong to a bygone era. Isolationism in foreign affairs is also *anachronistic* (both forms of the adjective are used); it was at a previous time in our history that we felt we could withdraw from the rest of the world, protected by our two oceans. Certain other attitudes, just at random, are equally *anachronous* today: that woman's place is in the home, that nervousness can be cured by a "sea change," that children should be harshly punished for minor transgressions so they will grow up law-abiding, etc. They are *anachronous* because in earlier times they were widely held but now are almost obsolete.

Anachronisms may also be things or events that are out of time because they rightly belong to the future rather than the present. Most of Jules Verne's novels dealt with *anachronisms* (submarines, not yet invented in his day, for example). The most-quoted incident is Shakespeare's Julius Caesar glancing at a clock, a gadget unknown in ancient Rome.

28. Haters

    misogyny (mə-SAH'-jə-nee)
    misogamy (mə-SOG'-ə-mee)
    misanthropy (mə-SAN'-thrə-pee)
    misogynous (mə-SAH'-jə-nəs)
    misogynist (mə-SAH'-jə-nist)
    gynecologist (guy'-nə-KOL'-e-jist; first syllable also jin- *or* jine)
    misogamist (mə-SOG'-ə-mist)
    monogamy (mə-NOG'-ə-mee)
    bigamy (BIG'-ə-mee)
    polygamy (pə-LIG'-ə-mee)
    misanthrope (MIS'-ən-thrope)
    misanthropic (mis'-ən-THROP'-ik)
    anthropology (an'-thrə-POL'-ə-jee)

The Greek verb *misein,* to hate, appears in three important English words: *misogyny,* aversion to, and distrust of, women; *misogamy,* hatred of marriage; and *misanthropy,* dislike of one's fellow man combined with a resultant avoidance of human society.

Distrust of, and contempt for, the gentler sex appears to have afflicted many of the world's early philosophers, if their writings are valid evidence. Aristotle suggested that "Woman may be said to be an inferior man." * One Latin poet, Catullus, claimed that "The vows that a woman makes to her lover are only fit to be written on air," while another, Juvenal, insisted that "Though a woman may be burning herself, she delights in her lover's torment."

* I am indebted for this and the following quotations to *A New Dictionary of Quotations,* edited by H. L. Mencken (Alfred A. Knopf, Inc.).

The German philosopher, Nietzsche: "Thou goest to women? Don't forget thy whip." The French novelist, Alexandre Dumas: "The Bible says that woman was the last thing God made. Evidently He made her on Saturday night. She reveals His fatigue." The British poet, Rudyard Kipling: "The female of the species is more deadly than the male."

National proverbs are equally *misogynous*. From the Japanese: "A woman's tongue is only three inches long, but it can kill a man six feet high." From the Persian: "Woman is a calamity, but every house must have its curse." From the Russian: "When the Devil fails himself, he sends a woman as his agent."

But enough. Such passionate hatred must hide an even more passionate love. The true *misogynist*, who shuns females in fact rather than merely taunting them in words, is probably a deeply disturbed personality who never satisfactorily worked out his oedipal relationship to his mother.

The *gyn-* of *misogyny* is, as you would guess, the Greek root for *woman*, found also in *gynecologist*, the medical doctor whose specialty is the treatment of female ailments.

The *misogamist* is that person, male or female, who tenaciously clings to bachelorhood—there is no aversion to the opposite sex, necessarily, but there *is* a deep-seated dread of a permanent, legal relationship. The root *gam-*, marriage, is found also in *monogamy*, the common custom of one marriage at a time; *bigamy*, the crime of contracting a further marriage before a previous union has been legally dissolved; and *polygamy*, that institution, once practiced by the Mormons, in which one man has, simultaneously, a number of wives.

The *misanthrope* is that bitter, cynical, antisocial creature who seems to loathe all humankind. The savage satirist Swift, author of *Gulliver's Travels,* is usually called *misanthropic*. The root *anthrop-*, mankind, is found also in *anthropology*, the science that is concerned with the development, culture, etc. of the human race from primitive times to the present.

29. *What We Hate Most*

anathema (ə-NATH′-ə-mə)

Think of something or someone you dislike so intensely that

even to let the name enter your mind is odious and repulsive to you. For instance, what? Lying, cheating, thievery, immorality, if your ethics are high? Republicans if you're a Democrat, Democrats if you're a Republican? Alcoholics if you're a teetotaler, narcotics pushers if you have teen-age children, cats if you're a mouse, fish if you're a worm? Such objects, abstractions, or people are *anathema* to you.

The language pattern in which the word is used is almost always the same—the person, thing, or idea loathed is *anathema* to the one who feels the loathing.

30. More Hate

antipathy (an-TIP′-ə-thee)
antipathetic (an′-tee-pə-THET′-ək)

There are positive feelings—and there are negative feelings.

On the one hand, there are attraction, infatuation, desire, friendliness, acceptance, affection, warmth, love—in no particular order.

On the other hand (and it is a commentary of some sort on either human relationships or human language that negative words spring more readily to mind), there are dislike, antagonism, aversion, enmity, hostility, animosity, hatred, loathing, repulsion, rancor, repugnance, abhorrence, revulsion.

There is sympathy and there is *antipathy.*

Etymologically, these two words are directly opposed. Both are built on Greek *pathein,* to feel. *Sympathy* is a feeling *with* (*sym-*), *antipathy,* a feeling *against* (*anti-*). But *antipathy* describes a much stronger emotion than its etymology indicates. It is a constitutional hatred combined with active hostility and, often, avoidance. If you have an *antipathy* toward someone, you will show your deep, perhaps ineradicable, repugnance in no uncertain ways; everything in you cries out against him and what he stands for; you will make every effort not to be near him.

You can feel *antipathy* (or, to use the adjective, *antipathetic*) toward people, groups, institutions, countries, abstract qualities, or even certain foods that may be repulsive to you.

FOURTH DAY'S TESTS

I. Match words and definitions.

A   *B*

	A		B
1.	acerb	*a.*	passive in acceptance
2.	nepotic	*b.*	out of time
3.	acquiescent	*c.*	feeling aversion or dislike
4.	nebulous	*d.*	hating females
5.	anachronous	*e.*	illegally wed to more than one spouse
6.	misogynous	*f.*	pertaining to favoritism to relatives
7.	misanthropic	*g.*	pertaining to that custom that permits a man more than one wife
8.	antipathetic		
9.	bigamous	*h.*	hating all mankind
10.	polygamous	*i.*	vague, unclear, obscure, cloudy
		j.	sharp and sour in disposition or temper

II. Write the word, starting as indicated, that fits the definition.

1. Object of hatred, loathing, revulsion   a——————
2. Science of the development of man   a——————
3. One who hates everyone   m——————
4. Favoritism to one's relatives   n——————
5. Hatred of marriage   m——————
6. Medical specialist in female disorders   g——————
7. To accept without enthusiasm   a——————
8. An event, attitude, object, etc., not in the proper time   a——————
9. One who hates women   m——————
10. Crime of taking another spouse before the legal dissolution of a former marriage   b——————

III. What is the English meaning of each root?

1. Latin *nepos*   ——————
2. Latin *nebula*   ——————
3. Greek *misein*   ——————

4. Greek *gyn-* _____
5. Greek *gam-* _____
6. Greek *anthrop-* _____
7. Greek *pathein* _____
8. Greek *sym-* _____
9. Greek *anti-* _____

ANSWERS:

I. 1—j, 2—f, 3—a, 4—i, 5—b, 6—d, 7—h, 8—c, 9—e, 10—g.
II. 1—anathema *or* antipathy, 2—anthropology, 3—misanthrope, 4—nepotism, 5—misogamy, 6—gynecologist, 7—acquiesce, 8—anachronism, 9—misogynist, 10—bigamy.
III. 1—nephew; 2—cloud; 3—to hate; 4—woman; 5—marriage; 6—mankind; 7—to feel; 8—with; 9—against.

FIFTH DAY

31. The Importance of Others

altruist (AL'-trōō-ist)	egoism (EE'-gō-iz-əm)
altruistic (al'-trōō-IS'-tik)	egoist (EE'-gō-ist)
altruism (AL'-trōō-iz-əm)	egoistic (ee'gō-IS'-tik)

Who comes first, you or the other fellow? The other fellow? You're an *altruist*.

Does a mother put her child's welfare above her own? Is a husband more interested in making his wife happy than in achieving happiness for himself? Such a mother and such a husband are *altruistic*.

When we operate out of *altruistic* motives, we are indifferent to our own needs and selfish desires—it is the other person's interests that we are dedicated to serving. Idealistic, unreal? The *altruist* is an idealist of the first water; true *altruism* is as unreal as it is rare and beautiful.

The word derives from Latin *alter,* another; its opposite, *egoism,* is from Latin *ego,* I. To an *egoist,* it's *I* who count, not the others. The adjective is *egoistic*.

32. Of Death and Dying

moribund (MAWR'-ə-bund)	mortician (mawr-TISH'-ən)
mortal (MAWR'-təl)	mortuary (MAWR'-chŏŏ-er'-ee)
immortal (im-MAWR'-təl)	

Everything that lives finally dies—plants, animals, people, even customs, businesses, institutions, governments, far-flung empires. This, apparently, is one of the first laws of life.

Some things give evidence of death long before the final moments. A business that sustains losses year after year, a government riddled with graft and corruption and without power over its citizens, any institution that no longer exhibits any vitality or vigor—these are all *moribund,* show signs of dying, of being almost (though not quite) dead. A person, in medical parlance, is *moribund* when almost all evidence of life is gone, and it is now only a question of minutes or seconds before every vital process ceases.

The root *mori* is the Latin verb *to die;* the derivative root *mort-,* death, occurs frequently in English words. Human beings are *mortal*—for them death is finally inevitable. The Greeks and Romans considered their gods *immortal*—not subject to death. A *mortician* (euphemism for *undertaker*) manages funeral, or death, arrangements. A *mortuary* is literally a place for the dead, the place where dead bodies are kept before burial.

33. *Our World*

mundane (MUN'-dayn)
demimonde (DEM'-ee-mond')
demimondaine (dem'-ee-mon-DAYN')
haut monde (Ō' MŌND, the -N nasalized, as in French)
hauteur (hō-TUR')
subterranean (sub'-tə-RAY'-nee-ən)
terrestrial (tə-RES'-tree-əl)
terra firma (TER'-ə FUR'-mə)

There is the world here below, as the philosophers put it, and the heavens above. And part of living in our world is concerned with the everyday aspects of staying alive—with money, and food, and shelter, and working, and with other ordinary activities and things that make up the commonplace, routine business of existence.

Not very exciting, perhaps. Even a bit boring, if you like. But essential, inescapable. Nothing very spiritual, here, no poetic flights of imagination, no soaring into the wild blue yonder—just solid, down-to-earth, practical matters that, somewhat apologetically, we call *mundane.* And why *mundane?* The root is *mundus,* a Latin word for the world or earth we live on, a root found also, with a change of the internal vowel from *u* to *o,* in two words borrowed from the French: *demimonde* and *haut monde.*

The *demimonde* is literally the half-world, actually that class of society made up of women whose sexual behavior is too free, too uninhibited, too much a flagrant violation of cultural restrictions to be quite acceptable. A woman of this half-world is a *demimondaine*

—she is by no means a harlot, a prostitute, a streetwalker, or a call girl. But she moves in circles in which the women have "reputations," have lost social caste, because they easily attach themselves as mistresses to one man after another.

The *haut monde,* on the other hand, is the very top layer of society, Society with a capital *S,* the Four Hundred, the social elite, literally the high world. Often the use of this phrase indicates just a trace of contempt (perhaps envious contempt) for this world with all its wealth, snobbery, exclusiveness, and unearned prerogatives and perquisites, and so it is a label not generally used for themselves by the people who belong to it.

The *haut* in *haut monde* is the French word for *high,* found also in *hauteur,* a disdainful, arrogant pride and snobbery that give its possessor an air of overweening and intolerable haughtiness—he (or she) is too high, too good, too special to mingle with the common people.

Another Latin word for world or earth is *terra,* found as a root in, for example, *subterranean,* under the earth; *terrestrial,* pertaining to this earth; *territory,* a section of the earth; and *terra firma,* firm earth, i.e., solid ground.

34. Hardness

adamant (AD′-ə-mənt *or* AD′-ə-mant′)

In ancient times, *adamant* was the name given to the diamond because it was the hardest substance known. The word comes from a Greek adjective meaning *not to be subdued.*

And that is how some people are in the face of almost irresistible temptation or entreaty—not to be subdued. They are *adamant,* hard as nails (or as a diamond, which is harder), never yielding, not budging an inch, standing firm against every pressure.

35. Relief from Pain

anodyne (AN′-ə-dine)

Pain has ever been an affliction that human beings have sought to escape; or, failing complete escape, to relieve as much as possible. Hence aspirin, and opium, and morphine, and balms and unguents of every sort.

Pain can be mental as well as physical, and sometimes all the more distressing when it attacks the mind instead of the body. Hence alcohol, narcotics, overeating, and other soothing means of temporary forgetfulness.

The Greek word for *pain* is *odyne,* the prefix *an-* means *without*—so an *anodyne* is a pain remover. And, literally, aspirin and other drugs may be called *anodynes,* but the word is just as frequently used in a figurative sense to denote something that soothes, that allays anxiety or conflict or discontent or emotional distress of any sort without in any way eliminating or attacking the cause. Thus the Roman circuses were *anodynes* for the seething populace, or, to jump some centuries, Hoover's encouraging "Prosperity is just around the corner" during the blackest part of the Great Depression was no more than an *anodyne.* Atheists claim that religion is an *anodyne,* psychiatrists point out that some people use sex, shopping sprees, television watching, or gorging on rich desserts as an *anodyne.*

Call something an *anodyne* (in the figurative sense) and you show that you've seen through it and have nothing but contempt for it. This will not be of any real or lasting help, you are saying; its only purpose is to soothe for the moment and keep things calm.

36. Flowing Like Honey

mellifluous (mə-LIF′-lōō-əs)   efflux (EF′-fluks)
flux (FLUKS)   affluent (AF′-lōō-ənt)
influx (IN′-fluks)

What is sweeter than honey? Very little, if we judge by the evidence of language rather than our taste buds. We call someone we love *Honey,* we use *honeyed* words to show affection or to seduce by flattery, we speak of that golden period directly after marriage as the *honeymoon,* we have named a particularly sweet and delicious melon *honeydew.*

And if sounds or tones or words or phrases flow like honey, must they not be smooth, sweet, lovely, pleasant to listen to, perhaps seductive and in every way delightful? They must be, surely. When we describe sounds, etc. as *mellifluous,* or when we apply this adjective to anything else that evokes an auditory reaction (a voice, singing, music, bells, a guitar or violin, and so on), we are saying, etymologically, that we hear honey (Latin, *mellis*) flowing (Latin, *fluere*).

Fluere, to flow, is found in a number of English words. A *fluid* is a substance which, unlike a solid, can flow. *Influence* is the power (at least etymologically) to flow into a person or thing and affect him or it. Anything *superfluous* flows over the top. *Flux* is a constant flowing or changing. *Influx* (as of visitors, customers, tourists, etc.) is a flowing in, while *efflux* is a flowing out. And if someone is *affluent,* money and other material riches appear always to flow toward him.

37. Making Every Word Count

laconic (lə-KON′-ik)   laconicism (lə-KON′-ə-siz-əm)
taciturn (TAS′-ə-turn)   taciturnity (tas′-ə-TUR′-nə-tee)
laconism (LAK′-ə-niz-əm)

A *laconic* answer is brief. So brief, so to the point, so concise, so meticulously pruned of every unnecessary word or syllable that it is pregnant with meaning. As a result, it often has an air of abruptness, curtness, or veiled hostility.

The word derives from Laconia, ancient name for Sparta, and we know how austere and severely simple a life a Spartan was supposed to lead; how highly disciplined, stoical, sparing of all excess he had to be.

The story is told that when Philip of Macedonia was besieging Laconia (or Sparta), he sent this message to the beleaguered king: "If we capture your city, we will burn it to the ground." The messenger returned to Philip with a one-word, *laconic,* reply: "If!"

So *laconic* remarks or statements may be so highly condensed that they are, paradoxically, ambiguous or even momentarily mystifying. As in the case of the man standing at a crowded lunch counter who asked for a ham sandwich. "Eat it here or take it with you?" the counterman asked with perfect logic, since the customer was not seated. "Both," was the *laconic* retort.

A person may be described as *laconic* if he generally expresses himself in the pithy, terse, no-words-wasted manner I have indicated; he may also be described as hard to live with, even though brevity of speech is hailed as a virtue.

Laconic should not be confused with *taciturn.* A *taciturn* person is silent or uncommunicative by habit and temperament; he is unsociable, engaging in conversation only if he can't avoid it, and then grudgingly. When you talk to him you are lucky to get any kind of verbal response at all, for generally he prefers to make noncommittal grunts.

The nouns are *laconism* or *laconicism,* and *taciturnity.*

38. Gina Lollobrigida, Sophia Loren, et al.

aphrodisiac (af'-rə-DIZ'-ee-ak)
anaphrodisiac (an-af'-rə-DIZ'-ee-ak)

What incites sexual desire? Men, say the psychologists, are more quickly and easily aroused than women—a pretty girl, an exposed limb, a curving bodice, heady perfume, a seductive glance, words in a book or pictures on the screen, memories or fantasies or imagination can immediately stimulate the male. Women, in general, are not so instantaneously responsive to similar phenomena. For them the candlelight, the champagne, the soft music, the endearing words, the long, careful campaigning, etc., etc., are essential, or certainly helpful.

In any case, anything, including the list above, that sets off a positive sexual response is called an *aphrodisiac*—so named, as you might guess, after Aphrodite, the Greek goddess of love and beauty (the same deity who was called Venus by the ancient Romans).

Certain drugs and foods supposedly also have *aphrodisiac* properties—cantharides (or Spanish fly), spices, oysters, secret love potions, etc.—but there is no medical evidence that these have any effect. For some people, alcohol may be indirectly *aphrodisiac,* insofar as it dulls or removes certain inhibitions. For most men, of course, the greatest *aphrodisiac* is a female; for most women, a male.

Those drugs, foods, agents, or phenomena that dull sexual appetites (saltpeter, for example, has this unearned reputation) are *anaphrodisiac; an-,* as you will recall, is the Greek negative prefix.

FIFTH DAY'S TESTS

I. Match words and definitions.

A	B
1. moribund	*a.* certain to die eventually
2. mortal	*b.* underground
3. mundane	*c.* sweetly flowing
4. subterranean	*d.* uncommunicative
5. adamant	*e.* sexually stimulating
6. mellifluous	*f.* terse, pithy, to-the-point
7. laconic	*g.* dying
8. taciturn	*h.* firm, unyielding
9. aphrodisiac	*i.* interested in the welfare of others
10. altruistic	*j.* worldly, down-to-earth, not spiritual

II. Write the word, starting as indicated, that fits the definition.

1. Interest in one's own welfare exclusively   e_____
2. Place for the dead   m_____
3. The half-world of sexually uninhibited women   d_____
4. The world of high society   h_____
5. Arrogant pride   h_____
6. Pain reliever   a_____
7. That which reduces sexual desire   a_____
8. Inflow   i_____
9. Outflow   e_____
10. Wealthy, prosperous   a_____

III. What is the English meaning of each root?

1. Latin *mellis*   _____
2. Latin *fluere*   _____
3. Latin *alter*   _____
4. Greek *an-*   _____
5. Latin *mori*   _____
6. Latin *mundus*   _____

7. Latin *terra* _____

8. French *haut* _____

9. Latin *ego* _____

10. Latin *mort-*

ANSWERS:

I. 1—g, 2—a, 3—j, 4—b, 5—h, 6—c, 7—f, 8—d, 9—e, 10—i.

II. 1—egoism, 2—mortuary, 3—demimonde, 4—haut monde, 5—hauteur, 6—anodyne, 7—anaphrodisiac, 8—influx, 9—efflux, 10—affluent.

III. 1—honey; 2—to flow; 3—other; 4—without, not; 5—to die; 6—world, earth; 7—world, earth; 8—high; 9—I; 10—death.

39. Dull, Duller, Dullest

cliché (klee-SHAY′)	bromide (BRŌ′-mide)
platitude (PLAT′-ə-tōͦod)	bromidic (brō-MID′-ik)

There are times we are disposed to forgive triteness—not everybody has a flair for presenting an idea in an original, novel, or sparkling manner. We hear *clichés* all around us in everyday conversation, for in the ready give-and-take of personal communication there is usually no time, and generally no urgent necessity, to find electric or startling combinations of words in which to couch our every thought.

But then there is the person who delivers himself (with such pomposity, usually, and such evident self-relish, that "delivers himself" is the apt verb to use) of an idea so obvious, or so pathetically banal, and in language so commonplace and unimaginative, that he might greatly have furthered the cause of civilization by merely remaining still.

Try to get the picture.

A commonplace statement (whether in speaking or writing) made in hackneyed, overused phraseology (hackneyed now through overuse, though new and interesting and original when first invented by someone else, such as Mark Twain's delightful reflection that everyone complains about the weather but no one does anything about it) is a *cliché.* And *clichés,* I have suggested, are often pardonable in conversation.

But the *cliché* uttered as if it were the momentous saying of the year, as if it were so novel that no one else could possibly have been creative enough to so phrase it—that is a *platitude,* and most inexcusable.

And the *platitude* that is particularly wearisome and annoying, that gives the listener little or no credit for intelligence, that is delivered with an air of ridiculous self-importance that would make one want to throttle the speaker if one were not so amused—that is a *bromide.*

(In medicine, *bromides* were once popular as sedatives and tranquilizers; the connection between ideas is not hard to see.)

Bromide usually designates remarks or statements, but it may also be used for the person addicted to *bromidic* utterances.

40. When the Source Is in Doubt

apocryphal (ə-POK′-rə-fəl)

Certain writings have been, say the scholars, falsely attributed to Biblical characters, and therefore are not admissible to the New Testament. These are called *Apocrypha,* a name applied also to the fourteen books of the Septuagint (the Greek Old Testament), which Protestants do not accept as canonical.

And so the adjective *apocryphal* designates any statement, story, explanation, or writing whose genuineness is in grave question, or which is ascribed to an author or source who perhaps had nothing to do with its creation. When you say, "This is perhaps *apocryphal,*" you indicate that there is no clear proof or evidence that the person credited with it is indeed responsible.

41. It Looks Safe—but Watch Out!

residue (REZ′-ə-doō)
subside (səb-SIDE′)
insidious (in-SID′-ee-əs)

The root *sid-* is from the Latin verb *sedere,* to sit. Etymologically, when you *preside,* you sit before, or in front of, the other members of a group; you *reside* at that place in which you sit again and again; a *residue* is what is left sitting when everything else is gone; when something *subsides* it sits under, or at the bottom, instead of rising and being active.

Insidious too, by etymology, describes a sitting—a sitting concealed in ambush, waiting to attack. In actual use the word has a number of similar meanings, all relating more or less to the idea of an ambush.

Thus *insidious* designs, plans, questions, etc. are sly, wily, sneaky, calculated to trap or deceive. *Insidious* actions aim to undermine, or are treacherous, but in a stealthy, surreptitious way.

And *insidious* conditions are those which operate at first slowly, inconspicuously, below the surface, until suddenly they burst forth and, almost too late, we realize their danger or menace. We have been beguiled, deceived, lulled into what we now realize was a false sense of security—in short, we've been had.

Cancer, for example, is an *insidious* disease—the symptoms often do not appear until the malignancy has spread beyond control. The Nazis *insidiously,* and by subterfuge, built up their army despite the restrictions of the treaty that Germany had signed after World War I. Our opponent's *insidious* move in chess appears harmless, or purely defensive, or in any case nothing to worry about. Then, half a dozen moves later, we suddenly see the inevitable checkmate and realize, in humiliation and frustration, that the "harmless" move was the deceptive keystone of the lethal attack.

42. Beyond the Power of Words

ineffable (in-EF'-ə-bəl)   indescribable (in'-də-SKRY'-bə-bəl)
affable (AF'-ə-bəl)   unspeakable (un-SPEE'-kə-bəl)

Latin *fari,* to speak, plus the prefix *ex-,* out (changed, here, to the more pronounceable *ef-*) are the major building blocks of the English word *ineffable,* which thus, strictly, means *unable to be spoken out.*

But the structural elements of a word give one, often, only the literal denotation; most words through centuries of use take on color, flavor, and added connotations not accounted for in the dry and scientific etymology. Thus *affable,* from the same *fari,* has parts that add up to *able to be spoken to* (*af-* is a respelling of *ad,* to, and *-able* is a suffix meaning *able to be*)—and of course an *affable* person is one to whom it is easy to speak, but much more also. He is friendly, approachable, agreeably and warmly courteous, easygoing, likable. He has an air that welcomes advances, that says in effect, "Come talk to me, I'm nice to get along with."

So, too, with *ineffable,* which beyond its surface denotation suggests a quality so subtle or elusive, or so ethereal or spiritual, that mere words are incapable of describing it fully or accurately— as *ineffable* sadness, pathos, poignancy, tenderness, loveliness, beauty, etc.

Now we could call all these things *indescribable,* but this is a neutral, comparatively colorless adjective, lacking the rich connotations of *ineffable,* and attaching to qualities we either like or dislike. *Ineffable,* however, always shows a positive, sympathetic, or admiring attitude.

On the other hand, *unspeakable* (almost exactly equivalent in structure to *ineffable,* but built on native roots) most often is applied to qualities, experiences, or things to which we respond negatively; we are saying, when we call them *unspeakable,* that they are too disgusting, foul, or horrible to be fully described by words—as *unspeakable* brutality, filth, degradation, crimes, etc., or the *unspeakable* and humiliating experiences victims were subjected to in the Nazi concentration camps.

43. Pettiness as a Way of Life

cavil (KAV'-əl)

You have doubtless met, perhaps had the misfortune to work for, people who simply cannot be pleased.

Not because their standards are unreasonably high (that would be bad enough), or because they are annoyingly rigid in their expectations (equally hard to live with), but rather (and this is close to maddening) because their objections to what you do, or say, or suggest, or plan are unfailingly picayune. They take exception to the most petty, most trivial details; their criticisms seem almost frivolous except that they are made with such a straight face.

These people are *cavilers.* They *cavil* about such niggling trifles that they have obviously long since lost sight of broad aims and major purposes. And of course when they raise each cranky objection they say, piously, "I don't mean to *cavil,* I assure you, *but . . .*"

44. Flagwaver

chauvinism (SHŌ'-və-niz-əm)
chauvinist (SHŌ'-və-nist)
chauvinistic (shō'-və-NIS'-tik)

Nicolas Chauvin, way back in the times of Napoleon I, was such a mulish, blatant, irritating propagandist for French imperialism, by then a lost cause, that his name became a jestingstock not only in his own country but throughout much of the world.

Thus is a kind of immortality witlessly gained—that same

name once laughed at by so many is the origin of the word *chauvinism.*

Chauvinism is an exaggerated, blind, and warlike super-patriotism that unreasonably sees no good in any country but one's own. The *chauvinist* is a flagwaver in the most bigoted sense of that term.

People can be *chauvinistic,* in addition, about their religion, their neighborhood, their anything that is different from (i.e., as they see it, vastly superior to) someone else's.

Do they drive a foreign car? They boast tiresomely about its unique attributes, treating with condescension or contempt any domestic make of automobile. Are they male *chauvinists?* Women are weak, stupid, untrustworthy, despicable, inferior. Are they *chauvinistic* about the college they hail as their alma mater? All others are not worth talking about, let alone attending.

Chauvinists, to understate it, are not particularly broadminded.

45. No Fun

austere (aw-STEER′)
austerity (aw-STER′-ə-tee)

Remove all the ornaments, luxuries, refinements, and pleasant indulgences from life, leaving only those things absolutely essential for survival. That's when you have *austerity.*

Austere, also, is that form of existence based on abstinence or asceticism—avoidance of rich food, alcoholic beverages, and other fleshly pleasures.

Austere, in addition, is anything severely simple, unadorned, without flounce, furbelow, or frippery. Too, any mode of behavior governed by a strict moral code or rigorous and Spartan self-denial. Or, finally, anything stern, harsh, unmellowed, unsoftened, such as the *austere* realities of poverty, the *austere* countenance of a judge, the *austere* demands of economic competition, etc.

All these faces of *austerity,* whether the untempered simplicity of physical appearance, the self-denial of creature pleasures, the strictness of morality, or any of the others, exhibit one common element—harshness. And this makes etymological sense, for *austere* comes from Greek *austeros,* harsh.

46. Antidote to Austerity

badinage (BAD'-ə-nəj *or* bad'-ə-NAHZH')
persiflage (PUR'-sə-flahzh')

But, come, life is not necessarily austere, not always serious, humorless, harsh!

There must be some fun, some things purely for pleasure, if we are to retain our humanness.

And some of the fun, the frippery, the lightness are found in *badinage*—in, for example, the gay teasing of lovers, in the playful banter of drawing-room conversation, in the camaraderie and joking of well-fed men around the card table (excepting, of course, the heavy losers), in the repartee and punning of scintillating talkers. Important? No. But fun! And any of this is called *badinage*.

A very close synonym is *persiflage,* which, like *badinage,* is also light, gay, frivolous, witty talk or conversation.

47. No Point in Praying

inexorable (in-EKS'-ər-ə-bəl)
adamant (AD'-ə-mənt *or* AD'-ə-mant')
obdurate (OB'-dŏŏ-rət)
inflexible (in-FLEK'-sə-bəl)

The Latin verb to pray is *oro.* Hence, someone who cannot be moved by prayer, who is deaf to entreaty, is *inexorable,* etymologically *unable to be prayed to.*

Here, then, is a person who has made up his mind about a course of action. Nothing we say can influence him—he is *adamant,* hard as a diamond. He is *obdurate*—his heart has no softness, no room for pity, mercy, or even sympathy. He is *inflexible*—he won't bend or yield one inch, one cubit. He is *inexorable*—pray, beg, plead, get on your knees, nothing will avail to alter his decision.

When we call a man *inexorable* we generally imply that he has some power to affect our lives in a way we would like to pray him out of, if only we could. And when we speak of *inexorable* fate, justice, or wrath, or the *inexorable* demands of life or time, we impute to abstractions the same kind of imperviousness to our pleas.

48. Curse You, Jack Dalton!

execrable (EKS′-ə-krə-bəl)

What do we curse? Generally those things we hate or find beneath contempt. And so if we call something *execrable* (etymologically, worthy of curses) we indicate that it is so bad it is hateful, abominable, despicable, detestable—curse it, away with it! In a condensed way that is what we are saying when we refer to *execrable* gall, crimes, sins, murder, lies, etc.

However, words, like people, have a tendency to lose some of their strength or violence as they grow older. Hence, today, *execrable* is also applied to taste, quality, style, sense of humor, etc., in which instances we are saying that such things are so inferior that, exaggerating for the sake of effect, they deserve nothing but curses.

49. Four Ways to Be Dull

insipid (in-SIP′-əd)   insipidity (in′-sə-PID′-ə-tee)
banal (BAY′-nəl)   banality (bə-NAL′-ə-tee)
inane (in-AYN′)   inanity (in-AN′-ə-tee)
jejune (jə-JŌŌN′)

Imagine food utterly lacking in salt, a condiment almost universally used to bring out the natural flavor and pungency of meat, fish, vegetables, grains, etc. How will it taste? Flat, dull, pleasureless, unstimulating to the appetite.

Now imagine a person equally devoid of "salt," or, as we are more likely to say, spice. He (or she) similarly is flat, commonplace, flavorless, colorless, unattractive—barren of interest, distinction, piquancy, substance, or character.

Insipid, which means, etymologically, without taste or flavor, applies both literally to what we eat or drink and figuratively to people, their ideas, their language, their artistic efforts, etc.

A man or woman can be *inspid,* as also a book, story, play, poem, painting, college course, lecture, etc., etc. Not to mention overrefined white bread, frozen TV dinners, instant coffee, weak tea, overcooked spaghetti, and so on without end.

Insipid does not mean stupid, though it might easily be so construed from context, and no doubt a stupid person is often *insipid.* And the word should not be used to describe those things or persons which synonyms like *banal, inane,* or *jejune* characterize more precisely.

Insipid means flavorless, in any sense of the latter word.

Banal stresses commonplaceness, triteness, lack of imagination or novelty. *Banal* language or style is full of the same old tired clichés or bromides. A person or anything he says or does can be called *banal.*

Inane especially indicates emptiness of meaning or point. A conclusion, remark, statement, idea, etc. that makes little sense or is silly or foolish is *inane.*

Jejune suggests sterility, barrenness, lack of substance to satisfy the mind, spirit, or emotions. Language, literary style, or any kind of artistic creation may be described as *jejune* if it is so disappointingly juiceless, meager, thin, unstimulating that one can find no mental satisfaction or nourishment in it.

All these adjectives make the final implication of dullness, flatness, and lack of interest, but each one emphasizes a somewhat different cause.

The noun forms are *inspidity, banality, inanity.*

SIXTH DAY'S TESTS

I. Match words and definitions.

A	*B*
1. insipid	*a.* full of traps
2. apocryphal	*b.* friendly; genial; easy to approach and talk to
3. insidious	
4. ineffable	*c.* unyielding; firm against entreaty or prayer
5. affable	
6. austere	*d.* flavorless, dull
7. inexorable	*e.* so bad as to deserve curses
8. execrable	*f.* severely simple; ascetic; without luxuries
9. bromidic	*g.* hackneyed, trite, commonplace
10. chauvinistic	*h.* of doubtful authenticity
	i. superpatriotic
	j. too subtle, elusive, ethereal, etc. to be described

II. Write the word, starting as indicated, that fits the definition.

1. Commonplaceness; complete lack of novelty, imaginativeness, etc.   b_____

2. Hackeneyed statement uttered as if momentous or novel   p_____

3. To find petty faults or objections   c_____

4. Light, gay, clever, or mildly teasing conversation   b_____

p_____

5. Pointlessness   i_____

6. What's left; what sinks down at the bottom   r_____

7. Sterile, barren, meager, too thin to be satisfying   j_____

8. Too horrible or foul to mention or speak about   u_____

9. Unmoved by pity, mercy, etc.   o_____

10. Hackney, trite, overused phrase   c_____

III. What is the English meaning of each root?

1. Latin *sedere* (*sid-*)   _____
2. Latin *oro*   _____
3. Greek *austeros*   _____
4. Latin *fari*   _____
5. Latin *ex-*   _____

ANSWERS:

I. 1—d, 2—h, 3—a, 4—j, 5—b, 6—f, 7—c, 8—e, 9—g, 10—i.

II. 1—banality, 2—platitude, 3—cavil, 4—badinage, persiflage, 5—inanity, 6—residue, 7—jejune, 8—unspeakable, 9—obdurate, 10—cliché.

III. 1—to sit; 2—to pray; 3—harsh; 4—to speak; 5—out.

50. *One End Moo*

bovine (BŌ'-vine)

How stupid can you be? Well, as stupid as a cow, an ox, or a bull, all members of the family known biologically as *Bovidae*.

Is a cow stupid? Well, surely she's not as foxy as the fox, as humanlike in mentality as the dolphin, as wise as the owl. To the untrained human eye, the cow *seems* stupid—also patient, stolid, slow-moving, phlegmatic, dull, utterly emotionless. In short, cowlike or oxlike. (True, we say "dumb as an ox," not "dumb as a cow," but that doubtless is out of respect to the fair sex.)

So if we call a person *bovine,* we attribute to him (or, often, her) any or all of the qualities we fancy in a cow, with stupidity leading all the rest.

Applied to a bona fide member of *Bovidae,* of course, *bovine* means none of these things—it is only a scientific and objective categorization, as in Ogden Nash's famous rhyme:

> The cow is of the *bovine* ilk,
> One end moo, the other end milk.

51. *There It Is—or Is It?*

evanescent (ev'-ə-NES'-ənt)
evanescence (ev'-ə-NES'-ənce)
evanesce (ev'-ə-NES')

"Now you see it, now you don't" applies admirably to anything we call *evanescent,* so fleeting, so momentary, so quickly vanishing is it. An *evanescent* feeling, reaction, etc. lasts for so short a time that you hardly realize it's there before it's gone. By implication, then, it must also be remarkably fragile, delicate, subtle, intangible—almost, but not quite, imperceptible or impalpable. The noun is *evanescence,* the verb to *evanesce.*

52. Playboy

dilettante (dil'-ə-TAN'-tee)
dilettanti, pl. (dil'-ə-TAN'-tee)

The Italian verb *to delight* or *give pleasure* is *dilettare*—and if you dabble superficially in any of the arts merely for your own amusement, pleasure, or delight, you're a *dilettante,* a term, unfortunately, of mild disparagement.

"If you have talent, as obviously you do," someone who calls you a *dilettante* is saying, "why aren't you more serious about your music, or painting, or writing, etc.?"

Since this is an Italian import despite its French appearance, the recommended pronunciation is the more sophisticated one; but enough educated people say dil'-ə-TAHNT' to make this form also acceptable. The word can be pluralized either by adding an *-s,* or by using the foreign ending—*dilettanti.*

53. Two Extremes

ennui (AHN'-wee)
joie de vivre (ZHWAH' də VEE'-vrə)

The French import *ennui* describes a special emotional state that cannot adequately be described by any other single word in the English language.

Many feelings are condensed into its two syllables. The preliminary factors are inactivity and a lack of involvement in anything that can capture one's interest, evoke one's enthusiasm, or inspire one with the joy and excitement of just being alive. The result is a spirit-crushing tedium so vast, combined with a floating, generalized dissatisfaction so enormous, that one is left floundering in a sea of mental and physical depression, languor, and lethargy. Life is wearying, empty, one big nothing; boredom envelops and smothers one like a cloak. This is *ennui,* and you can have it.

And the direct opposite? What phrase designates that quality of zestfulness and relish and exhilaration with which some people react to every experience as if it were an adventure, so that they wake up bright-eyed, singing, eager to greet the new day? Let's turn to the French again: *joie de vivre,* literally *joy of life,* i.e., excitement in living and being alive.

54. Finished Product

consummate, adj. (kən-SUM′-ət)
to consummate, v. (KON′-sə-mayt)

Are you absolutely flawless in your skill or technique? Then you're *consummate*—or, as a popular song put it some decades ago, you're the tops.

Your genius of performance, by the way, need not be in a praiseworthy area. You can be a *consummate* liar, swindler, or seducer; then no one holds a candle to your gift for lying, swindling, or seducing.

More likely you'd prefer to be known for your *consummate* artistry at the keyboard, your *consummate* skill as a writer, teacher, or actor, your *consummate* genius for making money, or the *consummate* fulfillment you've found in your marriage or in your profession.

The word comes from the Latin verb *consummare,* to finish, complete, or bring to perfection—hence our own verb *consummate,* as in *consummate* a deal, a contract, a marriage, or an arrangement.

55. No Energy Left

enervated, adj. (EN′-ər-vay′-təd)
enervation (en′-ər-VAY′-shən)
enervate, v. (EN′-ər-vayt)

Think first of such dynamic qualities as strength, power, force, energy, vigor, and vitality. Now imagine any circumstances that might completely rob one of these qualities—perhaps disease, physical exhaustion, intense heat, starvation, intolerable mental or emotional stress. Then how does one feel? Limp, spent, weak, debilitated, empty, so languid, droopy, full of lassitude that the merest thought of vigorous action is painful. One is then *enervated.* (This word looks as if it's related to *energy,* but isn't. It comes from Latin *e-,* a shortened form of *ex-,* out, and *nervus,* nerve, sinew, strength, while *energy* is built on Greek *ergon,* work.)

In a different but equally current use, *enervation* may imply the weakening of moral strength or vigor, as from an excess of luxury, indulgence, idleness, pleasure, etc. Thus, paradoxically, both exhausting effort and total lack of it can be *enervating*. The verb, of course, is to *enervate*.

56. Dat Ole Debbil Conscience Again

contrite (kən-TRITE′)   trite (TRITE)
attrition (ə-TRISH′-ən)   contrition (kən-TRISH′-ən)

When you have *compunctions,* as I have said, your conscience is pierced; when you are *contrite* your conscience has been rubbed raw, at least etymologically, for the word comes from the Latin verb *to rub,* from which root we also get *attrition,* a wearing away by friction or rubbing; and *trite,* rubbed thin by overuse, as a cliché or other *trite* phrase.

Whether you feel *compunction* or *contrition,* you suffer from guilt, but *contrition* is a stronger and more lasting emotion, and though you can have *compunctions* before acting (and so, perhaps, refrain), you are *contrite* only after the deed is done. Additionally, there is the implication, when you are truly *contrite* over something, that you feel sufficiently remorseful to wish to make amends.

57. Puzzlements, Deliberate and Otherwise

cryptic (KRIP′-tik)   cryptography (krip-TOG′-rə-fee)
crypt (KRIPT)   enigmatic (en′-əg-MAT′-ik)

There is a verb *kryptein,* in Greek, meaning *to hide.*

And when the meaning of something, whether expressed in words or by any other means, is hidden from us because it is deliberately intended to puzzle, perplex, mystify, or baffle, then, building on the classical root, we call it *cryptic.*

(Also from the same verb come *crypt,* an underground burial vault—in which the corpse is, so to speak, hidden away—and *cryptography,* the art of using or breaking secret codes, i.e., writing in which the meaning is hidden.)

Thus a glance may be *cryptic.* What does it mean, what's really behind it? (And the glancer, you may be sure, doesn't wish us to know.) Or, similarly, a smile, a message, a warning, a phrase, a remark, an answer. Someone who is *cryptic* aims to keep his own secrets, to express just enough to challenge the other person's curiosity—but not one bit more, lest he satisfy it!

Enigmatic, from a Greek verb meaning *to speak in riddles,* is essentially the same as *cryptic,* except that the *enigmatic* person is mysterious without necessarily intending to be so. Mona Lisa's smile is *enigmatic* (we can't quite figure it out), but we do not imply, when we use this word, that the woman has with malice aforethought set out to mystify us.

58. No Genius

asinine (AS'-ə-nine)
fatuous (FACH'-ŏŏ-əs)
fatuity (fə-TOO'-ə-tee)

Obviously not all men are created equal—at least not in mental endowment. People who are less intelligent than the average, or who are less capable of rational or sensible judgment than one normally expects of human beings, do not merit, and should not, I suppose, receive, our contempt. And yet words like *stupid, silly* (except when used affectionately), and *foolish* certainly show that we not only disapprove of, but actually look down upon, those we so describe. Even terms like *moronic, imbecilic,* and *idiotic,* which properly only designate ascending degrees of feeble-mindedness, for which the victim is certainly not to be held responsible, are loosely used to show our annoyance and feelings of superiority.

If we call someone *asinine,* we are saying that he is as stupid as an ass, that most unthinking and imperceptive of beasts. And if we say he is *fatuous,* we imply that he is not only stupid, silly, foolish, moronic, imbecilic, idiotic, asinine, inane, empty-headed, and unreasoning; but in addition (and now we feel that our contempt is well deserved), totally unaware of his deficiencies and therefore irritatingly smug, self-satisfied, almost proud of himself. The noun is *fatuity.*

59. Love, Sex, and Money

cupidity (kyŏŏ-PID'-ə-tee)
concupiscence (kon-KYOO'-pə-sənce)
concupiscent (kon-KYOO'-pə-sənt)

Cupid is the Roman god of love. Love creates desire—or the other way around, if you prefer. Both the name Cupid and our word *cupidity* derive from the same Latin verb *cupio,* to wish or want, but the desire in *cupidity* is not a bit spiritual, emotional, or sexual—it's bedrock materialism.

Cupidity is a compelling passion for wealth, an intense, over-riding greed for money, possessions, things—for stocks and bonds and gold and silver and diamonds and land and cars, etc., etc.

It is, in short, a compulsion to *have.*

Concupiscence, from the same Latin verb, brings us back somewhat closer to Cupid. With this word we refer to purely sexual desire, irrespective of love, tenderness, or emotional warmth. It is a less judgmental term than *lust,* less indicative of contempt, but otherwise identical in meaning with it. The adjective is *concupiscent.*

60. *For Tender Ears Only*

euphemism (YOO'-fə-miz-əm)
euphemistic (yoo-fə-MIS'-tik)

Words are a tricky business. They are not things themselves, but only symbols of things, yet they have such power that people often mistake them for what they symbolize.

And so there are those who, considering the *fact* of death or insanity or sexual activity or toilet functions disagreeable, prefer not to say, or even hear or read, the *words* that accurately and directly describe these or other (to them) unpleasant aspects of life.

And so they use, and are offended if others fail to use, *euphemisms*—words or phrases like *the body, the remains,* or *the departed* for corpse; *pass away, depart, breathe one's last,* or *expire* for die; *some buttons missing,* or *screws loose,* or *a mental case* for insane or psychotic; *powder room, little girls' room, washroom, the utilities,* etc. for toilet; *intimacies, an affair, sleeping together,* etc. for sexual intercourse; *woman of easy virtue, painted lady, fille de joie,* etc. for prostitute. The meaning is perfectly clear, but the expression is indirect, more delicate, less graphic, hence not so close to the thing itself.

Eu- is a Greek root meaning *good; pheme* means *voice* or *sound.* A *euphemistic* expression, etymologically, gives a good sound to something that is otherwise considered bad.

61. *Are You in a Hurry or Just Bored?*

cursory (KUR'-sə-ree)
perfunctory (pər-FUNK'-tə-ree)
cursorily (KUR'-sə-rə-lee)
perfunctorily (pər-FUNK'-tə-rə-lee)

If you're in a hurry you can't pay much attention to details. You are quick rather than thorough. You want to get a job over with because time presses you, and so you skip here and there; you are no more than superficial.

So an examination, reading, investigation, search, study, etc. in which only the surface is skimmed, in which there is no finicky concentration on anything minor, in which a somewhat careless haste is the distinguishing characteristic, is *cursory*. Fair enough, considering that the word is ultimately derived from Latin *curro,* to run.

It could be worse, however. You may do some things with the heavy, bored air that shouts your indifference or irritation—you are merely going through the motions because routine requires it, or to please someone, but you're not a bit involved, not even interested, your heart just isn't in it. You do it because you have to, and the quicker you get it over with the happier you'll be. The adjective that exactly describes such actions is *perfunctory*.

The adverbs are *cursorily* and *perfunctorily*.

62. *How Not to Mean What You Say*

equivocal (ə-KWIV'-ə-kəl)
equivocate (ə-KWIV'-ə-kayt)
equivocation (ə-kwiv'-ə-KAY'-shən)
unequivocal (un-ə-KWIV'-ə-kəl)

Do you wish to confuse or mislead people? Here is the guaranteed method:

Say things in such a way that your listeners may, if they so desire, draw a false impression of your meaning or intentions, even though your exact words, if examined carefully, don't back up their conclusions. Do not be clear or direct, remain subtly vague, somewhat ambiguous, leave yourself an escape hatch without emphasizing the point. Hedge a little, be just a mite evasive, while nevertheless sounding absolutely sincere. If you can simultaneously manage an open and frank countenance, so much the better.

In a single word, be *equivocal.* Or, if you prefer a verb, *equivocate*—that is, etymologically, speak with equal (*equi-*) voice (*voc-*) out of both sides of your mouth.

The kind of slippery, devious individuals you can never pin down are masters of *equivocation.* The negative adjective, *unequivocal,* is precisely the opposite—direct, clear, straightforward, not in the slightest degree ambiguous or difficult to understand.

63. All About Faith

diffident (DIF'-ə-dent)   infidelity (in'-fə-DEL'-ə-tee)
diffidence (DIF'-ə-dənce)   infidel (IN'-fə-dəl)
fidelity (fə-DEL'-ə-tee)

If you have faith in yourself, you're confident. But if you're conspicuously lacking in such faith, if you distrust your abilities, your opinions, the impression you make on others, then you're *diffident.* When *diffidence* is your chief characteristic, asserting yourself is painful, probably emotionally impossible, and so you seem shy, even timid. You're hesitant about expressing with any conviction or strength what *you* feel, what *you* think, what *you* want or need or expect—and so most of the time you appear not only modest but downright self-depreciatory.

Both *confident* and *diffident* are built on the Latin *fides,* faith, as are also *fidelity,* faithfulness; *infidelity,* unfaithfulness, often sexual unfaithfulness to one's husband or wife, i.e., adultery; *infidel,* one who does not adhere to the accepted faith or religion; *confide,* to have enough faith in someone to entrust him with your secrets; and *Fido,* a name sometimes given to man's most faithful friend.

64. For Kangaroos

desultory (DES'-əl-taw'-ree)
desultorily (des'-əl-TAW'-rə-lee)

Do you lead a *desultory* kind of life? Are you *desultory* in your reading habits? Do you work *desultorily?*

If you say *yes* to one or more of these questions, you're a jumper. (*Desultory* derives from a Latin verb meaning jump down, just as *insult* comes from another form of the same verb, and signifies jump upon.)

You jump from one thing to another, never completing anything, acting without system or method or long-range plans, and following your whims and impulses whenever they beckon and wherever they lead. If your reading is *desultory,* it's random, haphazard—you dip into whatever you happen to pick up; you pick up whatever is around. If you work in a *desultory* manner, what (if anything) you accomplish is by chance, hit-or-miss—everything you do is aimless, lacking in final goals or concerted effort. You get no prize for either persistency or consistency and no admiration from others for your helter-skelter performance. Jumping, says the world, is for kangaroos; people who want to get somewhere should be organized and show some perseverance.

SEVENTH DAY'S TESTS

I. Match words and definitions.

<table>
<tr><td align="center">*A*</td><td align="center">*B*</td></tr>
<tr><td>1. bovine</td><td>*a.* completely worn out, exhausted</td></tr>
<tr><td>2. evanescent</td><td>*b.* hackneyed, overused, unimagina-</td></tr>
<tr><td>3. consummate (*adj.*)</td><td>tive</td></tr>
<tr><td>4. enervated</td><td>*c.* lustful, sexually desirous</td></tr>
<tr><td>5. contrite</td><td>*d.* hidden or puzzling in meaning</td></tr>
<tr><td>6. trite</td><td>*e.* superficial, careless, not thorough</td></tr>
<tr><td>7. cryptic</td><td>*f.* absolutely clear, unambiguous</td></tr>
<tr><td>8. concupiscent</td><td>*g.* stupid, patient, phlegmatic</td></tr>
<tr><td>9. cursory</td><td>*h.* remorseful, conscience-stricken</td></tr>
<tr><td>10. unequivocal</td><td>*i.* extremely skillful</td></tr>
<tr><td></td><td>*j.* lasting for a very short time</td></tr>
</table>

II. Write the word, starting as indicated, that fits the definition.

1. One who dabbles in an art for his own amusement   d_____
2. Sexual unfaithfulness   i_____

3. Loyalty   f_____
4. Desire for wealth or material possessions   c_____
5. Stupidity   f_____
6. Complete boredom, discontent, lack of interest in life   e_____
7. A word or phrase indirectly expressing an idea that might be offensive   e_____
8. To complete, put the final touches (to)   c_____
9. To be vague, purposely ambiguous   e_____
10. Joy of life   j_____
11. Lack of faith in oneself   d_____
12. Jumping aimlessly from one thing to another   d_____
13. Done without interest and merely as a matter of routine   p_____
14. As stupid as an ass   a_____
15. Puzzling, mystifying   e_____

III. What is the English meaning of each root?

1. Latin *voc-*   _____
2. Latin *fides*   _____
3. Latin *equi-*   _____
4. Greek *eu-*   _____
5. Greek *pheme*   _____
6. Latin *cupio*   _____
7. Latin *curro*   _____
8. Greek *kryptein*   _____

ANSWERS:

I. 1—g, 2—j, 3—i, 4—a, 5—h, 6—b, 7—d, 8—c, 9—e, 10—f.
II. 1—dilettante, 2—infidelity, 3—fidelity, 4—cupidity, 5—fatuity, 6—ennui, 7—euphemism, 8—consummate, 9—equivocate, 10—joie de vivre, 11—diffidence, 12—desultory, 13—perfunctory, 14—asinine, 15—enigmatic.
III. 1—voice; 2—faith; 3—equal; 4—good; 5—voice, sound; 6—to wish, want; 7—to run; 8—to hide.

Index